Religion on Trial

Donald Dutton, Ph.D.

Copyright © 2019 Donald Dutton, Ph.D.
https://drdondutton.com

All rights reserved. No part of this book may be used or reproduced by any means, graphic, electronic, or mechanical, including photocopying, recording, taping or by any information storage retrieval system without the written permission of the author except in the case of brief quotations embodied in critical articles and reviews.

Cover Design and Interior Formatting
by Iryna Spica, Spica Book Design
www.spicabookdesign.com

ISBNs: 978-1-77374-048-5 (Print)
978-1-77374-049-2 (E-book)

Escondido Press
P.O. Box 112194 – 119140
V6K 4R8
Vancouver, B.C.
Canada

Acknowledgments

Many people encouraged me in the writing of this book: Daniel Sonkin, Art and Elaine Aron, Michael Bond, Ehor Boyanowsky, and Vivian Yun. My wife Marta, who, despite being raised Catholic, did not throw me out of the house. Finally, Gordon Thomas and Cascadia's Ben Coles, for enabling me to publish this book on my own terms, and Michelle Balfour for an assiduous job of editing.

Table of Contents

	Introduction............................ vii	
1	The Epistemology of a Cult: Prophecies and Predictions.................. 1	
2	The Origin of Early Christianity: Birth, Sex, and Death...................... 43	
3	The Archaeology of Religion: The Judeo-Christian God of the Old Testament 75	
4	The Christian New Testament and the Basis of Christian Dogma............... 98	
5	Islam and the Arab Conquests............. 134	
6	The Legacy of Christianity: The Past is Prologue...................... 164	
7	Some Notable Heretics: From Julian to String Theory............... 197	
8	The Heretics Part 2: Psychological, Political, Moral, and Cosmological Issues of Faith..... 223	
9	God in the Brain: The Developmental Psychology of Religious Belief.............. 251	
10	The Social Psychology of Belief Systems..... 280	
	Coda 315	
	About the Author 333	

Introduction

When I was eleven, I decided to go to church. My mother would say, "We should go to church," but we never went—or even really discussed religion, for that matter. My father, I suspect, had his doubts, but he never said one way or the other. There was a vague sense that I was Protestant—I wasn't Catholic, or I would already have been going to a separate Catholic school. I wasn't Jewish—the Jews still seemed exotic to me. I wasn't Muslim—I probably didn't even know what that was.

I began the process of church shopping: going to Presbyterian, United, and Anglican services. The Anglicans served real wine. I was hooked.

I began a series of bible study breakfasts with the Minister at my local Anglican church in north Toronto. They were innocuous enough—mostly selected bible readings and their implications for modern life. I was confirmed and then got to participate in the service—the "blood and flesh of Christ"—although, unlike the Catholics, Anglicans believed these were symbolic, nothing more.

All was going well until one fateful day in Sunday bible study class. I was fourteen. The assistant Minister was speaking that day about the virgin birth and Jesus' parents, Joseph and Mary. I asked him, since Mary was married, how did he know it was a virgin birth? He took affront to my curiosity and refused to even answer. I walked out and never came back.

The years went by, and I rarely thought about religion. If asked, I said I was agnostic. When I got to university and took a double major of philosophy and psychology, the philosophers focused my thinking, especially the British empiricists, Locke, Berkeley, and Hume. I was trained as a social scientist, and did my graduate work in social psychology. I spent some time reading studies of cults, but never any studies of mainstream religion.

One such study, by Stanley Schachter, Leon Festinger, and Kurt Back, was called *When Prophecy Fails*. It was an insider's investigation of a doomsday cult. I began to see the forces involved in generating groupthink—the shared dogma of cults—but religion was still walled off, a world away.

My professional career led me into the study of violence, both domestic and political. I wrote a book on domestic violence and another on genocide, and was struck by the powerful role that beliefs play in generating all forms of violence: whether it is an (often erroneous) belief that a partner was unfaithful, or the belief that a group of people are less than human and do not deserve humane treatment.

I have always been driven by the challenge of trying to answer initially puzzling questions. Why would a man murder the woman he once loved? How can a soldier kill a helpless infant? So much of our motivation, for better or worse, derives from the beliefs that we hold as true but which, in fact, are not well-founded.

Eventually, this problem I have with curiosity—what Paul and Saint Augustine called "the disease of curiosity"— refocused on the dangling religious questions of my youth. How did the Christian church know that it was a virgin birth? Did they have proof in the day, or was it just the explanation that was used? In the latter case, it doesn't mean it was correct: it just means that it was all they knew. Over a thousand years later, the Black Plague was still explained as being caused by constellations and the positions of stars—clearly, they still did not know enough, such as the existence of the bacterium *Yersinia pestis*.

We have seen an escalation of technological and scientific knowledge in our lifetimes and forget how little was known when the desert religions of the Middle East—Christianity, Judaism, and Islam—were written down. They had no geography, no psychology, and no archaeology. Nothing was known about the distant past or distant places, let alone about human cognition.

I have focused this book on the desert religions of Christianity, Judaism, and Islam because of their current internecine strife: the ongoing wars in the Middle East, Al Qaeda, ISIS, the PLO, and their spillage into terrorist acts.

I don't remember when the current turmoil in the Middle East began. I do remember the hostage taking at the Munich Olympics, but before 9/11, I wasn't paying much attention. I was at a psychology conference in San Diego on September 11th, 2001. I woke up with the television on and the sight of an aircraft flying into a high rise tower. Like many others, I was stunned.

I became interested in the origins of anti-Semitism in particular when I wrote my book on genocide and the Holocaust in 2007. Anti-Semitic views date back to the original Christian story about the resurrection, and its continuing blame of Jews for the death of Christ; overlooking, of course, that Jesus was a Jew and that the crucifixion was "all within god's plan."

It may well be that mankind will always find a way to divide and make war, but religion has provided an easy means of doing so, and even provides rewards for fighting. It has too easily targeted the damned: outsiders and infidels.

The discoveries I made during the writing of this book were revelations to me: that no copies existed of the original bible; that we know of it only through the writings of others; and that it was written in classical Greek, while the disciples were illiterate and spoke only Aramaic. How, then, could verbatim descriptions exist of Jesus' dialogues with his disciples?

I found that modern scholars date the writing of the Old Testament to the 7th Century BCE, and concluded that it was written to unify the two Jewish states of Judah and Israel. However, the apocryphal events it describes were from the 13th Century BCE. I also learned that many sections of the New Testament had been forged or re-written in line with developing Christian orthodoxy.

My plan in writing this book was to apply the scholarship I had learned during my social science career to the complex question of religion, with a focus on the foundations of Christianity, Judaism, and Islam. In so doing, I discovered many laudable scholars: Charles Freeman, Bart Ehrman, Elaine Pagels, Patricia Crone, Bertrand Russell, Israel Finkelstein, and Neil Silberman, amongst others.

The plan to publish was not so rosy: two academic publishers decided the book was a "trade book" (i.e. for general readership), while one agent decided the book was far too scholarly to be anything but an academic book. In the end, I used an independent publisher that gave me my freedom: to publish a book that both weighs the evidence of, and provides a psychological theory for, religious belief.

My intent in writing this book is not to offend people, but neither to shrink from the evidence. My socialization as a psychologist and a researcher allows me to follow the evidence, and I have done so. I realize that true believers will not like the confrontation of their beliefs, but I am not expecting them to change solely as a result of this book.

The model of belief that I examine shows how we are very conservative in our adoption of new beliefs: they have to fit in some way with the patterns of beliefs we have already adopted. It is similar to the concept of *stare decisis* in court: new rulings have to be reconciled with established court decisions. In this way, we tend not to change.

We want an explanation for the universe that resembles a story—one we can enunciate. Current scientific explanations of the universe—quantum physics and string theory—are too complex and counter-intuitive for us to apprehend. They are difficult for us to apply to our previously-held understandings of the world. For this reason, they do not supply a narrative that properly competes with religious teachings.

But how did these religions achieve this status in the first place? How did they get from being just the generic explanation used for a phenomenon we didn't understand to a culturally-understood and -accepted religious narrative? And what causes believers to remain, despite there being no evidence for the religion's doctrines and divisive nature? How do they reconcile these facts? These are the questions I seek to discuss, while applying the normal levels of skepticism used in court to judge the merits and acceptability of religious beliefs. In so doing, we will put religion, as it were, on trial.

CHAPTER 1

The Epistemology of a Cult: Prophecies and Predictions

In his review of anthropological studies of Pacific Islanders, David Attenborough described the birth of a belief system: "cargo cults."[1]

Groups of Pacific Islanders had taken note of the inexplicable and wondrous possessions of white people who had landed by ship on their islands in the aftermath of World War II. These wondrous articles were not made by the white people themselves, and when they needed repair they were sent away. No white man was ever seen working on them. Instead, new ones kept arriving as cargo in ships. The cargo, it was concluded, must be supernatural.

The white men were believed to engage in supernatural ceremonies, such as listening to small boxes that glowed with lights and emitted strange noises. These ceremonies must be the rituals that kept the cargo coming. Many of the cults claimed that a particular messiah would bring the cargo on the day an apocalypse arrived.

These cargo cults, as biologist Richard Dawkins describes them,[2] sprang up independently on various islands that were separated geographically and culturally, including New Caledonia, the Solomon Islands, Fiji, New Hebrides, and New Guinea. As Dawkins describes it, one such cult is still in existence.

Dawkins proposes that *"the independent flowering of so many independent but similar cults suggests some unifying features of human psychology in general"* (p 203). These unifying features are:

1) The amazing speed that a cult can spring up
2) How quickly the origination process can cover its tracks
3) The similarity of each cultic myth to myths elsewhere, and
4) Their similarity to the myths of other, older religions.

Faced with puzzling and momentous phenomena, the cargo cults evoked a mythology to explain the inexplicable. The mythology borrowed on concepts of the supernatural and a messiah. How might such a central conviction, for which there is no empirical evidence, establish and sustain a religious group?

While adherents of religions believe they have superior evidence than cults, cults too believe they have a hold on absolute truths. I shall argue in this book that the dynamics of cults also apply to religions, especially in their formative years.

And so, before we review the origin and perpetuation of the desert religions, we will examine the creation, maintenance, and demise of cults and other quasi-religious belief systems.

One such type of belief system can be found associated with moral panics. In his book, *Satanic Panic: The Creation of a Contemporary Legend*,[3] sociologist Jeffrey Victor examines modern legends: specifically, the belief in the Satanic sexual abuse of children. Victor points out how belief in these killer cults became widespread in the 1980s, especially amongst social workers and members of the helping professions.

A poll of social workers in California showed a majority believed in the existence of groups of Satanic child-killers, and had an elaborate central myth to describe this group (e.g. they were successful business people with ties to the police, and had practised Satanism across many generations). However, three investigations by state and federal agencies (including the FBI) turned up no evidence for Satanic ritual killings. In all cases where Satanic practice was alleged, the accused either wound up with not guilty verdicts or guilty verdicts to much lesser crimes.

The most expensive criminal investigation in California history, the McMartin preschool case, was one such example. In 1983, the McMartin staff were accused of sodomizing a woman's son, forcing sex between children and animals, and "flying in the air." The ensuing trial after the initial hysteria dragged on for years, resulting in no convictions and all charges being dropped. The initial complainant was diagnosed as a paranoid schizophrenic and died of alcoholism.

The Satanic Panic contagion occurred in modern times and amongst literate people, but the process was very much the same as with the cargo cults: it was a story that served a purpose. In this case, it posited the existence of a group that could be blamed for a general sense of anxiety over modern threats to children.

The moral panic described by Victor was limited to time (the 1980s) and space (mostly USA). In comparison, cargo cult beliefs lasted much longer and served psychological needs that were more sustaining than the moral panic myths of Satanic abuse. They do have a central feature in common, however: they were both elaborate sets of beliefs with no basis in fact. People can easily persuade themselves of delusional beliefs, especially when there is social support for those beliefs.

This is not a new phenomenon. One of the most popular and enduring collections in descriptive sociology is Charles Mackay's book, *Extraordinary Popular Delusions and the Madness of Crowds*.[4] Originally published in 1852, it chronicles historical mass delusions, including Nostradamus' "prophecies" and Pope Urban II's launch of the Crusades (based on delusional beliefs about Muslims).

Whether with a religion, cult, or moral panic, members have either experienced the inexplicable or seek to diffuse anxiety. Such groups evolve stories that "explain" the inexplicable or reduce anxiety by generating a source, blaming the source, and seeking remedies against the source. In each case, groups with invariable dogmas emerge.

A Brief History of Prophecies

The true "litmus test" of any belief system is how well it makes predictions or prophecies:[6] its ability to forecast events. Prophecy very much concerned the major desert religions (Christianity, Judaism, and Islam), although at different time periods.[7] Jesus was a prophet, as was Moses and Muhammad. In their case, prophecy was based on the belief that earth-shaking knowledge was being offered by god.

As we shall see, religion developed as an attempt to "appease the gods"—appease them and save the tribe from future storms, droughts, or famines. In the case of the Jews, prophecy was an attempt to reassure the tribe that god had a plan for them; as such, many "prophecies" were written retroactively (by about 600 years).

This hope that we can control the future is part of the human condition: it underlies our very perceptual systems. As a species, we perceive events in a way that allows us to believe that we have some control of the environment:[8] an objective that may have had evolutionary origins. It underlies our belief systems—for whether they are religious or scientific, all have a central tenet of future prediction and control. Religion offers hope for a better future, sometimes described in fundamentalist Christianity as an "end times" or second coming of Christ.*

Social psychologists Leon Festinger, Henry Riecken, and Stanley Schachter[5] performed an in-depth study of the development of the belief system within a doomsday cult—a cult that believed the world was going to end. In doing so, they provided several important insights into the development, perpetuation, and ultimate resolution of belief systems, especially the capacity of these systems to withstand disconfirmation.

According to the authors, the inspiration for their study was religious historical events and prophecies, including the

---

* Google searches of end times indicate that some fundamentalists see forest fires, the bird flu, and the dying of sea lions as signs of the coming Apocalypse.

crucifixion of Christ. They argued that followers who believed Christ was the messiah must have been traumatized and shaken by his crucifixion. Their prophecy failed cataclysmically. The shattering of any strongly-held belief such as theirs generates "cognitive dissonance": an aversive psychological state that can only be reduced by cognitively re-evaluating what has just transpired.[9]

There have been millennial movements throughout history predicting either the "End of Days," the second coming of Christ, or both.[10,11] These prophecies typically originated with one person who claimed to have mystical knowledge.

In his biographical history of Jesus,[12] Reza Aslan lists the numerous times that Jesus referred to the imminent coming of the kingdom of god. For example, in Mark 9:1, Jesus says *"I tell you there are those here who will not taste death until they have seen the Kingdom of God."* Hence, it was soon to arrive, during the lifetimes of current people. Azlan reads the sayings of Jesus to suggest that this kingdom of god was a real kingdom, to be established on earth with a real king (god).

In the 2nd Century, a priest in Phrygia (now central Turkey) called Montanus had a fixed conviction that the second coming of Christ (followed by the kingdom of god) was at hand, and that it would take place near what is now Ankara. He founded the *Illuminati*, a group given to ecstatic religious experiences. He then proclaimed himself the Holy Spirit incarnate and preached that Christians should practice asceticism and separate themselves from the world.

He developed followers (called Montanists) throughout Asia Minor, North Africa, and parts of Europe (p 46).[13] His authority for the claim of the second coming was unofficial, but he was eloquent and inspirational. He developed mobs of followers who made pilgrimages in such numbers that a whole new town had to be built to house them all.

When the date of the event came and went, followers appeared not to have relinquished their beliefs. On the contrary, they developed what they considered to be a new, elite form of Christianity, based on personal revelation (p 7).[12]

In the 16th Century, a Christian splinter group called the Anabaptists[14] forecast an "end time" scenario to occur in the year 1533. This would include the entire earth burning while a "kingdom of righteousness" was set up in the city of Strasbourg, France. As the belief took hold, many gave up all their worldly possessions and went to study with the movement's leaders.

When the time of the Apocalypse came and went, the Anabaptists increased their proselytizing—that is, they attempted to induce others to accept their own belief system—and began to send out missionaries, which they had never done before.

In the 17th Century, the Jews believed the messiah would come in the year 1648. A self-styled student of the cabala in Smyrna (in what is now Turkey) named Sabbati Zevi proclaimed himself to be the messiah and developed a small band of followers (called Sabbati). Again, despite the initial shock and disappointment, when the prophesied second coming did not occur Zevi took to proselytizing. He even travelled to large Jewish communities to generate more converts. The failure of the prophecy was rationalized as a necessary condition of future glorification of Sabbati.

With this rationalization now available to justify their previous commitments (many had left their homes, businesses, and villages to follow him), the proselytizing reached a higher, louder level. Zevi was widely accepted by Middle Eastern Jews as the new messiah (p 10).[12]

This new power appears to have allowed Zevi to attempt to depose the Sultan of Constantinople in 1666, leading to his arrest, imprisonment, and eventual forced conversion to Islam. His followers maintained the faith after his arrest; a smaller group even did so after his conversion, some of whom followed his example by also converting.

Festinger and his colleagues were fascinated by this apparent increase in "spreading the word" after a failed prophecy. They saw it as an attempt to reduce cognitive dissonance: the uneasy feeling that occurs when two beliefs do not "fit" psychologically. In this case, that the sacrifices one has made do not fit with the subsequent failed prophecy. It leads a person to ask: did I do all of that for nothing? This thought has negative effects for the self-image of a person who makes good decisions.

In 1818, American preacher William Miller became convinced that the world, as it was known, would end in 1843,[15,16] followed by the return of Christ (The second coming). He was convinced, apparently, by a statement in the book of Daniel (8:14), which said *"Unto two thousand and three hundred days, then shall the sanctuary be cleansed."* Miller took the "days" to be symbols for years and calculated the prophecy as being written in 457 BCE.

After another five years of study, Miller began to proselytize and won many adherents, including church ministers (who called themselves the Millerites). The movement swelled in both numbers and fervour as 1843 approached. By November 1842, the Millerites had held 30 "camp meetings," each attended by thousands, and had built a tabernacle in Boston.

They now published several newspapers, and set the precise time for the second coming as occurring between March 21, 1843 and March 21, 1844. Splinter groups developed that favoured different days within this one-year period.

As the critical year began without the prophecy being fulfilled, adherents focused on the latter part of the timeframe (1844), as suggested by the Jewish rather than the Christian calendar. When March 21, 1844 came and went, the Millerites were publicly ridiculed, and fringe followers fell away from the group.

The most committed, however, renewed their fervour, and outreach and conversions now expanded to international levels. The date was again revised to October 22, 1844. As Festinger put it, *"The two partial disconfirmations (April 23, 1843 and the end of 1843) and one complete and unequivocal disconfirmation (March 21, 1844) served simply to strengthen conviction that the Coming was near at hand and to increase the time and energy that Miller's adherents spent trying to convince others"* (p 19).

Followers in farming communities did not plough their fields because the end was near. One of the movement's newspapers stated that *"Some, going into their fields to cut their grass, found themselves entirely unable to proceed, and, conforming to their sense of duty, left their crops standing in the field, to show their faith by their works, and thus to condemn the world"* (The Advent Herald, Oct. 20, 1844, p 93; cited in Festinger et al., p 19).

Proselytizing reached a fever pitch in the weeks before October 22, 1844, despite (or because of) the prior disconfirmations. The "camp meetings" overflowed with new adherents. Followers gave up or sold worldly possessions.

When October 22, 1844 came and went, the Millerites finally accepted disconfirmation. They gave up their beliefs, and the movement disintegrated into dissention, controversy, and discord. As Festinger put it, *"Although there is a limit beyond which belief will not withstand disconfirmation, it is clear that the introduction of contrary evidence can serve to increase the conviction and enthusiasm of a believer"* (p 23).

Festinger also used another example: that of the crucifixion of Jesus, as described in the Christian bible. The description relies on a conventional orthodox Christian "historical account," called *The History of Christianity in the Light of Modern Knowledge*. It was written in 1929 by a number of church ministers, and yet still manages to include snippets of conversation between Christ and his disciples.

Festinger assumes from this "historical account" that the disciples really believed Jesus was the messiah, and left their everyday lives to follow him. Since Jewish sects of the day believed that the messiah could not be made to suffer, Jesus' crying out when crucified was a disconfirmation.

However, the same religious source states that Jesus had predicted that he would die in Jerusalem and would have to suffer. An alternative interpretation is that his followers' response to the crucifixion was to focus on a prophecy in the Old Testament, stating *"He [the messiah] will be taken from the land of the living and will be wounded for the sins of his people."*

Even within the narrow restrictions of Christian orthodoxy, there is debate as to whether the crucifixion constitutes a disconfirmation. In fact, one of the earliest debates in the Christian church focused on whether Jesus was a human or a god. If he was a god, one side argued, why did he suffer? But if he was human, then how could he be the messiah of Jewish legend?

Either way, Jesus' suffering for the sins of humanity became a central tenet of Christianity. Is this central aspect of Christian doctrine a result of cognitive dissonance? It certainly reduces dissonance by offering an explanation for the crucifixion: by providing a reason for why it happened, it makes the crucifixion historically necessary.

Cognitive Dissonance and Proselytizing

Festinger and his colleagues specified that certain criteria were needed to be met to see an increase in proselytizing after disconfirmation of a set of beliefs. They concluded that the following conditions lead to increased conviction following disconfirmation: first off, that the belief is held with deep conviction; that it is relevant to the believer's actions or behaviour; that it must have produced actions that are difficult to undo; that it is sufficiently specific, in such a way that it can be clearly disconfirmed; that the disconfirming evidence is recognized by the believer; and, finally, that the believer must have social support from other believers.

Festinger's explanation for proselytizing is that disconfirmation produces a state of cognitive dissonance: a psychological discomfort produced by a contradiction between one's pre-existing actions and beliefs and any subsequent disconfirmation. The magnitude of this state of cognitive dissonance depends on the importance of the beliefs to the individual and the magnitude of their commitment and actions.

Festinger describes a "central belief" and its accompanying ideology (such as a religion's core tenets) as being of major importance. For a true believer, religious beliefs provide a framework of assumptions into which more narrow, or transient, beliefs must fit. Moral notions, ideas of who is in the group (believers) or outside the group (infidels), and what behaviours are acceptable toward the infidels are all narrower ideas than the original religious precepts.

This complex of ideas has a neurological basis, called a "cognitive web" or "cogweb,"[17] and has billions of neural connections. As such, it is resistant to change. Since the neural network is so hard to alter, one's perception of the disconfirming event must change instead.

In laboratory studies, research subjects who were induced to make dubious choices would enhance the consequences of those choices. Otherwise, the insult implied by their poor decision would impact on their self-esteem.

Even before our present knowledge of neural networks, American philosopher Willard van Orman Quine made a similar argument on the centrality of beliefs: that since central beliefs require too much cognitive work to change, new ideas must fit with the old, immutable ones.[18] Against this background in philosophy and neurobiology, proselytizing can be seen as a means of preserving one's central belief.

The five necessary elements that precede proselytizing work in concert: cognitive dissonance occurs when we have taken actions that commit us to the belief in question; the disconfirmation implies that we have been gullible or mindless, and the rationalization rescues us from this unwanted conclusion; the social support of others makes the rationalization more believable. The self-rationalization then becomes the reason for the proselytizing. If we can convince more people of its "truth," then the subjective correctness of our truth increases.

However, this explanation appears to require some success at generating converts in order to work.

Social Relations and the Epistemology of a Cult

Festinger and his colleagues found that all historical examples lacked enough information to enable a test of this theory. Therefore, when the opportunity arose to infiltrate a doomsday cult, they seized it.

Marian Keech, the pseudonym given to the cult's leader in Festinger's study, was a charismatic woman in the northern US who claimed to be receiving messages from "superior beings" on a planet called Clarion. They had told her that there were fault lines in the earth that would collapse on December 21, 1954, triggering a flood that would turn North American into a lake (p 31).[5] Festinger and his associates were specifically interested in how the group would cope with the resulting disconfirmation.

Marian Keech had long been interested in the mystical, as applied to the cosmos and her own nature; she had previously attended lectures in both theosophy and Dianetics (the precursor to Scientology).[*] As she described the latter, "*I prefer to call it 'Scientology' which is the art and science of taking someone back as far in his life as he can go*" (p 34).[5]

She also became interested in a popular phenomenon of the early 1950s: flying saucers. She became convinced that these saucers contained inhabitants who could communicate with humans.

---

[*] Scientology, a mix of bizarre fantasy and pop-psychology about freeing oneself from trauma in past lives, was developed by L. Ron Hubbard and sought status as a religion, which it received in the US (hence, no taxes). It is still considered controversial in many countries (including France and Germany).

Sometime after she had immersed herself in these pursuits, Mrs. Keech awoke one morning with a tingling sensation in her arm and began to write: a type of automatic (involuntary) writing. She described the writing as "strangely familiar," and (mentally) asked the author of the writing to identify himself; he responded that he was her departed father. This was her first direct experience with the occult.*

Eventually, she began to receive messages from other beings. The first of these only described himself as her "Elder Brother," then as *"other spiritual beings who dwelt on the planets Clarion and Cerus"* (p 36).[5] Eventually, she received messages from a being who called himself Sananda, *"who was destined to become her most important source of information and instruction, as well as her most principal link with orthodox Christian revelation … Sananda identified himself as the contemporary identity of the historical Jesus"* (p 36).[5] She referred to these collective voices as "the Guardians."

At Easter, Mrs. Keech received a message that the Guardians were planning an "earthly liaison," and that she should tell other mortals about this plan (p 37).[5] These messages that she should "spread the news" (p 38)[5] were repeated.

Initially, she told only her husband, who was unreceptive but did not attempt to dissuade her. Then she linked into a group of housewives who met to discuss Scientology and

---

* She took her father's message to her mother, who reprimanded her and told her to stop such nonsense (p 35). She persevered however, and sat each day awaiting a message, which only occasionally arrived. It was during these early days that she first began to receive messages from other beings. She prayed at this stage (indicating her initial religious upbringing) that she would not fall into the wrong hands.

the occult. They were joined by a lecturer on flying saucers and a former Michigan physician, called "Dr. Armstrong" by Festinger. Dr. Armstrong, along with his wife, attended many of the talks on flying saucers, and identified themselves as members of a "non-denominational Protestant church" (p 39-41).[5]

The Armstrongs believed in the existence of a spirit world, whose masters could communicate and instruct the people of earth. They were convinced that extrasensory migration (movement without bodily change or motion) had occurred and subscribed to many occult beliefs, including reincarnation. They, too, were convinced that flying saucers were real (p 42-43).[5] The "meeting of minds" with the Armstrongs appears to have increased Mrs. Keech's confidence that her messages were foretelling a real truth. The frequency of the involuntary messages she received increased to ten a day (p 43).[5]

The belief system they developed claimed that there was a universe of planets beyond the solar system, where beings of superior intelligence (the Guardians) lived. These beings existed at higher vibration frequencies than humans, so their actions were carried out by thought rather than physical activity. They therefore communicated telepathically, and had learned to transcend death (p 43-46).[5] The Guardians were benign and sought to decrease conflict on earth.*

Predictions of a flood on Earth began slowly, but eventually became more explicit. It was clear to Mrs. Keech that the Guardians were coming to save the Earth by gathering up "certain dwellers" (p 46).[5] In their messages to her, the Guardians

---

* Note: similar to the spaceman in the 1951 film The Day the Earth Stood Still

included "*fulminations against warmongers, scientists, nonbelievers and materialists*" and exhortations to cease thinking, since "*There is no advantage to thinking when we are studying the teaching of the Creator*" (p 47).[5] She was advised to "*be still of the five senses*" and focus instead on direct knowledge of the Father, the Creator (p 47).[5]

Messages from the Guardians began to refer to specific future events and potential meetings with extraterrestrials already on earth; the Guardians had already been in contact with individuals from Earth (all in the US). Although they were coming toward earth and had been detected by astronomers, they were simply mistaken for sunspots.

One message directed Mrs. Keech to a military air base at a specific date. She attended with the Armstrongs and ten other acquaintances (she had not yet begun evangelizing, but word had leaked out through her typist). All of them drove to a road near the airfield. Nothing happened, except that they were approached while waiting by a strange, unknown man.

The following day, it was revealed to Mrs. Keech during her automatic writing sessions that this stranger was an alien. She became further convinced that she had been selected. Of the ten who had waited at the airfield with her, only five remained as disciples—the others dropped out.

Mrs. Keech's writing now extended to 14 hours a day, and began to feature a description of the earth's origin, dividing it into the forces of Light and Evil. Scientists were part of the latter, blamed as they were for inventing atomic bombs. The Guardians "*were over West Virginia and taking listings of the world's industrial people that make war material and profit from war assets*" (p 45).[5] It was the "*ignorance of Universal Laws that makes all misery of the Earth*" (p 45).[5]

Festinger points out (p 54)[5] that all of this material was present in popular magazines and books of the time. There was a popular belief in the flying saucers, as well as a potential nuclear catastrophe.* Mrs. Keech's prophecies reflected this Zeitgeist, and began to include descriptions of a coming apocalypse: the flood that would alter North America.

Mrs. Armstrong had taken to typing out Mrs. Keech's automatic writings, and Dr. Armstrong began to mimeograph and distribute them. They sent out a press release to newspapers on August 30, 1954, and began public outreach.

The initial response to this information was negligible. However, it was through this release of limited information that Festinger and his colleagues learned of Mrs. Keech and visited her to find out more.

They described her as not making any attempt to persuade them on the initial visit. They did learn, however, from Mrs. Armstrong, that a small group had formed to witness the approaching flood, although *"we believe Mrs. Keech had only a few followers at this point [mid-October, 1954]"* (p 63).[5]

The Armstrongs were more motivated to obtain followers, mostly through their community church and the discussions held there of Christian mysticism (p 67).[5] They communicated the content of Mrs. Keech's writings to this group and to a mailing list (who received mimeographed text) of about 150-250 people.

---

* According to a 2013 poll, 29% of Americans believed aliens existed (Public Policy Polling, Raleigh, North Carolina). In comparison, alien-resistance.org claims (by citing polls[5] performed by CNN and Scripps in 2008) that 33% of persons polled believe aliens have visited earth, 10% they have seen a UFO and 3% claim they had been abducted. The site also argues that belief in UFOs is higher today than in the 1950s.

Initially, they sent out only pre-prediction writings and were selective in their preaching. They seemed to have a policy of "passive recruiting," by which they would respond to interested individuals (whom they called "Seekers") but not spread the word beyond their initial press release. They believed that those who were ready would be sent to them, and that they should not force their beliefs on others (p 71).[5] Doubters were just not ready, but Seekers were.

Taking an active role in the cult meetings would be problematic for the researchers, since they did not want to influence the group's process. Therefore, Festinger and his colleagues did not introduce themselves as social scientists, but instead as potential converts.

By November 1954, Festinger had observers successfully infiltrate the group. To gain entry, one recounted to Mrs. Keech a dream she'd had: of standing near the base of a hill, where she saw a man surrounded by an aura of light and torrents of water. The man, however, pulled her up to safety (p 70).[5] This generated instant entry.

The Seekers in Mrs. Keech's group at that point were described as *"college students ... young people of religious bent"* (p 71).[5] A group meeting was described by an observer as members sitting quietly with closed eyes, trying to get in touch with their inner voice and with Christian prayers. Dr. Armstrong led the meeting, reading the latest "lesson from Mrs. Keech" (p 72)[5] and a reinstatement of the group belief system.

Group discussion explored the identities those present had in prior incarnations. This included the identity they had when Jesus was on the earth. One of the Seekers, given the name "Cleo," was informed that her biblical identity had been Martha, wife of Lazarus (p 77).[5] Dr. Armstrong let it be known that someone in the room had been identified as Joseph, and that Mrs. Keech had been Mary, mother of Jesus, in her previous incarnation (p 74).[5] In a later session, another group member, who was asked to act as a medium, channelled the voice of the Creator Himself (p 98).[5]

Mrs. Keech set December 21, 1954* as the day for the flood which would engulf North America and, eventually, the rest of the world (p 74).[5] At the end of the meeting, everyone present signed a letter to then-US President Dwight Eisenhower, asking him to release information the government had on flying saucers (p 72).[5]

Festinger's observers attended all group meetings from the middle of November to December 20, 1954. During this time, 33 people attended the meetings, of which 8 were true believers: devoted individuals who had taken committing actions. These actions were consistent with the beliefs and difficult or impossible to undo, such as quitting a job, dropping friendships, arguing with disbelieving parents, or dropping out of school (p 107).[5]

As the days before the flood diminished, several events occurred: for one thing, the group had received some publicity, and both Mrs. Keech and Dr. Armstrong were asked to speak to those outside of their followers (albeit to a group that was interested in flying saucers). On this occasion, and all other media events during this time, they did not encourage converts or even mention the specific date for the flood.

---

* Along with their architectural achievements, the Mayans left us with calendars that, some argue, predicted the end of the world on December 21, 2012. December 21 is the winter solstice. Some religious historians argue that the date for Christmas was based on this earlier date.

By mid-December, a series of disconfirmations occurred: the group had believed they would be picked up by a flying saucer days before the flood. The Seekers spent one cold night outside awaiting a pick-up. When it never occurred, they rationalized it as having been "just a drill" (p 148):[5] practice events to show the Guardians that the earthlings really were ready. Some members defected from the group with these early disconfirmations.

The public began to react, and in some cases, play pranks on the Seekers. One prank phone call led Mrs. Keech to proclaim to the group, "He is coming, He is coming" (p 152).[5] A group of outsiders came to the Keech house and conferred intently with Mrs. Keech. She told her followers that the outsiders were spacemen; the one skeptic (whose continuing attendance was not explained) in the group said they were college students. As Festinger and colleagues remarked, "The net result of this attack on the belief system and the prophecy was to strengthen it" (p 155).[5]

Fifteen people waited at Mrs. Keech's house on the evening of December 20th for a flying saucer to pick them up at midnight. Many removed any metal they had on them (zippers, glasses, tooth fillings) to enable space travel.

As midnight passed, the group became increasingly tense. A few "interpretations" of the delays were offered and rejected. Then Marian Keech came up with a message from god at 4:45 am (she was now channelling the Creator). It said that the goodness that the group displayed had saved the world from the flood; they had saved the world because they believed. Immediately, Marian Keech began to call the press, resulting in a tsunami of such calls.

The Festinger study focused primarily on the paradoxical reaction of the group's increased proselytizing after the disconfirmation of their prediction. While it seems clear that enormous dissonance must have been experienced, even if temporarily, by this group—they had taken committing actions, and waited for a spaceship that never came—the final condition that Festinger required for dissonance reduction was never met.

Festinger was quite clear on the relationship of proselytizing to dissonance reduction: *"If more and more people can be persuaded that the system of belief is correct, then clearly it must be, after all, correct"* (p 28).[5] It is a form of social reality, where group belief becomes absolute.

However, in this case, no one was persuaded by the post-disconfirmation proselytizing. The press had never been "converts," even before the disconfirmation, and the proselytizing just brought more humiliation to the group (p 174)[5] in the form of public skepticism. If you can't convince the press that the world will end based on your prophecy, how can you convince them, after the fact, that the world was spared from it because of you?

The group had been the object of pranks before the disconfirmation and was, for obvious reasons, not winning any converts after its failure. No one joined the group after the post-disconfirmation proclamations began. No one outside of their following spread the word, although some newspapers reported the disconfirmation. Several people continued to contact the group after the disconfirmation, and these people were immediately labelled as the "Chosen," by the remaining members. However, none of them appeared to join the group or come to espouse group beliefs.

The proselytizing was a desperate act by a group searching for any signs consistent with their beliefs: literally grasping at straws. If dissonance was reduced, it must have been through a more intra-psychic process than Festinger had imagined, because there was no payoff through social reactions. We have to consider the possibility that Festinger's own prophecy—his hypothetical mechanism for dissonance reduction—also failed.

Mrs. Keech moved to Arizona, where she rejoined Scientology. According to letters she later sent to the study's authors, she maintained her convictions regarding her prophecy.

There have been about 170 documented, high-profile prophesies of a world-ending apocalypse between 634 BCE and 2012. Apocalypse predictors included Pope Sylvester II, Pope Innocent III, and Nostradamus, as well as mathematicians, astrologers, Herbert W. Armstrong (founder of the Worldwide Church of God),* Christian Television Preacher Pat Robertson, and Christian book author Tim LaHaye.

The media-hyped prediction that the world would end in December of 2012 was seconded by Warren Jeffs, the president of the Fundamentalist Church of the Latter Day Saints. Jeffs is currently serving life in prison (life plus 20 years) in Texas for aggravated sexual assault of children. While in prison, Jeffs wrote a book that he purported to be the revelations of Jesus Christ, as delivered to him. It included a command to set Jeffs free.

The Group Dynamics of Belief Systems in Cults

Although a fact that was largely overlooked by its authors, the Festinger study was important for shedding some light on the influence processes that occur in cults to shape and

---

* Not to be dissuaded in the face of disconfirmation, Armstrong revised his date for the apocalypse 4 times.

form beliefs. The cult's "message" (their central beliefs) as it was presented, could only be accepted by those who were "ready." It was a notion of being evolved and, in that sense, better persons than the "unready." Hence, those who joined the group experienced a sense of being elite, of knowing something that the unready did not know.

This sense bound the Seekers to the cult and enhanced the influence of the group. The implicit message was: if you accepted Mrs. Keech's latest message, you were attuned; if you were skeptical, you were not. Therefore, status in the group became commensurate with dogmatic acceptance. Apart from those who did drop out, there was only one member of the cult who doubted the prophecy.

Many groups generate influence to central tenets by equating the knowledge system of the group with some elite status: typically, it is a non-empirical system of receiving knowledge. There is an "in-group" who has the message; the others can only get into the in-group by believing and espousing the dogma.

An adjunct to this precept is that in all religious groups and cults there is a claim of secret knowledge, known only to those in the in-group. The existence of this knowledge must be accepted on faith.

Social psychologists have explained group consensus as occurring by three processes,[19] which describe the groups' dynamics. The first is the matter of who is drawn to a particular group; in Festinger's study, most of the believers were either students or persons drawn from other, similar groups. These similar groups were primarily church groups interested in Christian mysticism and flying saucers (headed by Dr. Armstrong).

Other studies have found that young people join cults searching for an identity or answers to questions about the meaning of life.[20] A prediction of a world-changing event clearly focuses the meaning of life into an issue of survival. An interest in mysticism indicates that one sees rational processes as limited and subscribes to a "higher knowledge" available only through non-rational means. In Mrs. Keech's case, it was information revealed to her and communicated through her "automatic writing."

The second process at work within groups is known as group dynamics: people become more homogenized to the group's central dogma by virtue of the information they are exposed to and no longer exposed to (i.e. corrective information) by being in the group. This process of informational shaping is known as social reality.[19, 21]

Finally, people within groups with extreme views are shaped by the new status they find within the group. The need for status is universal in all social groupings. Those who are a little more extreme than the mainstream group belief are accorded more status within the group; hence the group inches toward a more extreme position as others clamour for status. It is the status and connection with similar others, rather than the group ideology per se, that binds a person to the group.

In his study of people who had escaped cults in the 1970s, investigative reporter Wayne Sage found that cult members who were "deprogrammed" by their parents—kidnapped by a "professional deprogrammer" in a controversial phenomenon that involved forcefully confronting them about their cult philosophy—reported that it was not the cult's views per se, but the sense of belonging and status in the group, that was important.[20]

This was illustrated in Mrs. Keech's group by a woman named "Bertha," who challenged Mrs. Keech for leadership of the group. She claimed to receive messages from the Creator (rather than Sananda, Mrs. Keech's source) and was to be the designated mother of Christ, who was not yet reborn. This woman had little status outside the group, but was ambitious and upwardly mobile within it. She came to believe the information she channelled, to the extent that she had a hysterical childbirth within the group.

All of these social processes were operative in Keech's prophecy group, as they are in real-world religions. The prophecy group was the product of a social backdrop: a Zeitgeist in the post-World War II culture of anxiety about the new nuclear bomb, the effects of radiation on the planet, the potential for an escape to outer space, and the desire for a saviour.

Several films from this era illustrate this Zeitgeist, including *The Day the Earth Stood Still* (1951), in which a spaceman comes to earth to warn the earthlings about a coming nuclear catastrophe; he proves his identity to a scientist by solving a complicated mathematical calculation. Another film from that era, *When Worlds Collide* (1951), focused on the coming end of the earth via collision with another planet, and the subsequent plans to load up a spaceship and escape. In 1951 alone, fifteen sci-fi movies were released with spaceman/end of earth themes.[22]

This Zeitgeist also included beliefs that spacemen had already landed or crashed (e.g. in Roswell, New Mexico) and that the government was covering up this fact. The Internet Movie Database lists 50 "sci-fi" films with that theme, the genre having originated in the 1950s.

It seems that themes from this Zeitgeist were woven into the central beliefs of the Seekers: a group seeking hidden knowledge and salvation. Themes and tropes from any given Zeitgeist occasionally coalesce into a narrative that can form part of a central tenet for a group. It did so with Mrs. Keech's group, and has also done so with Christianity, Judaism, and Islam.

When the messages Mrs. Keech "received" became focused on group concerns (i.e. the problematic disconfirmation) and her own need to respond to doubts regarding her credibility, it became even more evident that the origin of the messages was within her. She tailored the messages to fit the group's concerns and her own needs.

The initial "revealed plan" of flying saucers and a flood indicated another aspect of her projected thought: all of the planned landings and events were to occur within the United States, the only country Mrs. Keech and her followers knew. Their own limited map of the universe was the blueprint for the prophecy.

We often hear protesters with a religious bent who claim to know the mind of god. "god hates gays" is a common protest sign of anti-homosexual groups, as though god, and not the sign carrier, is the hater. In such ways, god becomes a projection-phenomenon; it gives unwarranted authority to the worst impulses of the pathological.

The geography is also important; in projections onto a god, the "chosen" group is always the geographic and cultural in-group of the believer. No one ever seems to ask why the god chose only this particular group.

Belief Perseverance

This phenomenon that Festinger and his colleagues documented with Marian Keech's cult was later studied by other social psychologists, including Charles Lord, Lee Ross, and Mark Lepper. It was given the name "belief perseverance:"[23] where beliefs sustain themselves despite contradictory evidence.

In controlled lab studies on this phenomenon, subjects with strong beliefs regarding the effectiveness of the death penalty to deter future violent crimes were presented with two methodologically equivalent studies: one that found evidence for deterrence and one that did not. Those who held a prior belief in the death penalty were more critical of the method used in the study that found no quantifiable effect. Those who believed there was no effect were critical of the study finding one. Each group became more extreme in the direction of their prior belief after exposure to the study opposing it.

The authors described this effect as biased assimilation—in other words, that we tend to select data that confirms our beliefs and disregard or disparage the rest. This produces belief perseverance, the persistence of beliefs through exposure to disconfirming data.

The Seekers and Religion

Marian Keech's mindset was an amalgam of Christianity and Scientology; the latter provided the basis for pseudo-psychological "insights," and, more importantly, the system for structuring a cult around hidden knowledge that granted status within the group. Christianity influenced the theme of salvation via the Guardians (e.g. guardian angels), messages from Sananda (the contemporary Jesus) and eventually, the Creator. The only power struggle described between Mrs. Keech and another follower was over which of them was really the mother of Jesus.*

The solution to their disconfirmation was, in effect, also influenced by Christianity: by using the Abraham-Isaac solution from the Christian bible (Genesis 22; 1-13). Abraham was spared from having to kill his son, Isaac, by god because he showed a willingness to do it (and hence, showed his fear of god).

This "test of faith" is a central Christian tenet: the classic Christian explanation for how faith saves. According to the Christian Apologetics and Research Ministry website, "*There is a very close parallel between the sacrifice of Isaac and the sacrifice of Jesus. Furthermore, you should be able to see that Abraham represented God the Father. Isaac represented God the Son. And the servant represented the God the Holy Spirit. The sacrifice of Christ was typified in the sacrifice of Isaac.*"

So, why did Abraham offer his son Isaac? He did so out of obedience, believing that god could raise him from the dead.

Christian beliefs contain a built-in explanation for disconfirmation, such as when prayers are not answered or a second coming does not occur. That explanation is that "god works in mysterious ways," and thus faith in god is paramount.

In 1997, a cult in San Diego called Heaven's Gate took the prophecy issue to the limit by committing mass suicide in anticipation of their doomsday. The group, led by Marshall Applewhite, had a central dogma that was a blend of

---

* Neither woman had been able to conceive, which carried a stigma in the 1950s; this may have been at least partially behind what drove these women to this specific claim.

Christianity and New Age beliefs. The Christian aspect came from the book of Revelation 11:3, and contained themes of apocalypse and salvation: a type of "end time" where the earth was to be recycled (wiped clean and rejuvenated).

This coming apocalypse was inescapable, so the group decided to leave their vehicles (bodies) behind. They saw this as a test of faith (comparable to the Abraham-Isaac solution), which they described in Applewhite's video, taken just before all 39 members of the group committed suicide using alcohol and barbiturates.

Similar to Mrs. Keech, Applewhite claimed that a comet (Hale-Bopp, which orbits the sun every 4,200 years) was approaching the earth, trailed by a space ship. As with the Seekers, Heaven's Gate believed their souls would board the spaceship, which would take them to a higher level of existence.

In his study of prophecy groups and thinking, cultural historian Paul Boyer links the exponential proliferation of end times groups to the invention of the atomic bomb. Boyer tracks the lengthy history of apocalyptic predictions, and they show a spike after 1948. After the bomb was first used in WWII, apocalyptic prophecy expanded exponentially and became explicitly linked to the bomb.[13]

Predicting the End

Prophecy is not limited to cults like Applewhite's and Keech's but is also central to Christian Evangelical thinking.* Author Tim LaHaye sells huge numbers of books predicting the end

---

* Not coincidently, fundamentalist Christian groups were central in contributing to the social hysteria surrounding Satanic cults[3] in the 1990s.

time is near, arguing that it is predicted by the Christian bible.[24] In his co-edited book, *The Popular Handbook on the Rapture*, LaHaye argues that 1,000 prophecies are made in the bible's scriptures and "over 500 have become fulfilled" (p 15).[24]

The "fulfillment" of these prophecies is elastic, to say the least. LaHaye gives Daniel's interpretation of the King's dream in Babylon as an example of a fulfilled prophecy from the Old Testament: Daniel 2:40, which refers to four future kingdoms followed by the kingdom of god. Christian fundamentalists see this as a prophecy for the end times, when Jesus will return to earth.

LaHaye posits that the *"Babylonian Kingdom, Medo/Persian Empire, Greek Empire and Roman Empire"* (p 17)[24] are the four kingdoms. He claims that *"history is unfolding exactly the way God said it would,"* and could very well reach its zenith in the twenty-first century (p 17).[24]

Of course, there is no way to prove that the kingdoms mentioned by Daniel are the same kingdoms LaHaye describes. In the same timeframe, there has also been the kingdom of the Mongol Empire, the Han Dynasty (which lasted 400 years), the Umayyad Caliphate, the Abbasid Caliphate, the Spanish Empire, the Portuguese Empire, the British Empire, the Russian Empire, the French Colonial Empire, the Yuan Dynasty, the Ming Dynasty, the Tang Dynasty, and the Maya (amongst others). Kingdoms come and go. Stretching or adjusting the evidence to fit the gospel is LaHaye's *modus operandi*.

The Book of Daniel, on which LaHaye and so much prophecy depends, was actually written (by an unknown author) around 167 BCE, but was presented as a four-hundred-year-old text. In this way, events that had already occurred (e.g. Alexander's Conquests, the wars of the Seleucids and the

Ptolemies, Antiochus' persecutions) could be presented as fulfilled prophecies.

The point in doing this was to *"assure faithful Jews reeling under assaults from external enemies that all these events were part of a divine plan that would culminate in the destruction of Israel's foes and the establishment of a righteous and everlasting kingdom"* (p 31).[24] This context is important in understanding the reality of the "prophecies" LaHaye depicts—they were not really prophecies, but were retrospective depictions to serve a political purpose.

LaHaye decries the secularism that pervades the world today, and claims that it is what leads to *"questioning the matter of the origin of the earth"* (p 21)[24] and the *"varying theories of evolution"* (p 21).[24] He calls this *"error-filled knowledge which has been programmed into students through a secular education system,"* (p 21)[24] which ignores that the bible's *"perfect track record of fulfilled prophecies prove man is wrong the bible right"* (p 21).[24] As Lahaye puts it, *"whenever one is confronted with 'the wisdom of man' that questions the Word of God, he had best take God's Word for what it says"* (p 21).[24]

This theme in Christianity, that only the bible contains the true history of man's origin, stems from Paul, who raised the concept of the "wisdom of the wise:" the idea that faith, not reason, should prevail (leading to, as historian Charles Freeman[8] put it, "the closing of the western mind" for 1000 years).

Among the fulfilled prophecies that LaHaye cites are 109 Messianic prophecies that Jesus fulfilled during his time on earth. Although LaHaye says he hasn't the time to list all 109, some of the most important are: being born of a virgin, being born in Bethlehem, having the power to heal, dying, and being resurrected.

Biblical scholar Bart Ehrman[26] also weighs in on the "prophecies" in the Old Testament regarding the coming of the messiah. Many of these "prophecies" were post-dictions, not predictions; that is, they resulted from Christians re-examining the Old Testament after Jesus' crucifixion. There were no Jewish prophecies that a messiah would suffer and die, so they simply took Old Testament passages that described suffering (e.g. Isaiah 53:1-6) and argued that they were referring to a messiah, even though no messiah was named in the originals (p 234).[26]

Similarly, Psalm 22:1-18, *"my God, my God, why have you forsaken me?"* has nothing to do with a messiah. However, Christians reread them after the fact and made them out as "predictions" that referred to Jesus.

Ehrman also examines the Gospel descriptions of Jesus. LaHaye attributes some of these "prophecies" to the book of Matthew, which was written (and rewritten) well after the life of Jesus on earth. It was based on orally-transmitted stories, and the extensive rewriting shaped it with the Old Testament "predictions" of a messiah in mind.

The Gospels that do describe Jesus being born in Bethlehem (Matthew and Luke) contradict each other on several key facts; it also seems much more likely that he was born in Nazareth, where he grew up. However, the writers of the Gospel wanted to shape the narrative to the "prediction" in the Old Testament that a saviour would come from Bethlehem.* The "predictions" that LaHaye described are, in fact, post-dictions, and the key event, the presence of Jesus as messiah, is highly

---

* Micah 5:2: But thou, Bethlehem Ephrathah, though thou be little among the thousands of Judah, yet out of thee shall come forth unto me that is to be ruler of Israel.

dubious; they are not prophesying about Jesus, but rather recounting Christian dogma.

The "fulfilled" prophecies lead to what LaHaye[24] calls *"God's Wonderful Plan for Our Future"* (p 25).[24] This future includes a Rapture following a Church Age, a Glorious Appearing, a Millennium, and a Great White Throne. The appeal is obvious: all human experience is god's plan, so one should feel no personal responsibility, anxiety over difficult choices, or remorse for bad decisions. The future will be wonderful. It's all good, and you're off the hook. LaHaye sells millions of books telling people what they want to hear. It worked for the Book of Daniel, and it works for LaHaye.

LaHaye takes the biblical accounts as a certainty, and states categorically that *"this plan will begin with the rapture of all believers"* (p 26).[24] It will be followed by 100 years of peace, where earth is ruled by Christ. Then there will be a new heaven and Earth (foretold in Revelation 21-22). As LaHaye puts it, *"the second coming of Christ is not an obscure teaching in the bible— it is one of the frequently mentioned future events recorded."* (p 26)[24] LaHaye claims it has been predicted 329 times.

Since *"Jesus' first coming was predicted 109 times and is one of the most certified facts in ancient history"* (p 26),[24] *"then it follows that the 329 predictions of our Lord's Second Coming make it all the more certain"* (p 26).[24] The sheer number of predictions is what generates his certainty.

This argument, of course, is absurd. The number of predictions has no bearing on the certainty of an event; it simply means that a lot of people will be either right or wrong. If it did have a bearing on certainty, we could win the lottery by repetitively "predicting" 10,000 times that we would win it. Wishing does not make it so.

If these predictions come from a small group of believers who influence each other, there is no independence in their predictions, rendering them even less reliable.[26] Even in cases where large numbers of people make predictions, the prediction can, and often does, go wrong.

In his book *Extraordinary Popular Delusions and the Madness of Crowds*,[4] Scottish author Charles Mackay documented historical examples of mass delusions. For example, mass numbers of people prophesied future events such as the Dutch Tulip Mania, where thousands of speculators foresaw the tulip as skyrocketing in value. They invested heavily, even buying "futures" on tulip bulbs. The mania and the price of tulips crashed and burned.

Mackay puts religious prophecies in the same company as these other social delusions. The second coming has been predicted repeatedly throughout the centuries and never confirmed. Like Mrs. Keech's prophecy, religion keeps getting it wrong. In so doing, though, it affords a glimpse into the motivations for religion: the illusion of control generated by forecasting future events.[8] It is a motive evident in humanity's earlier sacrifices to the gods: if we feed the rain god, the crops will be good.

Between 1982 and 2012, there have been numerous dates given for predicted second comings, and it has been publicly predicted around 40 times in the last 300 years.[26] Increases in end time thinking occur whenever general anxiety is high. In his book on end times predictions, Baumgartner[27] reviews millennial thinking in a variety of cults and social movements, including the Crusades, Nazism, Rastafarianism, James Jones, and the Manson Family.

As an example, Martin Luther believed the Pope was the Antichrist, and early Protestants were convinced that they were living in the last days. The proof was the rampant corruption in the church, the papacy's non-biblical authority, and the success of the infidel Turks in taking Constantinople in 1453.

In the latter part of the 15th Century (1455-1498), religion and astrology joined forces to predict the end of the world to come in 1524: a conjunction of all the major planets in the zodiac water sign Pisces meant that a great flood would occur.

In 1970, fundamentalist Hal Lindsey wrote a book called *The Late, Great Planet Earth,* in which he predicted the end of the world via nuclear holocaust.

Evangelical preacher Pat Robertson predicted Armageddon would occur in 1982, and the world would become increasingly apocalyptic as that year approached.[13] However, there was no evidence of him increasing his proselytizing after 1982; instead, he backpedalled: *"There is no way I am going to help the Lord bring the world to an end"* (p 138).[13]

Numerous interviews and quotes show that US President Ronald Reagan and his appointees strongly believed in the second coming. As Reagan told *Christian Life* magazine in 1968, *"Never in history have so many of the prophecies come true in such a relatively short time"* (p 142).[13] His Secretary of Defense, Caspar Weinberger, said in 1982, *"Yes I have read the Book of Revelation and yes, I believe the world is going to end— by an act of God, I hope, but every day I think time is running out"* (p 141).[13] At that time, the Antichrist was identified with the Soviet Union.

LaHaye is on record as predicting the apocalypse would occur on January 1, 2000, triggered by the Y2K bug. There would be economic chaos, followed by the rise of the Antichrist. He retracted this as the date approached.*

In 2015, the Islamic State of Iraq and Syria organization (sometimes called ISIS) had an end times prophecy that required "Rome" (e.g. the west) to be fighting them in the Syrian desert.[29]

Predictions of a second coming, as with those of an apocalypse, increase during times of world unrest and uncertainty. World events that seem insurmountable tend to trigger these predictions.

Prayer

The end times is not the only verifiable prophecy made by religion. The other is prayer. Whether or not prayers have been answered is an empirical question subject to measurement and verification.

Religious adherents do not test these results, but rather rationalize the prayers that have not been answered by using the phrase "god works in mysterious ways." However, the noted cardiologist Herbert Benson and a group of his colleagues subjected prayer to a carefully-designed experimental test aimed at the recovery of cardiac patients.[30]

Patients at six US hospitals, all recovering from a coronary artery bypass graft (CABG) were randomly assigned to 1 of 3 groups: 604 patients in the first group received intercessory

---

* The best summary statement on LaHaye's work is given by Christopher Hitchens in his excellent book, *God is Not Great*.[28] In it, he critiques that LaHaye's series "*was apparently generated by the old expedient of letting two orangutans loose on a word processor*" (p 56). Personally, I find LaHaye absurd, but not chaotic.

prayer (that god would intercede and make the patient well) after being informed that they may or may not receive prayer; 597 did not receive intercessory prayer, also after being informed that they may or may not receive prayer; and a final 601 received intercessory prayer after being informed that they would definitely receive prayer.

Intercessory prayer was provided for 14 days, starting the night before the CABG. The primary measure for success was the presence of any health complication that arose within 30 days of CABG.

The study was well-controlled; subjects were assigned to treatment conditions from the pool of CABG patients at random, so systematic differences (besides the prayer conditions) were eliminated. There were no differences between groups in demographics (all averaged 64 years of age and were about 80% male with similar health histories). About 80% of the members reported that they had religious affiliations. They had virtually identical cardiac health issues. The expectancy effect on patients of receiving prayer was controlled by having conditions where patients were told they either definitely would or may receive prayer.

In the end, there was no difference in recovery between the two groups that were told prayer was a possibility. However, the group that was given the expectation that they would definitely be prayed for showed an increase in the risk of complications—perhaps from added pressure to get well. Across all groups, slightly more than half had complications, but there were no differences according to prayer condition.

It must be added that although the evidence disconfirms the belief that prayer is effective, the process of praying and other "positive strategies" of religious coping is related to other adaptive functions, such as positive affect and heightened self-esteem.[31,32] The irony is that, although prayer doesn't work, if you don't know this and you pray you may feel better. It is the illusion that has psychological benefits. How would evolutionary theorists explain this? I suppose they could argue that evolution is a work in progress: we are not a finished product, and we have evolved somewhat from our illusionary past, but still have a ways to go.

Cultic and Religious Predictions

LaHaye and his co-writers appeal to the "Christian Right" and hold the iron-clad claim that the bible is the word of god. All of their "scholarship" is specious in nature, bending interpretations of biblical passages to fit the idea of a second coming. They never bother to address the difference between when the bible was written and when the events depicted occurred. Interpretations themselves are fluid, as illustrated by the repeated differing predictions of an apocalypse.

The Bible, the Torah, and the Koran were all written in times of extreme ignorance; nothing was known of the shape of the earth, dinosaurs, celestial orbits, the human body, psychology, or even the existence of other societies outside of the Middle East.

Accurate prediction of events, the "litmus test" of any belief system, has never been demonstrated by any religion. In science on the other hand, Mendeleev, a Russian chemist, predicted the periodic table of elements—including 4 elements unknown at the time of his prediction. He did so by organizing the atomic weights of existing elements and seeing patterns from which he extrapolated to the future.

Nikola Tesla, the inventor of alternating current, predicted in 1909 that personal wireless devices (e.g. cell phones) would exist. Darwin predicted the existence of a type of finch based purely on evolutionary principles; it was later found.

Theoretical physicists in the 20th Century, many of whom won the Nobel Prize, often predicted phenomena that were not empirically discovered until decades after their prediction. Robert Oppenheimer, for example, predicted interstellar objects that were not discovered until 40 years later, once the advent of radio telescopes and X-ray satellites allowed them to be seen.[33] Today, we operate a satellite on a comet and beam photos back from Pluto.

Science is astounding. Religion is frozen in time, rendered incapable of change by immutable dogmas.

The Seekers were a typical cult; they had an "infallible" leader who received mystical esoteric knowledge. Status in the group came from demonstrated loyalty to this supreme leader. Only those with such status were privy to inside knowledge. The cult made specific predictions about the coming end of the world, which, of course, were never fulfilled.

Social psychology and, to a lesser extent, sociology and anthropology have studied cults, but have rarely made the assertion that organized religion had much in common with cults. Yet when it comes to religion making predictions about the world, whether through a "doomsday" prediction or the assurance that prayer works, the prediction fails. This suggests that the very epistemology of religious knowledge may be flawed—that faith, is, in fact, not the equal of reason.

REFERENCES

1. Attenborough D. *Quest in paradise*. London: Lutterworth; 1960.
2. Dawkins R. *The god delusion*. Boston: Houghton Mifflin; 2006.
3. Victor JS. *Satanic panic*. La Salle: Open Court; 1993.
4. Mackay C. *Extraordinary popular delusions and the madness of crowds*. New York: Harmony Books; 1980.
5. Festinger L, Riecken H, Schachter S. *When prophecy fails*. Minneapolis: University of Minnesota Press; 1956.
6. Silver N. *The signal and the noise: why so may predictions fail but some don't*. New York: Penguin; 2012.
7. Hecht JM. *Doubt: A history*. New York: Harper One; 2004.
8. Langer E. The illusion of control. *Journal of Personality and Social Psychology*. 1975; 32:311-328.
9. Festinger L. *A theory of cognitive dissonance*. Stanford: Stanford University Press; 1957.
10. Hughes P. *A popular history of the catholic church*. New York: Doubleday; 1954.
11. Graetz H. *History of the jews*. Philadelphia: Jewish Publication Society of America; 1895.
12. Aslan R. *Zealot: the life and times of jesus of nazareth*. New York: Random House; 2013.
13. Boyer P. *When time shall be no more: prophecy belief in modern american culture*. Cambridge: Harvard University Press; 1992.
14. Heath R. *Anabaptism*. London: Alexander and Shepheard; 1895.

15. Sears CE. *Days of delusion: a strange bit of history.* New York: Houghton Mifflin; 1914.
16. Nichol FD. *The midnight cry.* Washington: Review and Herald Publishing; 1944.
17. Taylor K. *Brainwashing.* New York: Oxford University Press; 2004.
18. Quine WvO. *Ontological relativity and other essays.* New York: Columbia University Press; 1969.
19. Haslam SA, Reicher S. Beyond the banality of evil: Three dynamics on an interactive social psychology. *Personality and Social Psychology Bulletin.* 2007; 33:615-622.
20. Sage W. The war on the cults. *Human Behavior.* 1976; October:40-49.
21. Lamm H, Meyers D. Group-induced polarization of attitudes and behavior. *Advances in Experimental Social Psychology.* New York: Academic Press; 1978.
22. Clarens C. *An illustrated history of the horror film.* New York: G.P. Putnam's Sons; 1967.
23. Lord C, Ross L, Lepper MR. Biased assimilation and attitude polarization: The effects of prior theories and subsequently considered evidence. *Journal of Personality and Social Psychology.* 1979; 37:2098-2109.
24. LaHaye T, Ice T, Hindson E. *The popular handbook on the rapture.* Eugene: Harvest House Publishers; 2011.
25. Freeman C. *The closing of the western mind.* New York: Vintage Books; 2002.
26. Ehrman, B. (2009) *Jesus, Interrupted.* New York: Harper One; 2009.
27. Baumgartner FJ. *Longing for the end.* New York: St. Martin's Press; 1999.

28. Hitchens C. *God is not great: how religion poisons everything.* New York: Twelve; 2007.
29. Wood G. What ISIS really wants. *The Atlantic.* New York; 2015.
30. Benson H, Fusey D, Sherwood JB. Study of the therapeutic effects of intercessory prayer (STEP) in cardiac bypass patients: A multicenter randomized trial of uncertainty and certainty of receiving intercessory prayer. *American Heart Journal.* 2006; 151(4):934-942.
31. Ano GG, Vasconcelles EB. Religious coping and psychological adjustment to stress: A meta- analysis. *Journal of Clinical Psychology.* 2005; 61(4):461-480.
32. Pargament KI, Smith BW, Koenig HG, Perez L. Patterns of positive and neagtive coping with major life stressors. *Journal for the Scientific Study of Religion.* 1998; 37(4):710-724.
33. Rhodes R. *The making of the atomic bomb.* New York: Simon & Schuster; 1992.

CHAPTER 2

The Origin of Early Christianity: Birth, Sex, and Death

"Religions' single function is to give man access to powers which seem to control his destiny, and its single purpose is to induce those powers to be friendly to him ... nothing else is essential."
HL MENCKEN: TREATISE ON THE GODS 1930

Fundamentalist views of the bible are contradicted by years of scholarship that study the writing of the bible and the context in which it was written. Current scholarship includes studies of biblical society and textual studies (e.g. the styles of writing used in various time periods). The writing of the bible did not exist in a vacuum; there were many factors that influenced its writing. Consider, for instance, that Jesus was an illiterate Palestinian Jew, living in a time when people had no knowledge of the wider world around them. They had no cultural or geographic awareness beyond the Middle East. They did not know of the Americas, Europe, or Asia; they had no archaeology, anthropology, astronomy, psychology, or modern medicine, and only a rudimentary history. They lived in a culture of magic and superstition, and believed that the world was flat.[1]

For one thousand years before the Common Era (CE being the modern equivalent of AD, *Anno Domini*: "In the year of our Lord"), it was believed that all first-born sons were sons of gods, and human sacrifice, especially of these first-born sons, was common (p 18).[2] The accepted belief at the time was that a god's energy was depleted by the begetting of a child, so the sacrifice was necessary to replenish that energy.

Anyone who performed any extraordinary deeds was said to be a son of god: some examples include Alexander the Great (356-323 BCE), Augustus Caesar (63 BCE - 14 CE), Plato (427 BCE - 347 BCE) and Pythagoras (570-495 BCE).[3] In short, saying that Jesus was a "son of god" tells us more about the Zeitgeist of the times than it does about actual divinity. It tells us how people explained events to themselves, not how things actually were.

The origins of religion, not surprisingly, are related to a need to explain basic human phenomena: sex, birth, survival, and death. Early (pagan) religion was man's attempt to transcend fragility and mortality.[4,5] Anthropologist Ernest Becker argued in his great work, *The Denial of Death*,[4] that we avoid the terror of death by creating an illusion that we have some control over our environment. This was done in ancient times through the practice of sacrifices to the gods. They were made in order to avoid droughts or floods, enhance the harvest, or otherwise enhance control over our own mortality.

The expansion of consciousness in humans, generated by a larger cortex, carried with it the realization, and consequent terror, of death. Becker's great insight was how extensive, debilitating, and demoralizing this terror could be if not buffered. As far as we know, we are the only animal with an awareness of death, although elephants and some other animals appear to sense imminent death.[*]

Mankind has invented numerous buffers against death-terror in the form of belief systems that generate a sense of symbolic immortality. The sacrifice of "others" generated a sense of control over one's fate: a sense of power and escape from death. "Others" were defined as those outside the tribe, who did not believe what the tribe believed: infidels.[6,7]

Most religions have lower moral standards when it comes to actions taken against infidels; they are expendable, and in sacrificing them we both cheat death and reinforce the notion that only believers will triumph. For instance, the Maya sacrificed captives to Chak Muul, the rain god, to prevent drought.

The illusion that we could avoid death by increasing our sense of control was generated by man's "ingenuity:" our ability to use reason and imagination. Becker brought his training in both anthropology and psychoanalysis to bear on this ultimate question about the nature of humanity, and concluded *"it was man's ingenuity, rather than his animal nature, that has given his fellow creatures a bitter earthly fate"* (p 5).[5] Man's "ingenuity" was generated by the development of his pronounced frontal cortex (which governs language and symbolic reasoning).

---

[*] Or so we believe. Elephants appear to have a sense of death and leave the herd to walk off and die.[35] Also, as we discover more about the internal lives of animals, we become less exceptionalist in our view of humanity[36].

From it ensued the ability to contemplate his mortality, as well as planning the means to circumvent that mortality.

Becker saw this prime human motive, the denial of death, as the origin of religion. Man cannot tolerate the notion of a chaotic universe or his own death, and hence, he needs to invent a cause—including a "first cause"—to give the universe meaning and to give him a sense of control. This belief is a man-made illusion. As we shall see, the universe is chaotic, and current thinking in theoretical physics is that we are extremely lucky to have survived our fiery origins on this planet.[8]

By placating a god through sacrifice or benign actions, man created an illusion of control over his fate. Yet religion does not persist merely because it reduces anxiety. Anthropologist Pascal Boyer, in his thoughtful treatise *Religion Explained*,[9] points out that many religious beliefs create anxiety as well (e.g. anxiety about hell), and do not, Boyer claims, *"produce adequate comforting delusions against all situations of stress or fear"* (p 21/375 [Kindle E-book]).

In fact, any organism that was prone to such delusions would not survive long. The task, then, is to explain how religious thoughts provide enough comfort to allay anxiety.

In her book *A History of God*,[2] Karen Armstrong indicates that archaeological evidence for god first showed up about 14,000 years ago, although others place it sooner. Gobekli Tepe, in south-eastern Turkey, is currently considered the world's oldest religious structure, dating back to 9,000 BCE. The structure has many mysteries, one of which being its creation. It is made of huge stones—7 to 10 tons each—but is located at a site far away from any other known settlements and built at a time when the use of domesticated animals to pull heavy loads had not yet been developed. In building it, the ancients attempted to circumvent the fragility and mortality of earthly life by imitating the actions of the gods (p 5).[2] Similarly, Armstrong describes the Babylonian epic poem, the Enuma Elish, as a celebration of the gods over chaos (p 7).[2]

Primordial religion, as journalist Robert Wright calls it,[10] did not have the moral aspect central to modern religion; instead, it was motivated by the belief that the forces of nature were driven by minds or spirits, and could be influenced through negotiation or sacrifice (p 12).[10] For example, the native Haida of the Pacific Northwest believed that earthquakes happened when the sea god's dog shook himself (p 20),[10] not because of anything an individual had done.

Not coincidentally, the advent of early religion corresponded to the evolution of human brain size. This enhanced our capabilities to symbolize, as well as our capability to construct and communicate chains of elaborate ideas and intricate stories. These abilities culminated in an awareness of death and mortality.

Social psychologists Sheldon Solomon, Jeffrey Greenberg, and Thomas Pyszczynski[11] posed the question, *"what happened when a life form, crafted by billions of years of evolution to survive at almost any cost, recognized that it was destined to lose that war?"* (p 67)[11] Their answer was based on Becker's notion that death awareness is debilitating, and that humans have erected multi-layered defences against this awareness.

The foremost example is a belief in a god and an eternity in heaven. The origins of religion appear to coincide with the time archaeologists believe mankind first developed an awareness of mortality. It followed hundreds of thousands of years of the evolution of human consciousness, brain size, and social adaptation to larger groups. And with this evolution of consciousness came the awareness of death and existential dread.

Overwhelming fear of death would be an evolutionary dead-end, stifling the cognitive functioning necessary for survival and reproductive fitness. So, as Solomon and colleagues put it, "Our ancestors made a supremely adaptive, ingenious and imaginative leap: they created a supernatural world, one in which death was not inevitable or irrevocable" (p 67).[11] Excavations of archaeological sites dating back to 26,000 BCE show inhabitants elaborately dressed in burial sites, as if preparing for a special "life beyond."

Evidence consistent with a belief in the everlasting and supernatural coincide with other signs of advances in human cognition such as art, body adornment, elaborate graves, and the worship of deities. The shape and form given to human depictions of god reflect the temporal concerns of the tribe in which they lived.

Further evidence for fear of death as a generator of superstition comes from Malinowsky's[12] study of the Trobriand Islanders. The Islanders were broken into two groups: those who fished the inner lagoons, who relied on knowledge and skill; and those who braved the dangers of the open ocean, who developed superstitions for ensuring their safety and plentiful fish.

In her study of magical thinking, Professor Jane Risen[13] reports studies showing that Germans and Israelis living under stressful circumstances developed more superstitions than others in less stressful circumstances.

In their review of the coexistence of natural and supernatural explanations, Professor Cristine Legare and her colleagues[14] found that natural explanations were usually used to answer "how did this happen" questions, while supernatural explanations would often answer "why did this happen" questions. The answers for "why" a phenomenon occurs are more complicated, and require multiple natural explanations. Therefore a supernatural explanation is easier, even if not as satisfying to the skeptic.

Some religions, notably Christianity and Islam, have beliefs that further assuage the fear of death: the notion of everlasting life in heaven and reconnection with loved ones. There is no underestimating the power of this motive. One only has to look at the various Holy Wars to realize that many, both Christians and Muslims, have died throughout history to fulfill this belief.[7]

Solomon and colleagues have performed numerous ingenious experiments (what they called "terror management" research) where participants were either told to think about death and dying or were exposed to symbols of death. Meanwhile, control subjects were told to think about more mundane tasks, negative thoughts (but not ones involving death, e.g. going to the dentist), or were exposed to neutral symbols.

Exposure to death thoughts or symbolism made the participants adhere more strongly to their normative cultural beliefs, be more punitive to outsiders, and invest in a wide variety of "transcendent practices" (i.e. ones that promised a subjective feeling of immortality). The adherence to normative practices reinforces the idea that one's cultural worldview will survive the individual and hence, symbolically, we will survive as well. We cling to this notion like a life preserver on a stormy sea, although this process is largely unconscious.

Terror management research finds that dual-defences are erected against death.[15] The first type of defence involves the rational control of conscious thoughts. This is used most often when we are exposed to observable ideas or images of death. The second type is used when we are exposed to subliminal thoughts or images—ones that appear and disappear too quickly to be seen and processed rationally. These subliminal images of death trigger a heightened belief in the norms and mores of the socializing culture, and are thus called the "worldview defence." This latter defence suggests that an unconscious network of associations exists, which includes the cognitions instilled by socialization. These serve the function of reducing death anxiety.

At the centre of many sets of cultural beliefs is a set of religious beliefs. These beliefs serve many functions, including group identity (e.g. I am a Muslim), an enhanced trust in fellow believers,[16] and even a comforting belief in an afterlife, where we can be together with our dearly departed. This latter belief, called "attachment in perpetuity"[7] is the ultimate cognitive response to death terror. No thought is more reassuring than the notion that we will meet our beloved on the other side.

But even in religions that do not hold this central tenet, the very fact that religion represents a belief system that transcends human life expectancy allows it to serve as a form of distal defence against death terror.

Female Deities

The rise of monotheistic male gods started with the Mesopotamian god Aten in the 14th Century BCE, who took the form of a falcon-headed man. The reign of Amenhotep III in Egypt occurred around the same time. The deceased king was described as rising as a god to the heavens and uniting with the sun-disk.

This concept of the divine body merging with its maker may have been a precursor to the Christian myth of resurrection. In his book *Moses and Monotheism*, Freud suggested that Moses was in Egypt during Aten's worship and carried the idea of monotheism to Canaan, where it launched Judaeo-Christian civilization (p 94).[10]

Prior to this, god was worshipped as a female deity (the mother goddess)[17, 18, 20] who lived amongst the other gods (p 5).[2] The pagan cosmology was essentially polytheistic, with female deities sometimes inhabiting a place at or near the apex of the hierarchy of gods. Not coincidently, these beliefs were held by people who accorded women high status because of their perceived magical ability to create life.[18]

In the Palaeolithic period, when agriculture was just beginning, the cult of the mother goddess expressed a sense that the fertility that generated human life was actually sacred. Archaeologist Marija Gimbutas argued that, based on radiocarbon dating and other evidence,* female deities were worshipped for 20,000 years before patriarchal religions:[17] not as a sole goddess, but as one that existed as part of a polytheistic set of god-like creatures, including cosmic snakes and eggs (p 89).[17, 18]

In "Old Europe," as Gimbutas termed it (Eastern Europe from 7000-3500 BCE), complex civilizations developed that had well-defined religions; art and pottery of the times depicted

---

* Radiocarbon dating is used to date organic material (e.g. wood or leather), based on the decay of an unstable isotope, Carbon-14. The method is reliably accurate as far back as about 50,000 years ago. Its inventor, Willard Libby, won the Nobel Prize in Chemistry for its invention in 1960.

recurrent themes and abstract concepts. For example, moon and water symbolized the rotation of seasons and the perpetuation of life; the cross symbolized (in its pre-Christian form) the four corners of the world.

The mythologies of these early eras—Egyptian, Babylonian, Hindu, and Greek—preserved the myths of a universe created from a cosmic egg. The themes depicted water, from which a cosmic snake emerged. The snake created another cosmic egg from which the gods were born. Sometimes birds and snakes were represented as goddesses with female features and connected to symbols of fecundity. In some areas a bear goddess was worshipped.

These themes are found throughout the ancient east. Wright claims that a variety of polytheistic religions existed,[10] each with their pantheon of gods in a hierarchy. Slowly, and with a different pace in different areas, a male deity prevailed as the chief god, the one to whom we returned when we died.

The female deity was associated with birth and with fluid. The interpretation of these images in modern times may reflect modern values. However, one can't help but wonder how childbirth, with the release of amniotic fluid, must have been inexplicable to the ancients. Thus, gods were invented to explain the inexplicable.

Creation

The ancient Babylonians believed that the gods emerged from a watery waste; their epic creation poem, the Enuma Elish (written between the 18th and the 16th Century BCE and discovered in Turkey in the 19th Century CE) describes a chaos of eternal material: a sort of formless swamp, that lacked both boundary and identity (p 6).² It portrays the gods as emerging from this infinite watery waste of raw material.² This image closely resembled the swampy wastelands of Mesopotamia where they lived: floods constantly threatened human works, and a sense of fragility in the face of nature was pervasive.

We cannot rule out, however, the connection of the experience when the birth canal is breached and amniotic fluids escape to their consequent belief that all life stemmed from a watery source. What would the ancients, with no knowledge of human physiology, have made of the "breaking of waters" at birth? Since the entire process of conception and birth was magic to them, one can see how water might become a magical symbol of creation.

The Enuma Elish is believed to be the content of a once-recited ritual, perhaps of the Babylonian New Year. The emerging gods were initially inferior versions until Marduk, the sun god (son of Tiamat and Apsu) arrived and fought his mother for supremacy. The creation was a struggle against overwhelming odds and reads like a Greek tragedy. At this time, polytheism was still the prevailing view, and Marduk shared heaven with the goddess Sarpanit.

Recent research on the origins of the earth reinforce the notion that life emerged against overwhelming odds.⁸ Ancient man must have sensed the dread of existence, but could not have fully understood just how haphazard his existence really was. As an afterthought, Marduk created humanity to serve the gods (p 9).¹⁹

The Enuma Elish may be the source for the Genesis account of creation in the Hebrew bible. Marduk was the god of Babylon in the time of King Hammurabi (p 88).¹⁰ As Babylon extended its political power throughout Mesopotamia,

Marduk became the "chief god," although not the only god in Mesopotamia. This stage of religion frequently had a hierarchy of gods, called a monolatry.

Robert Wright sees the evolution of gods from polytheism, through this hierarchy of gods, to monotheism as indicative of an evolution in the human quest for intellectual order. In this evolution, Marduk became a "grand unified theory of nature" (p 88):[10] he was a step between the chaos of polytheism and later monotheism.

The transition phase was essentially worshipping one god while accepting the existence of other gods (but rejecting the worship of those of foreign origin). Gods were accepted for worship largely as a product of political alliances: my allies' gods are acceptable, my enemies' are not.

In any event, the marriage of politics and religion was beyond dispute, both in man's early days and in modern history; Catholics in Latin America are Catholic because of the Conquest, Muslims in Persia are Muslim because of the Islamic conquests. As Karen Armstrong said in her history of religion and violence, *"Ancient peoples would have found it impossible to see where 'religion' ended and 'politics' began"* (p 5/392 [Kindle]).[19]

Despite this universal connection of the religious and the political, Armstrong puts the blame for religious violence in her later book, *Fields of Blood*, on the politicizing of religion.[19]

The Egyptian Book of the Dead (1,500 BCE) described Egyptian creation myths as beginning with divinities of water, darkness, formlessness, and emptiness.[20] Every act of creation represented the thought of a high creator—god—and its expression in words. Primeval waters were divided, and a primeval hill (the Earth) arose from those waters. In the Egyptian belief system, there was a higher god (amongst many), who was the creator of all and kept the primeval waters at bay.

The Christian bible reflects these creation themes; its cosmology is a product of the times when it was written, with all the limitations of that period. For example, it views the Earth as immovable (Psalm 93:1, 96; 10), and that only earthquakes, which are the product of god, move the Earth. The rest of the visible universe, including the sun, moved around the Earth (Ecclesiastes 1:5, Job 9:7).* The stars were brought out each night by god (Isaiah 40:26).

Compare this to the Babylonian Enuma Elish (1,100 BCE), in which the god Marduk maintained the motions of the stars.[20] There was obviously no knowledge of modern cosmology in the Christian bible. Much later, the Catholic church threatened Galileo with torture for providing a cosmological view compatible with empirical observation, such as the Earth's shadow on the moon and the function of tides,[20] which were consistent with the view of Earth revolving around the sun.

Gimbutas argues that these recurrent themes—water, birds, eggs, and women—originated in the Paleolithic Era (which ended around 10,000 BCE) and persisted into the Neolithic Era (10,000 to 3500 BCE). Before 10,000 BCE, Proto-Indo-Europeans existed in small bands of hunter-gatherers.

---

* In the 16th Century, such notions were still moving the Catholic Church to oppose a new theory by Copernicus, who argued that the sun, not the Earth, was central (heliocentrism). Dominican Bishop Giovanni Tolosani wrote *On the Truth of Sacred Scripture*, a rebuttal to Copernicus' major work *De Revolutionibus*. In his book, the Bishop argued that Copernicus used "mere mathematical devices," which could not determine physical causes. Therefore, Copernicus should not use the inferior field of science to oppose the superior field of religion.

These people then developed an agricultural existence in the Middle East and Eastern Europe.

Wright describes modern hunter-gatherer societies as tending to be polytheistic and animistic, frequently with one god amongst many who has greater importance (p 17-19).[10] It is hypothesized that hunter-gatherers evolved into larger groups in order to better protect breastfeeding mothers with infants (p 64).[10] The larger groups also made it easier to ward off predators and obtain food; the hunting of food began the evolution of the greater cooperation required to kill larger, more dangerous animals.

This cooperation also required sexual exclusivity and the drive to protect this exclusivity from dominant males—hence the evolution of monogamy and marriage. Mankind became a social animal with rules of behaviour designed to reduce conflict within the group. The existing view of the gods was a projection of this social arrangement into a heavenly milieu.

Goddess to God

Early farming communities date back to the Levant (Jericho and West Bank), between 10,000 and 8800 BCE. By 6900 BCE, signs of domesticated cattle and pigs are found in archaeological digs. Also found are carved statues of god as a naked, pregnant woman, which archaeologists have found in many places in Europe, the Middle East, and India (p 5, 201).[2]

By the fifth and fourth millennia, this goddess was clothed, except for her abdomen. There usually lay images of the sacred serpent (p 201).[2] This form was also found in amulets, used to foster fecundity. Pregnancy was expressed with a dot impressed on the abdomen.

This goddess of Life and Death was the central deity from the seventh to the fifth millennium BCE, and was later transformed into the more recognizable ancient goddesses. She became known as Ishtar in Babylon, Isis in Egypt, and Gaia and Aphrodite in Greece.[17,18]

Ishtar was the goddess of love, war, fertility, and sexuality, and was the divine personification of the planet Venus. When Ishtar descended to the underworld, all sexual activity ceased on Earth. She is depicted as bad-tempered and petulant in the Epic of Gilgamesh, which is considered to be the first form of recorded literature (written in cuneiform script), dated around 1200 BCE.[22]

A second female deity represented untamed nature, the divine femininity of nature, and the protection of the weak. She was called Artemis and Kallisto in Greece, and Diana in Rome, and possessed attributes of both virginity and maternal protection. This goddess was present everywhere in nature, and sometimes took the form of a bear or a doe. Rousing her anger caused the death of women in childbirth.

Archaeologists may dispute the timing and exact location of the influences of gods and goddesses, but it is clear that mankind developed an image of god that was a projection from his own society and values; man in short, makes god.

When someone has only a single religious viewpoint, or has accepted the framework of one particular religion, this point is lost. When one examines religious beliefs across times and cultural periods, it becomes inescapable.

The religions of early cultures (e.g. Sumerian, Babylonian, Egyptian) had a panoply of gods, both male and female. Families in those times were depicted as circling a large female figure, with a smaller male figure at the periphery. These male and female principles were in historical opposition leading to an (d)evolved depiction of one god as male.

As Armstrong puts it, *"ancient philosophies were entranced by the order of the cosmos; they marvelled at the mysterious power that kept the heavenly bodies in their orbits and the seas within bounds and that ensured that the earth regularly came to life again after the dearth of winter"* (p 6/392 [Kindle]).[19]

This fascination with the creation of life may easily have extended to the female "magic" of birth. Man did not yet make the causal connection between sexual intercourse and pregnancy, so female fecundity was still a magical process.

In his encyclopedic review of sexual relations throughout history,[23] historian Amaury de Riencourt argued that magical, pre-rational thinking about sexuality gave way to cause and effect thinking. *"The gradual awareness of man's biological role in determining pregnancy, understood in terms of rough causality, implies that sometime between the fifth and third or second millennia BC (depending on culture and geographic location), man crossed a mental threshold from magico-symbolic thought processes to rational thinking: the same fact (connection between coitus and pregnancy) that had been observed for some time was now understood quite differently in causal, and no longer magical terms"* (p 33).[23]

This radical change in thought became reflected in religion. Goddess worship gave way first to patriarchy in Indo-European societies, and then to the patriarchal "desert religions:" Christianity, Judaism, and Islam. In short, god changed to represent the form believed to be the most powerful at the time. When women held the magical key to creation, god was cast as a woman. When patriarchy developed, god became male.

During the times in between, the power of life and death slowly moved from female to male. For instance, the Greek gods such as Zeus were believed to foster offspring, which they sometimes ate. The other gods weren't denied, but there was a clear focus on the one. The monolatry of Greek religion was a step toward monotheism.

Freud[26] believed god was an illusion—a projection of the human need to be protected. If man created god, the image of god would be in the human form that held the most contemporary power, viewed in the same terms as one viewed the top of the human hierarchy. This is the form most capable of protection.

In fact, this is what archaeology reveals. The reality of gods in the days of this early period may have been intense: mankind literally hallucinated gods in those days, according to psychologist Julian Jaynes.[25] Jaynes argues that our modern perception of internal dialogues between ourselves and another is clearly viewed as something we create in our own mind.

However, around 1000 BCE, people were unaware that the second voice came from within themselves. They thought the second voice was a god—usually a minor household god that offered them advice or orders (now called command hallucinations). The origin of these second voices was the right brain hemisphere, which concedes dominance to the side that controls audible speech.

Shifting Gender, Shifting Power

Based on the work of Marija Gimbutas,[17] Riane Eisler expanded the view of matriarchal religion. She argued that Christianity replaced female-oriented *"partnership societies with hierarchical ones where females were devalued. In societies with patriarchal religion, a dominator model evolved which entailed destroying all competition"* (p 98).[19] For Christianity, the competition included Judaism, pagan religion, and heresy.

Eisler idealized early society, and appeared to believe that those with matriarchal religions were non-violent. However, Canadian psychologist Steven Pinker,[26] on examining the archaeological data in his book, *The Better Angels of Our Nature*, estimates that on average violent deaths in all pre-state societies (hunter-gatherer, hunter-horticulturalist, and other tribal groups) accounted for 15% of all deaths, compared to 3% for modern states. Worshipping female deities did not curb violence.

For Eisler, it was the maleness of patriarchy that caused the problems. In comparison, de Riencourt described that Christianity initially held an appeal to women, despite the patriarchy.

Christianity altered thinking about sex; instead of the pagan condoning of prostitution, sex now fell under rigid standards and was confined to monogamous marriage. Furthermore, it brought marriage from the status of social contract to religious sacrament; it had become insoluble, and enhanced the dignity and security of wife and mother. De Riencourt suggests this was of enormous import to women: it acted against the double-standard to which they had been subjected. For this reason, many early Christians were female.

Part of the later anti-female perspective of Christianity seems embedded in Saint Augustine's view that sex represented a departure from an awareness of god. This loss is repeated throughout human history by "concupiscence." The temptress to engage in concupiscence was woman,[2] and Adam's original sin (seeking knowledge and, hence, turning from god) was passed on through generations by the act of sex (p 123-124).[2]

As Armstrong puts it, "*A religion which looks askance upon half the human race and which regards every involuntary motion of mind, heart and body as a symptom of fatal concupiscence can only alienate men and women from their condition*" (p 124).[2] Early Christian writers such as Saint Jerome and Tertullian literally loathed women (p 124),[2] and Paul loathed sex. Armstrong cites Augustine as "*clearly puzzled God made the female sex*" since, if it was good company and conversation that Adam needed, it would have been better to have two men together as friends (p 124).[2]

Christianity: Born from Political Turmoil

According to Jewish historian Josephus, the 1st Century CE was a time of political upheaval, Roman repression, and political powerlessness. Pontius Pilate, who had become Roman Prefect in 26 CE, was cruel, cold-hearted, and rigid (p 46-47),[27] and responded to any minor protest from the Jews with their slaughter. Pilate was so violent he was summoned to Rome to explain himself after massacring the Samaritans in 36 CE and was replaced as Prefect of Judaea.

However, during his ten-year term as governor, Pilate had already crucified thousands of Jews. At this time, the Jewish high priest was Caiaphas, a wealthy Jew appointed in 18 CE, who had a close working relationship with Pilate (p 48).[27]

Various rebel groups existed in Judaea at that time, including the Zealots and the Sicarii (dagger men) who assassinated both Romans and prominent Jewish families that cooperated with the Roman tyrants (p 57)[27] The term "zealot" stems from this determined and organized Jewish resistance to Roman rule.

During this century, many Jews proclaimed themselves to be the messiah who would lead the Jews from servitude. These included Judas the Galilean, his son Menahim (who assassinated a Jewish high priest in 56 CE),* Theudas (who worked miracles and was decapitated by the Romans), Jesus son of Anaias (p 53)[27] and Simon.

As a ray of optimism against overwhelming Roman power, the concept of the messiah was foremost in Jewish thought at this time. A Jewish rebellion occurred in 66 CE, generating a Roman attack and the rebellion's subsequent destruction and slaughter. Seven years after that, the Sicarii (a group of Jewish zealots) fled to Masada, where they famously committed mass suicide in 73 CE rather than be captured by the Roman army.

It is not surprising that the mindset of the times was a fervent wish that some individual would be sent by god to liberate the people.[27] The notion of a messiah had long been a part of religious folklore, even before Judaism or Christianity, and it became a virtual obsession during the Roman occupation of Judaea.

This backdrop of Roman occupation and repression of the Jews led to a near-obsession with the coming of a messiah who would deliver them from Roman control. There were several would-be messiahs at the time, but only one persuaded his followers that he was divine.

---

* Menahim declared himself to be the son of god, and because of this hubris, was tortured to death by the Jewish Temple priests (p 59).

Christianity Borrows from Older Religions

The Christian church was fighting for popularity in the 2nd and 3rd Centuries, and debate in the church included whether the resurrection was real or symbolic. As we saw above, the Egyptian religion already had themes of death and resurrection. What better way to gain a more widespread acceptance than to use those concepts that are already in place? The Jesus parable became a way for the Christian church to make these themes more vivid.

As de Riencourt puts it, *"In one of the most amazing campaigns ever recorded in the history of religions, pagan deities were transmuted wholesale into saints or angels, introducing a mild form of polytheism through the back door, the most important ones—Horus, Adonis, Attis, Mithra, Ba'al—were absorbed into Jesus while the Virgin incorporated Demeter, Diana, Isis, Venus and the Magna Mater ... the great ageless theme of the death and rebirth of the male God sacrificed in fertility cults was remade into the Crucifixion, Death and Resurrection of Christ; even the old festivals of the dead became All Soul's Day ... bit by bit, the church absorbed into itself and metabolized all the great religious themes of a past that would not be stamped out"* (p 152).[23]

Canadian biblical scholar Tom Harpur[30] also argues that Christianity simply took allegories from older religions and incorporated them. *"Either deliberately, in a competitive bid to win over the greatest numbers of the unlettered masses, or through wilful ignorance of the true, inner sense of the profound spiritual wisdom it had inherited from so many ancient sources, the Church took a literalist, popularized, historical approach to the sublime truth"* (p 2).[30]

To the Persians, the prophet Zoroaster was born of a virgin birth, and Perseus, Adonis, and Attis were all ancient gods born of virgins (p 157).[3] It may be that the story of Jesus was altered over time to incorporate these more popular, pre-existing features.

The pre-Christian Sumerians and Egyptians had, as a central tenet of their religion, the notion of an indwelling god or divine essence in the human (p 35).[30] In Babylonian myth, Marduk created mankind by mixing divine blood with dust; hence, mankind had divinity within it (p 9),[2] in that man and god derived from the same original substance.

Numerous pagan religions had a concept of a saviour, including Osiris, Horus, Krishna, Orpheus, and others. The Persian Zoroaster issued a prophecy: *"A virgin should conceive and bear a son and a star would appear at midday to signal the occurrence ... when you behold the star, follow it to where it leads you and adore the mysterious child, offering gifts with humility"* (p 37).[30]

The discovery of the Rosetta Stone* in 1799, which enabled the deciphering of ancient Egyptian hieroglyphics, allowed students of comparative religion to make the discovery of these connections to earlier religions. All of them have been strongly opposed by the Christian church (p 7).[30]

Harpur cites authors Freke and Gandy[32] when they state that the Jesus myth was based on pagan stories of a "god-man"

---

* The trilingual Rosetta Stone was inscribed with a decree issued at Memphis in 196 BCE by Ptolemy V. The decree said the same thing in three languages (Ancient Egyptian Hieroglyphic, Demotic and Ancient Greek). The complete transliteration was completed by Jean-Francois Champollion in 1822.

in various cultures, called Osiris, Dionysius, Adonis, Bacchus, and Mithras. The *"hero is the saviour of mankind, God incarnate, born of a virgin in a cave on December 25, has a star appear at this birth, is visited by magi from the east, turns water into wine at a wedding, heals the sick, casts out demons, performs miracles, is transfigured before his disciples, rides a donkey into a special city, is betrayed for thirty pieces of silver, is put to death on a cross, descends into hell, is resurrected on the third day, dies to redeem the world's sins, ascends into heaven and is seated beside God. He represents Christos, the divine soul of every human being"* (p 68).[32] Osiris was widely worshipped as the god of the dead until the suppression of the Egyptian religion during the rise of Christianity.

Robert Wright, in his book *The Evolution of God*,[10] says, *"Osiris, who had been a major God in Egypt for millennia, bore a striking resemblance to the Jesus described in the Nicene Creed. He inhabited the after world, and there he judges the recently deceased, granting eternal life to those who believed in him and lived by his code"* (p 121).[10] Wright describes this as a "marketing problem" for early Christian evangelists.[33]

The pagan religions that preceded Christianity shared many of the same central beliefs and doctrines. The first known use of the crucifix symbol, a being on a cross, was the sun god Orpheus on a cross from 300 BCE (p 45).[30]

British writer Gerald Massey states that the crucifix was not the sign of Christianity in the early centuries: it was a bare cross or a cross with a lamb. Not until circa 600 CE does the crucifix appear. Massey argued that the crucifix fosters an unspoken belief that suffering is good and must be complied with; hence, compliance and conformity.

In his examination of Egyptian religion,[28] Massey describes four scenes depicted in the Temple of Luxor, in the chapel built by Amenhotep III (1300 BCE). They depict:

1) A god (Taht) hailing a virgin queen and announcing to her that she is to give birth to the coming son of god
2) Another god giving new life
3) The newborn god-child supported by its mother and nurses, and
4) Three wise men offering gifts in adoration of the god-child (p 5)[28]

The scenes, Massey argues, were mythical in Egyptian religion—depicting a universal concept—but were copied and reproduced in the Christian Gospels. There, they were concentrated into a single person and said to have actually existed (p 38).[30]

The events described in Egyptian religion were thought of as timeless spiritual truths, as symbols. The Egyptian religion mentioned the "messianic son," represented by the sun itself, who came mythically as the manifestation of god; he then became matter. In the Egyptian ritual, this god came every day, but also cycled periodically during solstice and equinoxes.

Instead of a "second coming," the Egyptian god's "comings" were at specific parts of the lunar cycle. Natural phenomena were taken to be symbols of god's spiritual coming. As Harpur put it, *"there was no manic expectation of some supernatural, apocalyptic 'second coming.' It was happening to those who opened themselves to it here and now, step by step."* (p 40).[30]

Tom Harpur argues that Christianity changed dramatically in its first four centuries: from a cult with origins in pagan religions, where resurrection and virgin birth were symbolic themes, to a literalist movement with state power. In this latter form, the resurrection had become a historical event.

During this transformation, the thinkers who were revered at the beginning (early Christianity) became heretics by the end. The process included "downgrading" the original thoughts of resurrection as a symbolic event to a literal one that the common people could grasp. This belief system had greater appeal to the masses, and thus converted myth to history. Harpur cites Massey as saying, "*The mythos having been last published as human history, everything else was suppressed to support the fraud*" (p 56).[30]

According to theosophist Alvin Kuhn in his book, *The Shadow of the Third Century*,[29] Christian suppression of dissent included the murder of opponents of the "true religion," the mass burning of books (including pagan works, the Talmud, and the works of Maimonides, the renowned Jewish philosopher and theologian), and the destruction of libraries. Christian mobs destroyed libraries at Bibracte, Arles, and Alexandria, all of which contained scrolls and books of pagan philosophy. Harpur lists several pages of such repressions and book burnings. These "pious frauds" were held as acceptable by the church because the "cause was just" (p 58).[30]

Indicative of the fury of these Christian mobs was the murder of Hypatia, an early female philosopher, astronomer, and mathematician in Alexandria, who was stoned and torn apart with oyster shells in 451 CE. She was viewed as emblematic of the old intellectual order.

In light of this violent repression and mass destruction of all forms of "heresies," it seems like the Gnostic Gospels may have been hidden in an attempt to escape the onslaught. The Gospels, found at Nag Hammadi in 1945, depicted a very different view of Christ and Christianity. Charles Freeman also subscribes to this view,[34] noting that the Gnostic Gospels were hidden during the 4th Century, *"when imperial legislation required the burning of heretical books ... this may well have been the reason why they were hidden"* (p 147).[34]

In his work *Sapiens*, historian Yuval Harari[33] argues that religious intolerance began with monotheism. Since polytheists such as the Egyptians, Romans, and Aztecs believed in one supreme and disinterested power and many partial powers, they rarely tried to force conversions or punish alternate religions. The only god the Romans resisted was the monotheistic and evangelizing god of the Christians.

Even then, the Roman Empire did not require Christians to give up their rituals, only to pay respect to the empire's protective gods and the divinity of the emperor. When the Christians refused to pay political loyalty, the Romans began to persecute what they viewed as a subversive faction. Probably no more than a few thousand Christians were killed by the Romans, compared to millions later killed by fellow Christians in religious wars between Catholics and Protestants.

Suppression and power struggles characterized the early Christian church from the 1st to the 4th Century, and transformed it from an organization of debate and philosophical search to one of dogma and repression. The themes of earlier religions had now become "facts" about the life of Jesus.

Virtually all the original thinkers who had shared in the building of the Christian movement in the earliest times (e.g. Origen)* were proclaimed as heretics by the 3rd Century. Harpur calls this transformation of the early church a "crime of major magnitude" (p 65).[30]

It was this latter ethos that became codified by Constantine and the Nicaean Council, when Christian dogma was enshrined into Roman Law.[34] The only remaining argument at the Nicaean Council focused on whether Jesus was both divine and human—called Arianism—or that god, Jesus, and the Holy Ghost were all the same substance (the substance being unknown)—this later became known as the Holy Trinity. The Arians argued that Jesus had to have some humanity; otherwise, he would not have suffered on the cross. They were voted down.**

According to biblical scholar Bart Ehrman[31] the earliest existing manuscripts of the New Testament date from this later time—the late 3rd and 4th Century. The earliest (not existing) manuscripts are dated to 60-80 CE; at least 30 years after the death of Jesus. They were purportedly written in Greek. Ehrman[31] takes issue with the argument that Jesus evolved from pagan myth because there is no evidence for this claim—only the connection.

As a scholar of early Christianity and the New Testament, and capable of reading Aramaic, Hebrew, and Greek, Ehrman is well-positioned to assess the evidence. Ehrman argues that there

---

* Origen (184-253 CE) was an early Christian ascetic. He argued that Jesus was subordinate to god, a position called Arianism. This subordination gave Christ the capacity for human suffering (as he did on the cross). He also argued that everyone would be welcomed in heaven and that god was essentially good and forgiving. Described by Freeman[34] as an intellectual hero to Christians of the 3rd and 4th Centuries, Origen was branded a heretic by the 6th Century (p 186-189).

** In the 16th Century, polymath scientist Michael Servetus renewed the Arian argument. He was burnt at the stake.

is no evidence for resurrection in Egyptian theological views, and that Christianity developed out of Judaism, not Egyptian religion. However, Ehrman does not read Sanskrit or cuneiform hieroglyphics. He does not dispute the "pious fraud" that Harpur speaks of regarding the prosecution of non-Christian faiths; just the sourcing of Christianity to Egypt.

If Freud was right, Moses was exposed to Egyptian monotheism in Egypt and transmitted the notion back to Canaan. However, as we shall see, the "exodus" of the Jews from Egypt to Canaan is, in itself, dubious.

Various scholars of ancient religions see repetition of earlier myths in Christianity. Karen Armstrong, in her review of ancient religion[2] concluded, *"the death of a God, the quest of a goddess and the triumphant return to the religious sphere were constant religious themes in many cultures and would recur in the very different religion of the One God worshipped by Jews, Christians and Muslims"* (p 11).[2] The main issue seems not to be that Christianity developed from earlier religions, but specifically whether the source was Egyptian or Judaic.

Journalist Robert Wright[10] outlines two perspectives on religion (p 44).[10] One is that it serves as a bonding function for a social group. Its members come to believe in a "Big god" who watches their every move; therefore, they come to believe that others who also believe in this god will act honourably. This form of social trust became necessary when mankind moved to larger groups, and had to decide whether or not to trust anonymous strangers. In this vein, religion served an important social function.

The second perspective is that religion serves the powerful in any social hierarchy: an argument put forward by Karl Marx and by the anthropologist Paul Radin in his book

Primitive Religion. Religion numbs people to their exploitation; it has them instead focus on a future in heaven, and generates the fear of eternal punishment avoidable only through adherence to the precepts of the religion.

There is historical evidence for both functions, as well as for a third: to generate cohesiveness within a religious group through the focus on a shared enemy: the "unbelievers." In different times and places, these enemies are defined as atheists, Jews, Sunni Muslims, Shia Muslims, Protestants, or Catholics.

Religion: How Far It's Come

Religion originated as a set of beliefs about the supernatural, which assuaged man's newly developed terror of death. It helped social trust develop in larger, complex societies and was then elaborated into themes of creation and the governing of sexuality. Generically, religion survived because it offered an easily-grasped set of answers to baffling questions, generated an illusion of control over fate, and conferred status on co-believers to further group solidarity.

The historical concerns of religion, such as a virgin birth, resurrection, and immortality, were themes for millennia. In Christianity, they then became personified into one entity: Jesus. The age-old questions were "answered" by political fiat, directed by Constantine. As we shall see, there is evidence for a historical Jesus, but not for a Jesus Christ.

Early Christianity was a vibrant set of religious arguments questioning the virgin birth and the resurrection. All that questioning came to an abrupt halt when Christianity became the official religion of Rome. After four hundred years of sectarian in-fighting, the Christian creation myth was set in stone.

REFERENCES

1. Manchester W. *A world lit only by fire.* New York: Back Bay Books; 1992.
2. Armstrong K. *A history of god.* New York: Knopf; 1993.
3. Tobin P. The bible and modern scholarship. *The Christian delusion.* Amherst: Prometheus Press; 2010.
4. Becker E. *The denial of death.* New York: The Free Press; 1973.
5. Becker E. *Escape from evil.* New York: The Free Press; 1975.
6. Waller J. *Becoming evil: how ordinary people committ genocide and mass killing.* New York: Oxford University Press; 2002.
7. Dutton DG. *The psychology of genocide, massacres and extreme violence.* Westport: Praeger International; 2007.
8. Hawking S, Mlodinow L. *The grand design.* New York: Bantam Books; 2010.
9. Boyer P. *Religion explained: the evolutionary origins of religious thought.* New York: Basic Books; 2001.
10. Wright R. *The evolution of god.* New York: Little, Brown & Co.; 2009.
11. Solomon S, Greenberg J, Pyszcynski T. *The worm at the core: on the role of death in life.* New York: Random House; 2015.
12. Malinowsky B. *Magic, science, and religion and other essays.* Boston: Beacon Press; 1948.
13. Risen JL. Believing what we do not beleive: Acquiescence to superstitious beliefs and other powerful intutions. *Psychological Review.* 2016; 123(2):182-207.

14. Legare C, Evans EM, Rosengren KS, Harris PL. The coexistence of natural and supernatural explanations across cultures and development. *Child Development.* 2012; 83(3):779-793.
15. Pyszczynshi T, Greenberg J, Solomon S. A dual-process model of defense against conscious and unconscious death-related thoughts: An extension of terror management theory. *Psychological Review.* 1999; 106(4):835-845.
16. Norenzayan A. *Big gods: how religion transformed cooperation and conflict.* Princeton: Princeton University Press; 2013.
17. Gimbutas M. *Goddesses and gods of old europe 7000-3500 B.C.* Los Angeles: University of California Press; 1982.
18. Eisler R. *The chalice and the blade.* New York: Harper One; 1995.
19. Armstrong K. *Fields of blood: religion and the hisory of violence.* New York: Knopf; 2014.
20. Babinski ET. *The cosmology of the bible.* Amherst: Prometheus Press; 2010.
21. Freeman C. *The closing of the western mind.* New York: Vintage Books; 2002.
22. Guirand F. Assyro-babylonian mythology. *New Larousse Encyclopedia of Mythology.* London: Hamlyn; 1968.
23. de Riencourt A. *Sex and power in history.* New York: Delta; 1974.
24. Freud S. *The future of an illusion.* New York: W.W. Norton & Co.; 1961.
25. Jaynes J. *The origin of consciousness in the breakdown of the bicameral mind.* New York: Houghton Mifflin; 1976.
26. Pinker S. *The better angels of our nature: why violence has declined.* New York: Viking; 2011.

27 Aslan R. *Zealot: the life and times of jesus of nazareth*. New York: Random House; 2013.
28. Massey G. *Gerald massey's lectures*. Brooklyn: A&B Books Publishers; 1900/1998.
29. Kuhn AB. *Shadow of the third century: a reevaluation of christianity*. Kila: Kessinger Publishing; 1997.
30 Harpur T. *The pagan christ*. Toronto: Thomas Allen; 2004.
31 Ehrman B. *Did jesus exist? The historical argument for jesus of nazareth*. New York: Harper One; 2012.
32 Freke T, Gandy P. *The jesus mysteries: was the original jesus a pagan god?* New York: Three Rivers Press; 1999.
33 Harari Y. *Sapiens*. New York: Random House; 2014.
34. Freeman C. *A new history of early christianity*. New Haven: Yale University Press; 2009.
35 Masson JM, McCarthy S. *When elephants weep: the emotional lives of animals*. New York: Delta Press; 1995.
36 Safina C. *Beyond words: what animals think and feel*. New York: Henry Holt; 2015.

CHAPTER 3

The Archaeology of Religion: The Judeo-Christian God of the Old Testament

"A good world needs knowledge, kindliness, and courage; it does not need a regretful hankering after the past or a fettering of the free intelligence by words uttered long ago by ignorant men."
   BERTRAND RUSSELL, "WHY I AM NOT A CHRISTIAN".

The Judeo-Christian god Yahweh's very human attributes, especially jealousy and rage, are on constant display throughout the Old Testament. As god warns Moses in Exodus, *"Thou shalt worship no other God: for the Lord, whose name is Jealous, is a jealous God,"* (Exodus 34:14) *"You shall have no other gods before me,"* (Exodus 20:3) and *"Thou shalt not bow down thyself to them, nor serve them: for I the Lord am a jealous God, visiting the iniquity of the fathers upon children unto the third or fourth generation of those that hate me"* (Exodus 20:5).

Ezekiel tells a similar story: *"Thus saith the Lord: And I will set my jealousy against thee and they shall deal furiously with thee: they shall take away thy nose and thine ears and thy remnant shall fall by the sword: they will take thy sons and daughters and thy residue shall be devoured by fire"* (Ezekiel 23:25). Strange gods elicit a similar reaction: *"They have moved me to jealousy with that which is not God; they have provoked me to anger with their vanities"* (Deuteronomy 32:16, 21).

It strikes some as odd that this god, who is portrayed as the creator of the universe and omnipotent, is given to jealousy. If one is omnipotent, then what is there to be jealous about? Jealousy and rage seem more a product of the dominant social personality of people during those times.[1]

The image of god, be it a male or female entity, reflects the projection of mankind's self-image, which is reflected in the culture of the time. We create a god who has characteristics of ourselves because we are limited by our own concepts of "what is." We are thus unable to construe of god in any other way.

When concepts of a patriarchal male deity originated, the concept of who we were as a people was extremely limited. But these original concepts have influenced current concepts of god as envisioned by Christianity, Judaism, and Islam. We are limited by our own concepts of "what is:" our own descriptions of humanity and subsequent projections onto super-agents that think and feel.

The Christian Old Testament (or Hebrew bible) is described by Israeli archaeologists Israel Finkelstein and Neil

Silberman[2] as a collection of ancient writings—legend, poetry, philosophy, and history—written from the 9th to the 2nd Century BCE. It was originally written in Hebrew and Aramaic and consists of thirty-nine books, which were initially divided by author and length.*

Today, the Old Testament is traditionally divided into three main parts: the Torah, or Five Books of Moses (the Pentateuch); the Prophets; and the Writings.

The Prophets are divided into two main groups. The Former Prophets (i.e. Joshua, Judges, Samuel, and Kings) tells the story of the people of Israel from their crossing of the River Jordan. It covers the rises and falls of their kingdoms to their defeat and exile at the hands of the Assyrians and Babylonians. The Latter Prophets include Oracles, social teachings, and Messianic expectations from 850-500 BCE.

The Writings are a collection of homilies, poems, and prayers, composed in the 5th to the 2nd Century BCE. The Torah represents the essence of Jewish culture: the stories of the origin of the people and the moral lessons to be derived from it.

Of these writings, the Torah and the Former Prophets include historical works—in other words, writings that refer to events purported to have occurred. These include the destruction of the Temple of Jerusalem, the parting of the Dead Sea, the destruction of the walls of Jericho, the exodus of the Jews from Egypt, and others.

As Finkelstein and Silberman put it, the bible initially described the rise of the people of Israel, but differed from other creation myths (e.g. the Egyptian tales of Osiris, Isis, and

---

* Length being determined by the (then-standard) length of papyrus or parchment rolls.

Horus, or the Mesopotamian Gilgamesh epic) in that it was *"grounded in earthly history ... it is a divine drama played out before the eyes of humanity"* (p 8).² In the Hebrew bible, god communicates with humanity, but only one group of humanity. They are the chosen people—the Jews.

The story in the Hebrew bible begins with the Garden of Eden, and continues through the stories of Cain and Abel, the flood, Noah's ark, and then focuses on the family of Abraham, chosen by god to become the father of a great nation. Abraham is tested by god, who tells him to kill his son in order to assess his loyalty. God then spares the boy at the last moment. Jews and Christians see this parable as a test of faith; non-followers see it as proof that god is sadistic.

Abraham's son, Isaac, had a son of his own, Jacob, who wrestled with an angel and received the name Israel (which means "He who struggled with god"). Jacob names his son, Judah, as ruler of all (Genesis 49:8-10). Judah had twelve sons, who left their homeland for Egypt at the time of a great famine.

The story then takes on the elements of a historical saga. The god of Israel reveals his power in a demonstration against the pharaoh of Egypt. God then elects to make himself known to the world through Moses, who leads the children of Israel out of Egypt via the famous parting of the Red Sea. On Mount Sinai, he reveals his identity as YHWH (pronounced Yahweh), and gives humanity a code of law through Moses (The Ten Commandments: Exodus 20:1-17, Deuteronomy 5:4-21).

What became the basis for the Judeo-Christian code of conduct was not the first such code. Earlier legal codes include Hammurabi's Code (written during Hammurabi's tenure as King of Babylon from 1972 to 1750 BCE), the Code of Ur-Nammu (King of Ur, 2050 BCE), the Laws of Eshnunna (circa 1930 BCE) and the codex of Lipit-Ishtar of Isin (circa 1870 BCE).

The Ten Commandments, as they came to be known, included four rules governing man's relation to god (i.e. Thou shalt have no other gods before me, make any graven image, take god's name in vain, remember the Sabbath) and six governing man's relation to man (i.e. Honour your parents, thou shall not kill, commit adultery, steal, bear false witness against a neighbour, nor covet your neighbour's possessions).

There are no specific Commandments prohibiting physical abuse, of either spouses or children. Nor is slavery prohibited. In fact, god recommends it (e.g. Numbers, 31:18, Exodus 21:2 and 20-21, Leviticus 24:44, 25:45-46.). The hierarchy is clear: god is the highest authority, and parents are the intermediary authority between children and god. These Commandments provide the basis of the Judeo-Christian universal standards of right and wrong.

One of these "universal" standards is that non-believers have no human rights. This idea is expressed in the bible (*"You may treat your slaves like this but the people of Israel, your relatives, must never be treated this way."* Leviticus 25:46) and later in Papal Bulls, arguing that pagans and other non-believers should be searched out and reduced to "perpetual servitude" (p 194).[3] This was used by the Catholic church as a rationalization for slavery for many years.

As described in the text of the Old Testament, the people of Israel lived for two hundred years in two separate kingdoms (Judah and Israel), succumbing repeatedly to the lure of other gods besides Yahweh. In 586 BCE, they were conquered by the Babylonians and the Israelites were exiled. The conquest was explained as punishment for their infidelity in worshipping other gods. The religious community took it as divine law for the scrupulous adherence to religious ritual. The Hebrew bible emphasized personal responsibility to "keep the faith."

For centuries, followers of the bible took it for granted that the scriptures were divine revelation, as conveyed from god to an elite group of Israelite sages, prophets, and priests. Both Jewish and Christian religious authorities assumed that the Books of Moses (including Deuteronomy) were written by Moses himself (p 11).[2] Similarly, the prophets Samuel, King David, and King Solomon were believed to have been writers of Old Testament books.

However, by the 17th Century, textual analysis had made it clear that these older assumptions were incorrect. Moses,* for example, could not have written Deuteronomy, since it describes his own death (interestingly, earlier religious authorities never figured that out). Also, literary asides were contained in the texts that explained ancient place names; these asides sometimes noted that evidence of biblical events were still evident "to this day," indicating that some time had passed before the re-writing had occurred.

By the 19th Century, biblical scholars doubted Moses had any hand in writing the Torah. Several versions of the same stories existed within the Torah, suggesting several authors at work. The Book of Genesis, for example, has two different

---

* Biblical skeptic Paul Tobin[4] questions whether Moses ever existed. The story of his birth, escape from harm by being left to drift on the river in a papyrus basket, and subsequent rescue (Exodus 2:2-10) closely parallels the nativity story of the earlier Akkadian king Sargon. The Akkadians did have some cultural influence on both the Egyptians and Jews (p 154). Tobin sees Moses as a recycling of the earlier myth.

versions of creation (1:1-2:3 and 2:4-25), two conflicting versions of Adam's offspring* (Genesis 4:17-26 vs. 5:1-28), and two spliced and rearranged flood stories (Genesis 6:5 and 9:17). There are numerous duplicate and triplicate versions of events in the wanderings of the patriarchs, the exodus from Egypt, and the giving of the Ten Commandments.

These duplicates used different names to describe the god of Israel: Yahweh and Elohim. The latter god seemed most preoccupied with the southern territories (Judah) while Yahweh was most concerned with the northern territories (Israel).

There are also distinct uses of geographical terminology, religious symbols, and roles played by various tribes in the Yahweh and Elohim texts. This has led scholars to conclude that the Yahweh text (called the J text) originated in Jerusalem; it represented a perspective of someone writing in Judah soon after the time of King Solomon (circa 970-930 BCE). The E (Elohim) text seems to have been originally written in the north at around the same time. Some passages seem to have independent sources (including Deuteronomy).

Scholars now believe the current text is a redaction and constellation of these various source texts, made some time after the exile; however, scholars disagree when exactly these were made. The most recent time is said to be the 2nd Century BCE.

The book of Deuteronomy differs in terminology and theological stance from the other books. It is the only book to describe god as transcendent, and to prohibit sacrificial

---

* Adam, by the way, was described as living for 930 years.

worship anywhere but in the Temple of Jerusalem. It became, as Finkelstein and Silberman put it, *"the inspiration for a religious reform of unprecedented severity"* (p 13), and influenced the Former Prophets books (Joshua, Judges, Samuel, and Kings).

Initially, the practice of modern archaeology appeared supportive of Old Testament history when scholars with a strong biblical background began to excavate some of the bible's main locales, such as Jerusalem. American Congregationalist Minister Edward Robinson undertook two long explorations in Ottoman Palestine in 1838 and 1852, and pioneered techniques to link biblical geographical information with modern Arabic place names. Robinson began to systematically collate topography, biblical references, and archaeological remains, rather than merely relying on ecclesiastical traditions of various holy places. As a result, Robinson found dozens of ancient ruins with previously-forgotten biblical significance.

In the 1840s, archaeological excavations were undertaken throughout the broad plains between the Tigris and Euphrates rivers, uncovering places such as Nineveh and Babylon. Other excavations in Israel, Jordan, and neighbouring regions used new techniques to identify and date architectural styles, pottery forms, and other artifacts.

By the end of the 20th Century, it became clear that there was some historical basis to the Old Testament, but that there were *"way too many contradictions between the archaeological finds and the biblical narratives to suggest that the bible provided a precise description of what actually had occurred"* (p 21).[2]

Recent developments in archaeology date the writing of the Torah and Deuteronomy as somewhere in the 7th Century BCE, and argue that the historical events described are not supported by archaeological evidence. Instead, they appear to reflect the views of King Josiah of the Kingdom of Judah, and were written to provide ideological validation for particular political ambitions and religious reforms (p 14).[2] These biblical stories *"may have been based on certain historical kernels (but) they primarily reflect the ideology and the world view of the writers"* (p 23).[2]

As an example, camels in the stories of the patriarchs in Genesis are frequently described as beasts of burden (Genesis 37:25). However, the use of domesticated camels did not occur in the Middle East until the 7th Century BCE (p 37);[2] research has shown a dramatic increase in the number of camel bones at that time in the southern coastal plain of Israel. The bones were exclusively from mature animals, suggesting that they were from travelling beasts of burden, not from locally-produced herds with a mix of young and old animals. Therefore, it is doubtful that Genesis was written before the 7th Century.

Finkelstein and Silberman[2] cite German biblical scholar Julius Wellhausen as arguing that the Old Testament *"reflected the concerns of the later Israelite monarchy, which were projected onto the lives of legendary fathers in a largely mystical past. The bible stories should thus be regarded as a national mythology with no more historical basis than the Homeric saga of Odysseus's travels or Virgil's saga of Aeneas's founding of Rome"* (p 36).[2] Biblical scholars John van Seters and Thomas Thompson argued that even if the early texts contained some early traditions, the selection and arrangement of stories expressed a clear perspective by the bible's editors at the time of compilation (p 37).[2]

The archaeological evidence fails to support the existence of the patriarch Abraham, let alone confirm his conversations with god (p 28-33).[2] These dialogues with god, as with Moses' dialogues, were not witnessed and were reported centuries after the fact.

The archaeological evidence also fails to support two other major events in the Old Testament: the exodus and the Battle of Jericho. In the well-known exodus story, the Hebrews were forced into slavery by the new pharaoh (Exodus 1:12). They then escaped and were led by Moses to the Red Sea (Exodus 13:17-18), where the pharaoh had sent a force of "600 picked chariots" after them. The Red Sea parted to allow the Israelites to cross over Sinai on dry land, but then reformed to drown the pursuing Egyptian army (Exodus 15:1-18).

Finkelstein and Silberman[2] say the archaeological evidence confirms that immigrants did come from Canaan to Egypt, largely due to droughts and famine in Canaan (p 53).[2] There is also evidence of Egyptians forcibly expelling the immigrant Israelites (p 56).[2]

The references in the bible to Ramses as the Egyptian ruler locates the exodus to the 13th Century. Egyptian sources (stone carvings) mention Ramses II (1303-1213 BCE) as ruling in 1279-1213 BCE. His son, Merneptah, is described in a stone carving as leading a campaign into Canaan, in the course of which a people named Israel were decimated.

During that time, the Egyptians had established a series of forts along the eastern border of Egypt and closely monitored the movements of foreigners (p 59).[2] In fact, a late 13th Century papyrus exists with a record of these migrations. No mention exists of a movement of Israelites at that time (p 59),[2] yet the Canaan-Egypt border was closely controlled; if a group of Israelites had passed, a record should exist.

The records from that era are abundant, yet there is no mention of Israelites. Hence, no evidence for the biblical account of the exodus. At that time, Egypt was at the peak of its authority, and the dominant power in the world (p 60).[2] As Finkelstein and Silberman state, this cannot be ignored when considering the authenticity of the exodus: *"Putting aside the possibility of inspired miracles, one can hardly accept the idea of a flight of a large group of slaves from Egypt through the heavily guarded border fortifications into the desert and then Canaan in the time of such a formidable Egyptian presence. Any group escaping Egypt against the will of the pharaoh would have been easily tracked down not only by an Egyptian army chasing it from the delta but also by the Egyptian soldiers in the forts of the northern Sinai and in Canaan"* (p 61).[2]

It did, however, make for a good story, especially if the writer was trying to unite the Jewish people with wondrous tales of their origins. As Paul Tobin[4] points out, *"according to Exodus 12:40 the Israelites lived in Egypt for 430 years. Yet for all this time, there is simply no literary and archaeological evidence outside the Hebrew bible that records the sojourn of the Israelites in Egypt ... According to Exodus 12:37, there were six hundred thousand men, not counting the women and children, who left with Moses. We are also told this one million plus nation wandered for forty years in the wilderness (Joshua 5:6). Surely, more than a million people wandering around for forty years would have left some traces for the archaeologists to find. Yet not a single piece of archaeological evidence has been found"* (p 155).[4]

Repeated archaeological surveys in all regions of the Sinai have failed to yield any evidence of Israeli occupation; only the Egyptian forts left traces. There are no signs of ancient encampments, despite the fact that modern archaeological techniques are capable of tracing even the meagre remains of hunter-gatherers and pastoral nomads.*

Finkelstein and Silberman conclude that the exodus did not happen in the time and manner described in the bible (p 63).[2] There is no evidence suggesting an Israelite presence at sites where they were said to have camped for extended periods.

The events described in the bible of the Canaan tribes (e.g. Moab, Edom, Ammon) resisting the Israelites is also not likely. Archaeological evidence shows that those sites did exist, but were sparsely occupied at the time of the purported wandering of the Children of Israel (p 64).[2]

By contrast, there is considerable archaeological evidence for buildings at Troy and the Trojan wars of the 14th to 12th Century BCE. Archaeological digs have been done in the area of Troy since 1822 CE, and several layers of ruins have been discovered that date back as far as 3000 BCE. These have been given names consistent with chronological eras, with Troy VII matching the era of the Homeric legends.

Similarly, with the famous Battle of Jericho, no evidence exists. In the bible, the book of Joshua tells of the Jews military campaign in Canaan, where they cleared the area of paganism at god's command. But how could an army in rags, emerging after decades in the desert and travelling with women and children, overcome fortifications and mount an effective invasion?

Again, the archaeological evidence is telling: all the ancient cities mentioned in the conquest story (Jericho, Ai, Gibeon, Lachich, and Hazor) have been located and excavated,

---

* For example, archaeologists have found pastoral activity in the Sinai as far back as 3000 BCE, and evidence from the Hellenistic and Byzantine periods.

but all they show is that the Canaan cities and Jericho were mainly uninhabited, or were nothing more than small villages of a few huts and peasants living in the surrounding countryside. They were merely administrative strongholds; only the king and a few bureaucrats lived in such strongholds, and they had no fortifications. With Egypt being in charge of security for the entire province, there was no need for massive defensive walls (p 77).[2]

The biblical story suggests that the conquest of Canaan occurred between 1230 and 1222 BCE. There is considerable evidence from Egyptian texts on life in Canaan, including diplomatic letters, lists of conquered cities, scenes of sieges engraved on walls of temples, annals of Egyptian kings, literary works, and hymns. There is also extensive archaeological evidence for the Egyptian grip on Canaan in the 13th century: structures and courtyards had hieroglyphic inscriptions, and monuments to Egyptian kings from the 14th to 12th Centuries BCE were common. These show that the Egyptians had too much power in Canaan to have allowed the Jews conquests as described in the bible.

At the beginning of the 20th Century, many of the sites described in the biblical account were excavated. However, there was no evidence of fallen walls, burnt beams, or wholesale destruction. In the case of Jericho, there was no trace of a settlement of any kind in the 13th Century BCE. An earlier, 14th Century settlement existed, but it was small, poor, and unfortified. Likewise, it held no sign of destruction (p 82).

This was also true at Ai, where, according to the bible, Joshua carried out a clever ambush. Although the city matched its biblical description, there was no sign of a settlement there at the time of its supposed conquest.

In short, there were no walls discovered at Jericho, nor any other sign of the biblical battle. By way of comparison, it is telling that excavation of Troy (in what is now Turkey) did reveal extensive fortification and a battle fought around the time of the reported invasion in 1300 BCE (described by archaeologists as Troy VII) by the Greeks, as described in Homer's Iliad.[5] It seems probable that early biblical writers used known sites as locales for their stories, but that the stories themselves were fabrications; written, it seems, to fulfill a political goal of uniting the Jewish people from Israel and Judah.

An Alternative Explanation for the Old Testament

Finkelstein and Silberman[2] offer an alternative view for the Old Testament stories: one that takes into account the fact that although they could not have occurred as depicted in the bible, they still took place in identifiable locations.

The 13th Century BCE, when these stories were to have occurred, was a time of tumultuous change in the ancient world: the old Bronze Age kingdoms (Egypt and Anatolia) were being replaced by a new world order (including Mycenae). This appears to have been instigated by a mysterious group called the "Sea People"—migrants who came from the west by sea, leading to general upheaval.

The destruction of older cities in Canaan took over a century to occur. Since very few people were literate in those days, oral legends were started. These usually originated with an unusual geographic phenomenon (e.g. large ruins), which were described in ways that favoured heroic history.

For example, people living in the foothills of the Shepelah, impressed by the sheer size of a stone blocking the entrance to a mysterious cave near the town of Mekkedah, linked stories of their own hazy past with the stone; it was said to seal a cave where five ancient kings were buried (Joshua 10:16-27). Biblical stories that conclude with the note that the landmark could still be seen "to this very day" were probably legends of this kind (i.e. oral stories that grew and were written much later).

The Old Testament appears to have been written in the 7th Century BCE, and it reflected on the earlier chaotic events in the 13th Century. It was written when Israel was a divided community—Israel and Judah—and was an attempt to regenerate Jewish identity into one, unified sense. Thus, it appealed to heroic myths of Jewish I escape from Egyptian enslavement and subsequent military conquest.

As Finkelstein and Silberman point out, *"the book of Joshua is a classic literary expression of the yearnings and fantasies of a people at a certain time and place"* (p 95).[2] Archaeological evidence suggests that people in the land of Canaan underwent cyclical periods of dispersed, pastoral life followed by relative permanence in larger collectives.

The stories of the exodus were oral myths, compiled in later periods to serve the political benefit of Jewish unification. Unfortunately, this conclusion has political ramifications for Israelite notions of ancient nationhood; it appears that indigenous inhabitants of Canaan gradually developed an ethnic identity that could be called Israelite.

Finkelstein and Silberman realize that these findings also cast doubt on Israeli notions of themselves as an ancient nation (p 98).[2] There is no evidence of a unified invasion of Canaan under Joshua, or that the sagas of the patriarchs are anything but legends.

According to the authors,[2] several Canaanite tribes lived a pastoral, nomadic existence that changed dramatically around 1200 BCE (p 107).[2] The Canaanite cities were in a process of collapse. Suddenly, about 250 hilltop communities sprang up in the central hill region, far from the cities (p 107).[2] One group of these people became Israelites, while others (e.g. those in Ammon, Moab, Edom) did not.

The Israelites appear to have been Canaanites from the lower classes who took to the hills to avoid oppression. After being displaced, they amalgamated and set up a different tribe: one that was more egalitarian (based on archaeological finds) than the city. Only the tribe who became Israelites differed from the others in their refusal to eat pork; excavation of the sites reveal no pig bones in the Israelite communities, while surrounding communities reveal large numbers of pigs.

The Jewish aversion to pork preceded any religious proscription; monotheism and the traditions of exodus and the Covenant came later. Five hundred years before the composition of biblical text, the Jews chose, for reasons that are not clear, not to eat pork. Finkelstein and Silberman speculate that the proto-Israelites may have stopped eating pork merely because the surrounding people—their adversaries—did eat it, and they had begun to see themselves as different (p 120).[2] "*When modern Jews do the same, they are continuing the oldest archaeologically attested cultural practice of the people of Israel*" (p 120).[2]

Consistent with this alternative version of the origin of the Israelites is Shlomo Sand's book *The Invention of the Jewish People*,[6] which argues that the Jews are a historical-social invention. They bear no distinct differences in DNA from their Arabic neighbours; there is no Jewish race, nor typical Jewish appearance. The Jews are related genetically to the Kurds and, because of religious conversions and inter-marriage, no distinct DNA profile exists (p 275-280).[6]

Sand describes the feeding-frenzy of mistruths announced in the discovery of a "priestly" gene (the Cohen Gene) and the publicity given by an "identity-hungry Jewish press." He adds, *"so far, no research had found unique and unifying characteristics of Jewish heredity based on a random sampling of genetic material whose ethnic origin is not known in advance"* (p 279).[6] *"At most self-isolation, endogenous marriage and the long periods in the ghettoes had produced certain Jewish types. The Jews secluded social life had affected their behavior and even their physiognomy. Heredity and blood had nothing to do with it"* (p 269).[6]

Finkelstein and Silberman argue that archaeological evidence differs from the Old Testament version in another important way: the Israelites did not conquer Caanan; they evolved from Caanan. The "conquest" version was a creation myth that helped forge a new identity in the 7th Century, when Israel was attempting to join with Judah.

Yahweh, the Israelite god, was also absent in Caananite society and appears to have been an adaptation of an earlier Egyptian god. It was borrowed from a tribe that lived in a place called YWH, in Midian, near where the Israelites lived. The emancipation from Caananite city-states was attributed to a god—Yahweh. This god—the first monotheistic god, apart from Atun—helped form a collective identity amongst the disparate escaped tribes. When written down 600 years later, the name Yahweh was used.

The "invention" of the Jewish people, as Sand termed it, was not particular to Jews. Christian, and later Muslim, identities were equivalent, although requiring a stronger adherence to a central religious creed. One theory of the Inquisition was that it was an attempt to root out those who simply mouthed adherence: the *conversos,* or Jews who were forced to convert to Christianity, in Spain.[7]

In contrast to the other desert religions, Judaism has no history of missionaries and imperial conquest. The Jews seem to often be on the political defensive, while the Christians and Muslims both capitalized on their fortuitous historical circumstances to spread their religious ideas.

The Social Psychology of Rumour

If relatively-verifiable events such as the exodus and the Battle of Jericho are not supportable through archaeological evidence, then more private events, such as the conversations with god that are reported verbatim in the Old Testament, are even more dubious.

Social psychologist Gordon Allport performed a research study in the 1950s. In the study, he showed a picture of two men on a bus to a research subject. In the picture, a white man held a straight-razor[8-10] while facing a black man. They were standing as if they were having a conversation.

Allport had his research subjects look at the picture, and then tell another person what he had seen. The other person then did the same, passing along the received story through a series of five people in a chain of communication. Allport recorded what the last person said had been described to them: a black man holding a straight-razor.

Allport viewed the study as a demonstration of how racial attitudes affect reporting, but his results can be broadened to examine any attitudes that are emotionally-charged. We change stories to fit our preconceived notions, especially when those notions have importance to us. We use familiar narrative that is available in our culture.

Allport and his co-author, Leo Postman, described this process of selective reporting as "levelling:" where about 70% of details of the original picture are lost in 5-6 mouth-to-mouth retellings. The retained details operate through another process, "sharpening," that involves the distortion of specific details, usually those that are consistent with one's attitudes.

The authors found that stories passed on verbally had details that became assimilated into the principal theme: "*Falsifications of perception and memory they are, but they occur in the interests of putting together, bringing about a more coherent, consistent mental configuration*" (p 55).[10] "*Whenever a stimulus field is of potential importance to an individual, but at the same time is unclear, or susceptible to divergent interpretations, a subjective structuring process is started ... characterized as an effort to reduce the stimulus to a simple and meaningful structure that has adaptive significance for the individual in terms of his own interests and experience ... the longer the time that elapses and the more people involved in a serial report, the greater the change is likely to be, until the rumour has reached aphoristic brevity and is repeated by rote*" (p 57).[10]

In short, descriptions of unwitnessed conversations cannot be accurate (since they were not observed, they cannot meet the basic requirement of testimony: what the witness heard or saw). Instead, they merely reveal the attitudes of the storytellers.

Memory research is no more helpful to religious claims. Studies by psychologist Elizabeth Loftus[11] and others[12] find that human memory is notoriously unreliable. Memories can also be implanted through the wording used to ask questions about a past event. Loftus and others used this memory-biasing technique to lead people to recall broken glass, tape recorders, being lost in a shopping mall as a child, being abducted by aliens, having witnessed a demonic possession, or having been attacked by an animal. In one study,[13] research subjects were led to believe that they had an accurate memory from one day after birth. This is not possible; it's well before the development of autobiographical memory.

People fail to distinguish between information from an original event and from that posed by the questioner; instead, they blend the two sources of information into a single, cognitive structure: one "memory" that then elaborates on details from a central idea. Even in cases where people have personally witnessed a crime, their memory for the characteristics of the perpetrator is poor, rarely extending beyond the person's gender.[14]

In a comprehensive review of memory literature, Steven Jay Lynn and Kevin McConkey[12] cite research that shows poor recall for autobiographical events: only 15% of people who were young at the time of the Kennedy assassination could recall any details of the shooting, and only 3% could recall any personal information for the same time period.

The verbatim conversations between god and Moses or god and Abraham reported in the Old Testament, between Jesus and his disciples reported in the New Testament, and between Muhammad and the Archangel Gabriel in the Koran, all suffer from decades or even centuries elapsing between the purported event and the time of its writing.

Furthermore, there were no witnesses to each conversation; in the case of both the Christian and Islamic writings, all those involved had died before the first version was written down. With the Old Testament, around 600 years elapsed between the events depicted and the writing. The New Testament had a fifty-year difference. The revelations of Muhammad were not written down for 150 years after his death.[15] Try to recall a conversation you had from last month—it's virtually impossible to do. How, then, could there be any accuracy in recalling events that were not witnessed by the writers and had occurred years in the past?

It could be argued that religious stories were not merely serial reports, but several chains of communication emanating from one single source. But this simply reinforces the effect that Allport describes in his communication chain study, since all chains stem from a single source and can cross- contaminate each other. With multiple chains, one simply gets a lack of agreement at the end, or else experiences similar contamination thanks to one's embedded cultural attitudes.

The chance for any accuracy in verbatim conversations reported by the bible, Torah, or Koran is near zero. And this process is only considering the original writing; we are left wondering, then, what the effects of each re-writing are. For the Christian New Testament has been re-written several times, always with a snowballing conformity to dogma.

REFERENCES

1. Pinker S. *The better angels of our nature: why violence has declined.* New York: Viking; 2011.
2. Finkelstein I, Silberman N. *The bible unearthed: archaeology's new vision of ancient israel.* New York: Free Press; 2001.
3. Shermer M. *The moral arc.* New York: Henry Holt & Co.; 2015.
4. Tobin P. The bible and modern scholarship. *The christian delusion: why faith fails.* New York: Promethus Press; 2010.
5. Winkler M. *Troy: From homer's iliad to hollywood epic.* Oxford: Oxford University Press; 2007.
6. Sand S. *The invention of the jewish people.* London: Verso; 2009.
7. Sheset BI. Questions and responses of ben sheset. *Encyclopedia Judaica.* Tel Aviv: 2007.
8. Allport G, Postman LJ. The basic psychology of rumour. *Transactions of the New York Academy of Sciences.* 1945; Series 11(VII):61-81.
9. Allport G. *The nature of prejudice.* Reading: Addison Wesley; 1975.
10. Allport G, Postman LJ. The basic psychology of rumour. *Basic Studies in Social Psychology.* 1965; 47-58.
11. Loftus E. The reality of repressed memories. *American Psychologist.* 1993; 48(5):518-537.
12. Lynn SJ, McConkey KM. *Truth in memory.* New York: Guilford Press; 1998.

13. Spanos N, Burgess C, Burgess M, C. S, Blois WO. Creating false memories of infancy with hypnotic and non-hypnotic procedures. *Applied Cognitive Psychology.* 1999; 13:201-218.
14. Van Koppen PJ, Lochun SK. Portraying perpetrators: The validity of offender descriptions by witnesses. *Law and Human Behavior.* 1997; 21:661-685.
15. Crone P. *Slaves on horses.* London: Cambridge University Press; 1980.

CHAPTER 4

The Christian New Testament and the Basis of Christian Dogma

When one moves beyond the mindless certainty of fundamentalism, one can find a rich literature written by biblical scholars on the Christian New Testament. Unlike a number of Christian writers, these scholars[1-3] can read the languages of the bible: Hebrew, Aramaic, and Greek. What's more, these scholars have studied the context of society from when the bible was written. As such, they have a historical view of its conception, including the political rivalries in the early Christian church: rivalries that impinged upon and dictated the surviving text of the bible.

From the work of these scholars and others, several questions arise about Christian doctrine. One is the question of Jesus' existence. No one who wrote the bible had any firsthand knowledge of Jesus. The earliest Gospel (Mark) was written at least 40 years after his reported death:[3] around 65-70 CE (p 23).[2]

The actual authors of all four Gospels are unknown. But we do know that they were not disciples of Jesus, since they lived much later and wrote in classical Greek; Aramaic was the language of Jesus and his disciples. Classical Greek was the written language of educated people, and none of the disciples were literate, let alone educated. The names of the disciples were later connected to the Gospels arbitrarily by Gaulic Bishop Irenaeus* in 185 CE (p 74).[2]

Since these Gospels were written in Greek and no earlier versions existed, their authorship is dubious. The accounts of Jesus had been passed on by oral tradition, and thus subjected to the inaccuracies of that medium.

Why is it important to understand the context of the times? Because calling someone a "son of god" was relatively commonplace in those times; in fact, it was the typical explanation given for any person who committed exemplary action. "Miracles" were another common explanation in those times—there were many people who allegedly performed miracles, including several Jewish Holy Men (p 172).[3] They operated in a world where scientific causation was not understood, and thus many things appeared miraculous.

---

* Irenaeus was a church apologist who wrote extensively against the Gnostics, arguing that only the Church had the "official" version of the Gospels. The later finding of the Gnostic Gospels at Nag Hammadi in 1945 supported the Gnostic view, which was that an understanding of god was commensurate with self-awareness and insight. These texts, written on papyrus and sealed in an earthenware jar, have been dated to the 2nd Century. It is theorized that they were buried to escape destruction by orthodox Christians.

According to biblical scholar Bart Ehrman, Chairman of the Department of Religious Studies at the University of North Carolina, several "miracle workers" were in existence during biblical times. Apollonius of Tyana was said to be able to heal the sick, cast out demons, and raise the dead (p 172).[3] Hanina ben Dosa and Honi the Circle Drawer were also said to perform miracles (p 172).[3]

The coming of a messiah to radically alter society and free the Jews from servitude had been in the Jewish Zeitgeist for hundreds of years.[4] It was also common to believe that someone was a son of god—whether they were a first-born son or just a high achiever.[5] Alexander the Great was said to be the son of god, as were Augustus Caesar and Pythagoras (p 158).[6]

This was a world where people were illiterate: over 90% could not read or write,[7] and it was widely held that the world was flat and the centre of the universe. Spain was considered distant and exotic; the huge and longstanding society in China was unknown—let alone distant continents. The motives for human actions were thought of in religious, not psychological, terms. The notion of a son of god tells us more about the explanations used in those ignorant times than it does the divinity of the person described.

The biblical sources themselves are suspect; none of the original biblical scripts remain, and what we do have were repeatedly copied and recopied by hand, frequently with unfaithful results.[7] By and large, the rewritings tend to add material consistent with Christian dogma, or to suggest a factual basis for said dogma.

The existing copies of biblical texts date from the 4th

Century* (after Christianity had become the official state religion). The originals had ceased to exist even before the Nicaean Council produced the current foundation of Christian precepts (p 23).[2] That basis, it should be pointed out, was established by political wrangling amongst priests, each with their own theological and political agendas.

Ehrman's careful scholarship outlines the litany of contradictions in the bible and the Gospels.[3,7] Early Christians vigorously disputed the virgin birth and the resurrection—concepts that have more mundane explanations than those offered by Christian teachings. There were power struggles between factions even in early Christianity, and although a dominant version of Christian dogma survived, it was not the only version; it probably wasn't even the most truthful, just the one with the most powerful backers.[1]

Theologian Elaine Pagels[1] describes a different viewpoint on Jesus, one that comes from the Gnostic Gospels. The Gnostic Gospels are a series of documents written in Greek, bound in leather, and found in a sealed earthenware vase in 1945 at Nag Hammadi in Egypt. They have been dated between the 2nd and 4th Centuries CE.

This version portrayed Jesus as touting self-enlightenment and freedom from illusion as the guide to spiritual understanding, rather than the themes of sin and forgiveness

---

* In *Misquoting Jesus*, Ehrman lists the oldest and most important existing manuscripts. The oldest complete manuscript is the Syriac Sinaiticus (written in a form of Aramaic called Syriac) from the 4th Century (although some date it as from the 2nd Century). It was translated from the earlier Greek Gospels (which no longer exist). The Codex Vaticanus is from the 4th Century as well.[7,27]

adopted by the church. Self-awareness was portrayed as akin to an understanding of god (p xix-xxi),[1] and could be obtained by individual pursuits (even a mystical variety).

This Gnostic view of Christianity was declared "heretical" by early orthodoxy. However, the political struggle over the orthodox version eventually served church interests. Starting with Paul, it was claimed that Jesus revealed himself after the resurrection to Peter, who then conferred holy power to the church (Matthew 16:18-19): power that the Catholic church continues to claim.

The Gnostic view was that Christ's resurrection was in the form of a bright light, not flesh. That view, however, did not confer power to the church. Nor did the prospect of individual enlightenment provide the church with its gatekeeper capacity. The orthodox view aided the church to maintain a monopoly on power, both religious and political.

The first three centuries saw a struggle over these views. They were resolved in 325 CE, when Roman Emperor Constantine's Nicaean Council decreed the orthodoxy that is now Christian dogma. In short, modern Christian views are the result of a power struggle. The conclusion of that struggle decided which books constituted the "canon" authority, and revisions were subsequently made to match.

Struggles between groups of men generated these beliefs—not the word of a god. The beliefs were:

1) Consistent with the needs of the largest group at the time (the official Christian church)
2) Appealing to the people, making it easier to win converts
3) Preceded by the familiar themes of older religions (e.g. virgin birth and resurrection).

Bart Ehrman[*] has carefully detailed the forging, rewriting, and misquoting of early texts in the New Testament.[3,7, 8,9] These early texts include the four Gospels of the New Testament (Matthew, Mark, Luke, and John), which were written at the end of the 1st Century, decades after the life of Jesus. They were based on prior oral tradition without original copies. These Gospels report what appear to be verbatim accounts of conversations between Jesus and his disciples; verbatim accounts written, at best, decades after the alleged fact.

The New Testament books are filled with discrepancies, and sometimes outright contradictions. They were re-written numerous times,[7] and parallel, but inconsistent, versions exist. As Ehrman says, *"What we have are copies made later ... many centuries later ... there are more differences among our many manuscripts than there are words in the New Testament"* (p 10).[7]

The only existing copies date from the 4th Century and are written in Greek; that is, written by someone with an education, not one of Jesus' disciples (who were illiterate, lower-class peasants that spoke Aramaic).[3] These oldest versions are copies of copies. Repeat copies are prone to both error and purposeful attempts at rewriting (in this case, to make them conform to current doctrines). Scholars note that the authors of these Gospels

---

[*] The most amazing part is that Ehrman could persist in his uncovering of the forgery on the New Testament, apparently running headlong into a contradiction of his beliefs as a fundamentalist Christian. Ehrman did eventually leave the faith because he could not reconcile the Christian story with the visible suffering in the world. As far as the Christian bible is concerned, he has said, *"How does it help us to say the bible is the itinerant word of God if in fact, we don't have the words that God inspired but only the words copied, often incorrectly, by scribes ... when we don't have the originals, only error-ridden copies?"* (p 7).[7]

appeared ignorant of Palestinian geography or Jewish customs—suggesting that they might have been Christian converts who lived elsewhere.[4,7] For example, Erhman points out that the letters of Paul were actually written by Christians in the 2nd Century and ascribed to Paul in order to draw on his authority (p 23).[3]

Non-Christian Evidence for Jesus' Existence

There is only one mention of Jesus in a 1st Century, non-Christian source: a book by the Jewish historian Josephus in 90 CE. This mention appears to have been later augmented (i.e. rewritten) by Christian sources. Here is the quote from Josephus' text, cited by Ehrman (p 150)[3] with the later Christian additions in bold:

"At this time, there appeared Jesus, a wise man, **if indeed one should call him man**, he was a doer of startling deeds, a teacher of people who receive the truth with pleasure. And he gained a following both among many Jews and among many of Greek origin. **He was the messiah.** And when Pilate, because of an accusation made by the leading man among us, condemned him to the cross, those who had loved him previously did not cease to do so. **For he appeared to them on the third day, living again, just as the divine prophets had spoken of these and countless other things about him.** And up to this very day the tribe of Christians named after him has not died out." (Josephus' Antiquities 18.3.3)

Josephus' writings were not copied by Jews; he was considered a traitor in the Jews s' disastrous war with Rome that led to Jerusalem's destruction in 70 CE. They were copied instead by Christians (and added to). The quote above is the only mention of Jesus in Josephus' twenty-volume history of the Jewish people.

To someone raised to believe in Jesus' miracles, it should seem strange that he was not discussed in the decades after he existed. Greek and Roman sources have little to say about Jesus: there are no birth records, accounts of his trial or death, reflections on his significance, or disputes about his teachings (p 148).[3] There are numerous historical sources from the period: religious scholars, historians, philosophers, poets, natural scientists, thousands of private letters, and even inscriptions on buildings, but there is no 1st-Century source, of either Greek or Roman origin, that mentions Jesus (p 148).[3] As Ehrman describes it, *"He is never discussed, challenged, attacked, maligned or talked about in any way in any pagan source of the period"* (p 148).[3]

The earliest Roman reference to Jesus is in the writings of Pliny the Younger in 112 CE (p 31).[2] At the time, Pliny was the governor of a Roman province. He wrote to the Emperor Trajan, and mentioned a group of people called Christians who "worship Christ as a god" (p 149).[3] He said nothing more.

In 115 CE, Tacitus, the Roman historian, mentioned the fire in Rome set by Nero in the year 64. He mentioned "the Christians" who got their name from *"Christus ... who was executed at the hands of Pontius Pilate in the reign of Tiberius"* (Annals 15:44).[3] He goes on to say that the superstition of Christianity first appeared in Judea before spreading to Rome.

As Ehrman puts it, *"if we cast our net over the Greek and Roman sources for the first hundred years after Jesus' death (30-130 CE) these two brief references are all we find"* (p 149).[3] If Jesus performed the miracles claimed in the Christian Gospels, or stirred controversy, he should have at least been discussed in other sources. As it is, he appears to have been seen as little more than a cult leader by historians of that era.

Christian Sources

None of Jesus' disciples wrote Greek, the language of the first biblical text.[9] From the Gospels (and the Acts), we learn that they were illiterate, Palestinian Jewish peasants from rural Galilee (about 90% of the population was illiterate in those times). They were uneducated day labourers (fishermen and carpenters) who spoke Aramaic. There is some suggestion that Jesus could read (Luke 4:16-20) but none that he could write.

The Gospels are written anonymously, with names attached later by editors or scribes who thought these might be the original authors (p 103).[3] In some cases (e.g. in Matthew and John), the authors use the third-person about what "they" (i.e. Jesus and the disciples) were doing—not what "we" were doing (p 104).[3] This indicates that the authors were not disciples.

The oral tradition on which these Gospels are based is, in court, called "hearsay" evidence: in this case, third- or fourth-hand testimony at best. There are solid reasons why hearsay evidence is not allowable in court:* it is notoriously unreliable. In court, a witness must testify to what they saw or heard, not what someone else told them they had experienced. Why then, when we know hearsay is inherently untrustworthy, do we not demand more evidence for the basis for our religious beliefs?

Papias of Hierapolis, an early church father, contributed to the illusion that some disciples had written a Gospel;

---

* In 1603, Sir Walter Raleigh was found guilty of treason based solely on hearsay evidence. In response to the unpopular ruling, British courts changed the rules of evidence to require a more stringent code.[10] As a result, court rules of evidence were required to be more tightly-focused on fact, and hearsay was ruled unreliable.

however, Papias was largely discredited by later Christian authorities and scholars (p 107).[3] Ehrman also concluded that Papias was not a reliable source. The "authority" for the Gospels developed at the time of Papias, in the 2nd Century, rendering the competing Gospels as non-canonical (e.g. the Gospels attributed to Thomas, Peter, and Phillip).

Irenaeus (180 CE) also wrote a defence of the Gospels in rebuttal to the "heresies" attacking them. He attached the names of disciples to each Gospel. However, no Gospel was written by an eyewitness. The Gospel of John, who was a disciple, explicitly states it is not a first-hand account. Given the short life expectancy in those days, no eyewitnesses were likely even alive when the Gospels were supposedly written (about 47 years after the crucifixion).

As Charles Freeman puts it, the Gospel of Mark (or, more accurately, the Gospel attributed to Mark by Irenaeus) was written "sometime after 70 CE" (p 75)[4] by someone who wrote in Greek but was not a polished writer. He was probably Jewish (judging by his knowledge of the Old Testament), and had a muddled knowledge of Aramaic and the geography of Palestine (p 75).[4] He seemed to know about the fall of Jerusalem, which occurred in 70 CE, so it was obviously written after that date.

Ehrman points out that, apart from these New Testament Gospels, Jesus does not appear prominently in early Christian writings; for example, the apostle Paul says very little about Jesus, and very little about what Jesus did while he was alive (p 32).[2] The earliest existing written copy of the Gospels dates from the 4th Century, and has been re-written an unknown number of times.

DONALD DUTTON, PH.D.

The Virgin Birth

Contributing to the misunderstanding and debate behind the "virgin birth" are some problems with translation. Ehrman cites the Gospel of Matthew (1:23) as quoting Isaiah in the Old Testament saying, *"a virgin shall conceive and bear a son."*[3] Ehrman, however, points out that the translation from Hebrew to Greek from the Old to New Testament changed the meaning of what Isaiah said.

Isaiah (7:14) actually used the Hebrew word for "young woman," *alma*, not "virgin" (p 74).[4] The original passage in Isaiah read: *"Therefore the Lord himself shall give you a sign; Behold a young woman shall conceive, and bear a son and shall call his name Immanuel."* But in the New Testament Greek, the word for "virgin," *parthenos*, was used. Matthew (1:23) thus reads: *"Behold, a virgin shall be with child and shall bring forth a son; and they shall call him Emmanuel, which being translated, is God within us"*.

Now the English version of the Old Testament contains the "virgin" translation. Isaiah was talking about an event about to happen in his own community, not predicting a future messiah. This mistranslation is the origin of the Catholic cult of the virgin,[11] and subsequently establishes church perspectives on "virgins" and "whores," allowing women no middle ground.

The "anti-sin" message of the church, originating with Paul, elevated virginity to a holy ideal and transformed non-virgins into temptresses. It created a false dichotomy that still prevails (the Madonna- Whore dichotomy) and allows no acceptable expression of female sexuality in between.[11] [12]

Luke has his own version of the virgin birth: that god caused Mary to conceive, making her son the son of god. This was based on a revelation to her from the angel Gabriel. However, only Luke mentions this idea.

John has yet another version: that Jesus pre-existed the virgin birth (i.e. he was a being independent of god), and was "with god" before being born on Earth (John1:1-13). Ehrman sees John's version as dating back to Genesis and the Christian creation myth. John says nothing about a virgin birth, or about Joseph and Mary.

Of course, apart from the disparities in the Christian bible, virgin births were a way of explaining any unusual being in those times. In short, "virgin birth" tells us about an explanatory concept used by ignorant people, not about an actual event.

British writer Christopher Hitchens[13] finds it strange, given Jesus *"makes large claims for his heavenly father but never mentions that his mother is or was a virgin, and is repeatedly very rude and coarse to her when she makes an appearance"* (p 116).[13] The Catholic church has attempted to portray Joseph as an older man to avoid the thorny question of him having sex with his wife.

Jesus' Brothers

In Mark 6:3, the bible asks: *"Is not this the carpenter, the son of Mary, the brother of James and Joses and of Judas and Simon? ... and are not his sisters here with us?"* Matthew 13:55-57 also says *"Is this not the carpenter's son? Is this not his mother called Mary? And his brother James, and Joses, and Simon and Judas?"* At least two of the Gospels seem to agree on this point. However, the notion of Jesus having siblings further casts the virgin birth into doubt, so the Catholic church recast Jesus' brothers and sisters as "cousins," "brethren," or even as Joseph's children from an earlier marriage.

As Freeman[4] puts it, *"Mary came to absorb the attributes of pagan goddesses ... Rhea herself was associated with "virgin birth" stories, as was Isis"* (p 242-243).[4] Both Isis and Mary became virgins/ mother protectors emblemized by a rose. The doctrine of the Immaculate Conception was not announced by the Catholic church until 1852, and the notion that Mary did not die (the Assumption) in 1951.

The Forging of the Gospels

Based on his analysis, Ehrman claims that only eight of the 27 New Testament books go back to the original (named) author, and none of these are the Gospels. *"The Gospels ... were written decades later by people who didn't know Jesus, who lived in a different country or countries from Jesus, who spoke a different language from Jesus. They are different from each other in part because they didn't know each other, to some extent they had different sources of information, and they modified their stories on the basis of their own understandings of who Jesus was"* (p 24).[3] These differing versions allege, nevertheless, to report verbatim discussions between Jesus and his disciples.

As Ehrman puts it, *"the early Christian writers were busy and one of their common activities was to forge documents in the names of the apostles"* (p 122).[3] Forgery was a *"common phenomenon in the ancient world,"* and widely-discussed (Ehrman provides a list of 16 early authors who discuss forgery, including 7 Christian authors).

Forgery was not the only source of inaccuracies, however. Before the invention of the Gutenberg printing press, copying by hand was the only source of literary reproduction, and people made mistakes.

Modern technology available to current bible scholars includes data retrieval systems and computers to crunch out detailed evaluations of vocabulary and style. Where there are disconnects in style and/or word usage has now became apparent.

Such analysis convinced Ehrman that (with the exception of 1 Thessalonians), the letters of Paul were forged. For example, 2 Thessalonians has a main thesis that contradicts 1 Thessalonians. In 1 Thessalonians, "Paul" says that the second coming would be sudden and unexpected; in 2 Thessalonians, he says that it will not happen right away, and there will be clear-cut signs that the end is nigh; signs that had not yet appeared . In short, somewhere between the writing of 1 and 2 Thessalonians, prophecy failed again.

Ehrman suggests that 2 Thessalonians was written by some unknown author toward the end of the 1st Century: someone in Paul's church who was trying to calm the Christians who wondered why the second coming had not happened yet.

Some of Paul's other letters (e.g. Colossians and Ephesians) are not in Paul's writing style. He wrote short, simple sentences, while these are long and complex. In the "Pastoral Epistles" (attributed to Paul), 35% of the vocabulary occurs nowhere else in "Paul's" writings. The famous parable of the adulterous woman in John 7:53-8:12 (*"Let ye amongst you who is without sin cast the first stone"*) appears not to have been in the original:[7] it contains a number of words and phrases alien to the Gospel.

In the Gospel of Mark, the first Gospel to be written, there are several variations that describe Jesus healing a leper. Some of these described Jesus as angry (the oldest version, the Codex Bezae, dating from around 420 CE); others as feeling compassion.[7] Generally, the descriptive choice has moved toward the compassionate view, but it is not the more certain choice. Later Gospels, such as Matthew and John, omit the word "anger." However, Mark ascribes anger to Jesus three times, always in response to someone doubting his divine authority.

The Contradictions

Mark portrays Jesus as a physically and charismatically powerful authority figure and social outcast. Both Matthew and John ascribe compassion to him, and Luke portrays Jesus as imperturbable—dropping the earlier descriptions of anger, anguish, and despair that appear in Mark.

These later books revise Mark in the direction of Jesus as having no negative emotions.[11] The re-writing of the text appeared to make it simpler to understand and acceptable for the time it was rewritten. Given that this rewriting was so common, the weight Ehrman gives to "early texts" may not be warranted. So what if it's early (and conceivably closer to the source)? It's already been rewritten numerous times.

Apart from mistranslation and forgery, there were also theologically-motivated alterations of the text.[7] These were driven by the disputes of the scribes' day. Early Christians (2nd and 3rd Century) debated over many things: whether there was only one god (estimates ranged from 1 to 365); whether god had created the world; whether Jesus was human (Arianism), god-like, or a blend (Holy Trinity); whether his death generated salvation; and whether he had been born of a virgin. The orthodox view obviously prevailed: Jesus was proclaimed as being part of the Holy Trinity, as his mother being a virgin, and as having risen from the dead.

Ehrman[7] shows how biblical text was then revised to fit church orthodoxy on the issue of whether Jesus was god or human. The view came to predominate that Jesus was god-like. An early codex showing him described as follows: *"who was made manifest in the flesh"* (1 Timothy 3:16) was changed to *"God made manifest in the flesh,"* consistent with the prevailing view.

The Crucifixion and Resurrection

Scholars of the early church[2,4,11] agree that Jesus existed, but was not the Jesus Christ of the Christian myth. The notion that Christ rose from the dead has a much more mundane explanation, nicely outlined by Freeman.[4,11]

Caiaphas, the Jewish high priest who presided over the Sanhedrin (the Jewish council of elders) worked closely with Pontius Pilate. Caiaphas was the most threatened by Jesus' teachings and developing popularity. Jesus was a prophet and charismatic outsider. He threatened the status quo through his prophecies that society was about to be radically transformed by god's kingdom arriving on Earth.

This led to his crucifixion, masterminded by Caiaphas in 30 CE, as a way of dealing with this threat to the high priest's authority. The most likely reason for the animus toward Jesus was that Caiaphas feared the Romans would crack down if Jesus' stirring of the crowds escalated.

The Christian bible (Matthew) says that the (Jewish) priests took responsibility for Jesus' tomb after the crucifixion. Caiaphas wanted to thwart a burgeoning movement after Jesus' death. That meant having the body removed. He made sure that the tomb was open, and left a message with a "young man" that Jesus would reappear in Galilee to draw off the disciples. In short, Freeman explores the possibility that Caiaphas *"put in place a plan which would defuse the Jesus movement, or at least transfer it to Galilee"* (p 34).[4]

Descriptions of those who removed the body can be found in Matthew (28:11-15). Included is also how they offered a bribe to the soldiers who were guarding the body to say that his disciples had taken him to Galilee. Other post-crucifixion appearances of Jesus were to female disciples (Mark and John say it was Mary Magdalene) and may have grown out of rumour stemming from the surprise of women visiting his tomb, only to find it empty.

Clearly Caiaphas failed, but the plan was plausible, and he had the motive and opportunity to do it. As Freeman put it, *"It would have been important, of course, for the priests to emphasize that Jesus was no longer physically present but had 'risen.' Otherwise rumours might have persisted that his body was still to be found elsewhere in Jerusalem"* (p 33).[4]

It would have been priests who removed the body, and the description of their clothes as 'white' or 'dazzling' (as reported in some Gospel stories) corresponds to the white, linen robes worn by the junior priesthood. The bribe offered in Matthew (28:11-15) would have been a plausible cover if Caiaphas himself had the body removed.

The Gospel of Peter, discovered in the 19th Century, describes how soldiers saw two men enter an open tomb and emerge carrying a third man. Freeman cautions that this version goes on to describe the supporters as angels, but *"by the second century (when it was written), it may have 'grown in the telling."* Freeman apologises for his speculation, but this explanation is far more feasible than resurrection.

Again, rather than reflexively accepting the sightings of Jesus as fact, Freeman asks what frame of mind the disciples were in. They had just witnessed the mutilation and killing of a close friend, and feared that they might be picked up next. Freeman says that the various sightings of Jesus described in the Gospels (which vary from one account to another) could be ascribed to trauma, emotional exhaustion, and hallucination. Jesus' disciples went into hiding after the crucifixion,* believing they were being searched for by the authorities.

Psychologists Steven Lynn & Kevin McConkey[15] and sociologist Jeffrey Victor[16] reviewed research on trauma and how it interacts with hallucination and memory. Both reviews found evidence that prior trauma increases the likelihood of dissociation and depersonalization (feelings of unreality or of living in a dream-state) as reactions to present traumas.

Dissociative states are characterized by a disruption of the normal functions of consciousness (memory, identity, emotion, perception, body representation, motor control, and behaviour) and can include a confusion of inner voices with external stimuli. Depersonalization is an experience of unreality with respect to surroundings.[17] As Victor puts it, *"the content of what people experience in altered states of consciousness (such as produced by extreme anxiety or trauma) is shaped by prevailing cultural expectations"* (p 90).[16]

---

* The crucifixion was seen quite negatively by the disciples, and for many years afterward; Christians did not use the crucifix as their central symbol until 400 years had passed. The original Christian symbol was a lamb.

A similar phenomenon occurred with Elvis sightings: contagions of hallucination in the form of people claiming to have seen Elvis Presley, the rock and roll singer, in the years after his death in 1977. Two outbreaks occurred in Ottawa, Ontario and Kalamazoo, Michigan. A society was even formed of people who believed Presley was still alive in 2016, many of whom claimed to have seen him post 1977. This group has a central belief involving Presley's alleged reasons for wanting to drop out of public sight as part of their rationale.

In one case, a group of townspeople who believed in Satanic cults reported seeing such a cult performing rituals in the woods; they went to the police saying that the group was planning a human sacrifice. Further investigation indicated that it was a Halloween party by a group of "Goth" college students (p 177).[16] The "Satanic Panic" mindset of the early 1990s had shaped the townsfolk's perceptions.

Victor describes "rumour panics" as collective stress reactions that are a response to immediately threatening circumstances. Typically, the events he studied occurred in small towns in the US and had, as part of their core beliefs, the existence of Satanic rituals, kidnappings, and the murder of children. Satanic rumour panics sprung up in numerous newspapers around the same time (1988) and ended just as abruptly; a clear indicator of a social hysteria.

Victor reports a 1991 poll of California Social Workers, which revealed that 50% of those polled believed in a national conspiracy of multigenerational, Satanic baby-killers. FBI investigations produced no physical evidence for any ritual murder and missing child reports never generated the numbers required by these Satanic panic theories.

Victor ascribed the process to "groupthink,"[18] whereby a socially-produced reality becomes real for a group. Rapidly changing cultural values produce a cultural crisis, which increases communication of myths. The usual network to communicate these rumour panics was fundamentalist Christian groups who disseminated Satanic cult stories (p 64).[16]

Psychologists Leonard Newman and Roy Baumeister[19] describe reports of people who were "sure" they had been abducted by UFOs, and described aliens who had performed an operation on them. A Roper poll in 1992 found that 3.7 million Americans reported being abducted. However, no credible evidence for alien contact has ever been found.

The authors found that some people were "fantasy prone:" they had high levels of involvement in vivid fantasies and experienced difficulty in distinguishing those fantasies from reality. The story provided the person (and their therapist, if one was used) with a convincing explanation for their confused mental state.

Jesus' disciples had powerful reasons to want to believe that he was the messiah. The crucifixion disconfirmed these beliefs. The confusion surrounding the empty tomb provided enough ambiguity for a resurrection story to emerge—especially if one was purposefully planted by Caiaphas.

The crucifixion must also have traumatized disciples, shattering their belief that Jesus was an all-powerful messiah. These shattered assumptions of central beliefs are at the core of trauma.[20] If our central beliefs, the ones we use as a bedrock for our other, more limited beliefs, are contradicted, the result is traumatic. Acute anxiety is the usual response, accompanied by terror and the subsequent avoidance of the source of trauma.

Therefore, it is little wonder that we reject any sign of disconfirmation of central assumptions. These assumptions remain unchallenged and constitute a shared "intersubjectivity," to use Yuval Harari's term from his book, *Sapiens*. This intersubjectivity allows us to interact with strangers who we assume share our belief system.

Given the extensive rewriting of the bible, the resurrection myth seems more like a by-product of later church dogma. It caught on because it provided an explanation for the failed prophecy that Jesus was the messiah—failed because he never raised a triumphal army, became king, or drove the Romans out of the promised land (the traditional Jewish definitions of messiah); instead, he was crucified (p 235).[3] This created major cognitive dissonance, and the resurrection myth reduced that dissonance.[14] As Freeman puts it, "*a full historical account of the resurrection would need to examine the many accounts of charismatic leaders who had been "seen" by their followers after death.*"

Elaine Pagels[1] describes a battle over control of the resurrection story; the results favoured Peter's version of being the first to experience the resurrection. This claim would support the Catholic church's argument for apostolic succession, and led them to become the "Church of St. Peter." Pagans at the time dismissed the myth as a report of a hysterical woman (p 360),[11] while the 3rd Century Christian theologian Origen viewed the resurrection as an allegory; he claimed the literal version was intended only for the "simpleminded" (p 360).[1]

Even if we ignore the dubious nature of the crucifixion story, consider, as Christopher Hitchens asks us to do in his book, *God is not Great* (p 209),[13] the morality of the story if accepted as fact. "*I am told of a human sacrifice that took place* two thousand years ago, without my wishing it, and in circumstances so ghastly that had I been present and in possession of any influence, I would have been duty bound to try and stop it. In consequence of this murder, my own manifold sins are forgiven me" (p 209).[13]

In other words, in order to gain the benefit of this sacrifice, a Christian has to accept responsibility for it, even though they played no part in it. Furthermore, every time they decline this responsibility, or commit another sin, they are intensifying the agony of the original event.

A believer must also believe that the agony was necessary to compensate for an earlier crime that they also had no part in: the sin of Adam. Their own part in this is deemed the "original sin" and is inescapable. The Christian myth, both of genesis and the crucifixion, generates guilt for events that precede the life of the individual.

The Afterlife

According to Ehrman (p 261),[3] the Christian view of the afterlife was also invented as a reaction to a later disconfirmed prophecy. It is also full of contradictions: most contemporary Christians believe that the soul goes to an afterlife while the body remains in the grave, yet they also believe that the afterlife includes physical pain (hell) or pleasure (heaven). Reunification with loved ones would also require some ability to recognise these loved ones (for instance, having the appearance of a physical body to recognize).

The view of the afterlife in early Christianity stemmed from Judaism (the book of Job), and was an attempt to reconcile the bothersome notion of suffering on Earth with a notion of justice. It is an answer to the question, why do the righteous suffer? Because they will be redeemed in the afterlife (p 261).[3]

The notion developed that god had relinquished control of this world to cosmic forces of evil (p 262),[3] but soon he would intervene and make it right (the Apocalypse). This intervention would occur sometime after the resurrection of Jesus, in the end time. At this time, god would bodily raise the dead to give them an eternal reward—he would make them immortal (p 263).[3] This is the view expressed in the Old Testament (Daniel) and the New (Paul: 1 Thessalonians 4-5). This belief system rationalized injustice in a world designed by god and held out the promise of something better in heaven.

The transformation of the view began again as a result of the disconfirmation of a prophecy: Paul believed he would be alive for the second coming of Christ. In the last book of the New Testament (written after Paul's death), the prophecy was recast so that the divine calendar is not commensurate with the earthly calendar. The raising of the dead no longer meant the physical body. Now the message is that a person is judged not at the end of an age (Judgment Day) but at the end of one's life, when the soul enters heaven (p 265).[3]

The split between the end times, Judgment Day, and the kingdom of heaven was recast from two ages to two spheres: heaven and Earth. It no longer referred to a physical resurrection, but a division between the world of suffering on Earth and the world of ecstasy in heaven. This split is not found in the earliest Christian writings and appears to be a result of explaining the failed prophecy of Jesus' second coming during Paul's lifetime.

As Ehrman puts it, *"with the passing of time, the apocalyptic notion of the resurrection of the body becomes transformed in to the doctrine of the immortality of the soul"* (p 266).³ He concludes that *"orthodox Christian views emerged less as necessary consequences from the teachings of Jesus and his early followers than as doctrines that developed largely because of historical and cultural factors that influenced later Christians"* (p 267).³

Ehrman, who began as a born-again Christian, evolved into an agnostic. This stemmed from his inability *"to understand how a good and loving God could be in control of the world given the miserable lives that most people—even believers—are forced to endure here"* (p 273).³ He describes the bible as *"a human book from beginning to end ... written by different human authors at different times and in different places to address many different needs. Many of these authors no doubt felt they were inspired by God to say what they did, but they had their own perspectives ... beliefs, views, needs, understandings, theologies ... and these informed everything they said"* (p 11-12).⁷

The Authority of the Catholic Church

Viscount John Julius Norwich, British broadcaster and historian, points out (p 4)[21] that the sole foundation for the claims of the Catholic church stem from Matthew (16:18-19), and that the notion of a "church" appears only twice in all the Gospels; some biblical scholars believe even those to be a later interpolation.

The claim from Matthew 16:18-19 reports Jesus as saying, *"Thou art Peter, and on this rock I will build my church*

... *I will give unto thee the keys of the Kingdom of Heaven.*" On these few words, inscribed in Latin around the dome of the Basilica of St. Peter, rests the entire foundation of the Catholic church.[21] As Norwich notes, the word for "church" is used only twice in all four Gospels. It is for this reason that both uses are suspected of being later additions. Given the amount of rewriting that Ehrman chronicles, this is not surprising.

Whether it is a later addition or not, the veracity of this statement from Jesus is predicated on a verbatim quote allegedly made by Jesus to one other person (Peter): a person who did not write the original Gospel. In fact, Peter was dead when it was written (it is thought he died in Rome in 64 CE, Matthew was probably written around 95 CE). No one was present to hear this statement; it is hearsay from sixty years back. In fact, Jesus never even mentioned Rome in sayings attributed to him. However, this type of revision served the purposes of those in power.

Yuval Harari,[22] author of *Sapiens* and *Homo Deus*, describes how the Catholic church in medieval Europe enjoyed unlimited political authority. To justify this authority, the church referred to the Donation of Constantine—their claim that the Emperor Constantine had signed a decree on March 30, 315 granting Pope Sylvester I and his heirs perpetual control of the western part of the Roman Empire. This document served as a powerful propaganda tool whenever any challenge to church authority arose.

In 1441, a Catholic priest named Lorenzo Valla published a study based on the new technique of linguistic analysis. Valla analysed the style and grammar of the document, and showed that it included words that were unknown in 4th Century Latin. Furthermore, the date used on the document was two years off the historical dates for the consuls of that period. He concluded that the Donation of Constantine was probably forged somewhere around 400 years after Constantine's death.

According to Harari, historians now agree that the document was forged in the Papal Court during the 8th Century. The "authority" of the Catholic church in Europe is based on a lie.

Ehrman can be praised for his unflinching analysis of the New Testament and its revisions, but he describes the internecine church struggles as though they took place in a vacuum. In reality, as Freeman describes it, the orthodox view increasingly supported state power (p 251)[11] and wealth. The interplay of political and religious power played out for centuries, with religion offering redemption to state leaders and eventually benefitting from tax breaks as the "official religion."

Freeman describes the case of Roman Emperor Theodosius, who massacred thousands in Greece in response to anti-Roman rioting. The church leader of the day (Ambrose) allowed Theodosius to receive penance; in return, Theodosius passed laws banning all forms of pagan worship (p 225).[11] As Freeman states, "*encouraged* by the initiative, Christian mobs now began destroying the great shrines of the ancient world" (p 225).[11]

State and religious power became interconnected based on the perception that each had unique power: the state had legal and military power, while the church granted passage to heaven and redemption. In addition, they each had common enemies. By 438 CE, Rome had become a theocracy with laws against polytheists, Jews, pagans, and non-orthodox Christians.* Laws were passed promoting the burning of "heresies."

Christian dogma as we now know it was the result of this powerful coalition (p 253).²³ Theological "debates" (such as the nature of Jesus' divinity) were resolved by political power struggles (p 260).²³ Today's "truth" was yesterday's political victory.

The earliest claim from Christian writings of the New Testament being scripture is from Athanasius, Bishop of Alexandria in 367 CE (p 3);⁹ this is the approximate starting point of monolithic Christian creed. The principles Christians currently hold originated in that time period.[3,7]

The Jesus Seminar

As we have seen, scholars such as Bart Ehrman believe that there is sufficient evidence for an historical Jesus, but not for the "Christ" aspects of the story added by Christianity. The Jesus Seminar scholars arrived at many of the same conclusions.

The Jesus Seminar[23] is a group of scholars who attempted to reconstruct the life of the historical Jesus.[23] They asked who he was, what he did, and what he said using social anthropology, history, and textual analysis.

To begin, they used cross-cultural anthropological studies to set the general background. Then they narrowed in on the history of 1st Century Palestine and used textual analysis to focus on Jesus himself. They canvassed the records of the first

---

* To the point where capital punishment was given to those who made a sacrifice to a pagan deity.

four centuries for traditions about Jesus, and sifted through them by criteria such as multiple attestation (whether or not it appears in more than one independent source), distinctiveness, and orality.*

The seminar's reconstruction of the historical Jesus sees him as an itinerant Jewish faith healer who preached a gospel of liberation in startling parables and aphorisms. An iconoclast, Jesus broke with established Jewish theological doctrines in both his teachings and behaviours, often by turning common-sense ideas upside down. He would do this to confound the expectations of his audience: he preached that "heaven's imperial rule" (traditionally translated as "kingdom of god") was already present, but unseen; he depicted god as a loving father; he fraternized with outsiders and criticized the status quo.

According to the seminar, Jesus was a mortal man born of two human parents; he did not perform miracles, die as a substitute for sinners, or rise bodily from the dead. Sightings of a risen Jesus were nothing more than the visionary experiences of some of his disciples rather than physical encounters. They summarize their position as follows:

"Jesus of Nazareth was born during the reign of Herod the Great, his mother's name was Mary, and he had a human father whose name may not have been Joseph. He was born in Nazareth, not in Bethlehem, was an itinerant sage who shared meals with social outcasts, practiced faith healing without the use of ancient medicine or magic, relieving afflictions we now consider psychosomatic."

---

* Citations for each of these claims is available on the Jesus Seminar website.

He did not walk on water, feed the multitude with loaves and fishes, change water into wine, or raise Lazarus from the dead. He was arrested in Jerusalem and crucified by the Romans: executed as a public nuisance, not for claiming to be the son of god. The empty tomb was a fiction—Jesus was not raised bodily from the dead. Belief in the resurrection was based on the visionary experiences of Paul, Peter, and Mary Magdalene.[23]

In short, a picture very much like the one we have developed above.

Constantine and the State Religion

A defining change in the status of Christianity came with Constantine. Christianity had started off as a fringe religion whose adherents ran afoul of Roman law by refusing to honour the gods and the Holy Roman Emperor. As a result, in the reigns of Nero, Domitian, and Decius, they became Christian martyrs. However, with Constantine, Christianity became the official religion of the Roman Empire. From there, it was then transmitted to the countries that the Romans conquered.

This transformation was prompted by Constantine having a vision of a cross before a battle (Milvian Bridge in 312 CE) that the Romans then won. Constantine had had other visions, of Apollo and of the sun god (p 156),[11] but this one provided him with a rationale for including Christians in his political scheme. It also forged a fusion of Christianity and war success that was absent from the original views of Christian followers.

Jesus' image was also transformed from passivism to a warrior-like visage (p 177).[11] As Freeman states, "*This* *extraordinary transformation of Jesus' role is a mark of the extent to which Constantine forced Christianity into new channels*" (p 177).[4] In fact, it was this militarization of Christian beliefs that was later exploited by Saint Augustine* in his rationalization for Holy War (p 2).[24]

As Freeman puts it, "*there is no evidence that suggests that Constantine knew anything much about Christ or even of the requirements for Christian living*" (p 155).[4] In fact, he had his own son killed after a false rape accusation by his wife. He then had his wife killed by boiling her in a bath (229-230).[4]

From that point on, stature in the Christian church meant access to wealth and power. Intellectual diversity in religious matters now ceased to exist in the lands ruled by the Roman Empire. The questioning that had earmarked early Christianity became illegal in 381 CE by order of Theodosius, with horrendous penalties. Those pagans now classified as "insane and demented heretics" (p 249)[4] had to forfeit their churches to the new Christians. If they protested, they were expelled from the city.

By 527 CE, under the Emperor Justinian, the death penalty was decreed for anyone practising paganism (p 268).[11] Despite these harsh measures, pagans still practiced in the mountains, where they could not be detected (p 269).[4] These early pagan religions had no specific creed toward others (p

---

* Augustine wrote *Contra Faustum Manichaeum* (Reply to Faustus the Manichaean) from 408-410 CE. Faustus' heresy was that "*He supposed the Gospels, in their present form, to be not the works of the Apostles, but rather later Judaizing falsifiers*" (www.textmanuscripts.com). Faustus, it seems, was onto something. In his critique of Faustus, Augustine developed his notion of the Holy War, one fought against the enemies of the Pope (god's representative on Earth).

6).[8] But Christianity did: there was only one holy church, the Catholic church.

Hypatia, a female pagan philosopher and mathematician, was torn to pieces by a Christian mob in 415 CE (p 268).[11] Her death symbolized the end of Greek rationality and the beginning of 1,600 years of Christian theocracy: what Freeman called the "closing of the Western mind." The dumbing-down of rational inquiry* was replaced by "faith." What Augustine called the "disease of curiosity" (rational inquiry) was prohibited, to the point where works of the Greek scholars were no longer read.

Inevitably, this lust for power led to the Inquisition, where the Catholic church went looking for heresy in people's minds. Within a century of achieving power, any dissent from Christian Orthodoxy was punishable either by death or banishment. Roman Emperor Justinian passed laws in the 6th Century that made Christian baptism obligatory and specified "exclusion from the state" and seizure of property as punishments for non-compliance (p 268).[4]

Constantine effectively ended the power struggle within the church between the Arians and the Nicaeans. Within years of this becoming law, Christian mobs killed heretics and burned all heretic writing, including the libraries that housed them. As Freeman puts it, *"The archaeologist finds signs of Christian iconoclasm everywhere: the cutting out of phalluses*

---

* Venerable Bede, an English monk and historian living in England in the 7th-8th Century, adopted the term *Anno Domini* to refer to all dates from the birth of Christ. However, Bede was accused of heresy because he had worked out his own way of dating the origin of the Earth: 3,952 years before the birth of Christ. The Church was offended, because church authority put the Earth as 5,000 years old. Current radiometric dating puts the age of the Earth at about 4.5 billion years.

of Amun on Egyptian temples, the carving of crosses on pagan statues, the erasure of inscriptions of (pagan) gods' names, bathhouses converted into churches. The statue of Marcus Aurelius remained intact only because it was mistakenly believed to be Constantine ... the elimination of paganism was accompanied by a dampening down of emotions, dance and song so effective that we still lower our voices when we enter a church" (p 267).[11]

The Perseverance of Christianity

How is it that this dogma has endured for so long? There are, of course, numerous reasons, including political power, socialization of followers, and punishment of infidels. Church power became so absolute when intertwined with political power that it became insurmountable. However, another reason is the fear and effort involved in challenging a central belief that encompasses all we know.

New York Times writer Ross Douthat, in his book *Bad Religion: How We Became a Nation of Heretics*,[25] sees modern society as the problem that stains original Christian orthodoxy. Douthat is a Catholic and obviously well-read, so it is instructive to see how he treats the works of Ehrman, Pagels, and others.

Much of Douthat's argument is well taken: that the amalgamation of orthodoxy with unfettered capitalism has corrupted the Christian cult of the self and turned it into the cult of greed. Douthat makes it clear that he has retained his belief in the orthodox arguments of St Paul and the canonical texts that were written within fifty years of the crucifixion (p 167/339 [Kindle E-book]). His voluminous bibliography shows that he has been exposed to a broad spectrum of heretical ideas along the way, including Bart Ehrman, Elaine Pagels, and Sam Harris.

What is relevant here is how Douthat dismisses these thinkers. Pagels and Ehrman are lumped together with novelist Dan Brown and labelled "accommodationists," while Harris is labelled as a "polemicist." But in no case are any of their ideas revealed, discussed, taken seriously, or challenged. They are simply dismissed as part of a current Zeitgeist.

What enables this blanket dismissal? In this, one's preconceived notions get in the way, creating the unalterable belief that they are right and all critics are wrong. Douthat seems myopic to the notion that Paul's ideas, along with the rest of early Christianity, were also part of a social movement or Zeitgeist, one far less informed than those of the present. Douthat points out that biographies of Jesus penned by Victorian scholars were deeply autobiographical and said more about the author than about Jesus (as argued by Albert Schweitzer in his book, *The Quest for the Historical Jesus*).

However, Douthat fails to see this process as also happening with Paul or the founders of Christianity. He takes it as rock-solid evidence that the Gospels were selected from writings within 50 years of the crucifixion, as though that made them accurate.

Douthat advocates a "numinous" personal experience of god, and sees this as the sustenance of religion (220/339 [Kindle E-book]). As he puts it, Christian orthodoxy requires "commitment to mystery and paradox" since the truth about god surpasses rationality (p 9-10/339 [Kindle E-book]).

But this "numinous" experiential truth is too fraught with subjectivity; it is to the point where some would call it hallucinatory. Absolute truth may exist, but everything we know about the human brain and all we know about human social influence points to the opposite conclusion: that subjectivity generates beliefs that are falsely viewed as being objectively true.

This being the case, no numinous experience can be trusted as being representative of something outside of the self. Douthat demonstrates how intelligent, well-read people still generate belief perseverance,[26] often through simply failing to engage in questions raised by heresy. The systems that serve us best are those very systems that have attempted to reduce our subjective bias—the systems of science and the adversarial system in law. A religion that can tap into an emotional sphere is valuable so long as it does not attempt to deliver dogma whose basis is ephemeral and dubious.

Dogma-Free Christianity

Of course, not all Christians may be bothered by contradictions in dogma, or even be aware of the dogma at all. A Pew Survey in the US (2010) found that 90% surveyed believed in god, and 85% of these self-identified as Christians. Of these, a third believed Billy Graham (20th Century evangelist) delivered the Sermon on the Mount (Jesus' moral sayings in Matthew). Over half did not know Judaism was a religion, one in ten believed Joan of Arc was Noah's wife, and 20% believed Sodom and Gomorrah were a married couple.

Atheists scored higher than Christians on knowledge of the Christian bible. Instead, much like the cult members discussed in Chapter 1, the feelings associated with religious observance (belonging, family, and a worldview) were more important than information.

REFERENCES

1. Pagels E. *The gnostic gospels.* New York: Vintage Paperbacks; 1981.
2. Ehrman B. *Did jesus exist? The historical argument for jesus of nazareth.* New York: Harper One; 2012.
3. Ehrman B. *Jesus, interrupted.* New York: Harper One; 2009.
4. Freeman C. *A new history of early christianity.* New Haven: Yale University Press; 2009.
5. Armstrong K. *A history of god.* New York: Knopf; 1993.
6. Tobin P. The bible and modern scholarship. *The christian delusion.* Amherst: Prometheus Press; 2010.
7. Ehrman B. *Misquoting jesus: the story behind who changed the bible and why.* New York: Harper One; 2005.
8. Ehrman B. *Forged.* New York: Harper One; 2011.
9. Ehrman B. *Lost scriptures.* New York: Oxford University Press; 2003.
10. Kadri S. *The trial: a history from socates to o.j. simpson.* New York: Random House; 2005.
11. Freeman C. *The closing of the western mind.* New York: Vintage Books; 2002.
12. de Riencourt A. *Sex and power in history.* New York: Delta; 1974.
13. Hitchens C. *God is not great: how religion poisons everything.* New York: Twelve; 2007.
14. Festinger L, Riecken H, Schachter S. *When prophecy fails.* Minneapolis: University of Minnesota Press; 1956.
15. Lynn SJ, McConkey KM. *Truth in memory.* New York: Guilford Press; 1998.

16. Victor JS. *Satanic panic*. La Salle: Open Court; 1993.
17. American Psychiatric Association. Diagnostic and statistical manual of mental disorders; version V. Washington: American Psychiatric Association Pub; 2013.
18. Janis I. *Groupthink*. Boston: Houghton-Mifflin; 1982.
19. Newman L, Baumeister R. Abducted by aliens: Spurious reports on interplanetary masochism. *Truth in memory*. New York: The Guilford Press; 1998.
20. Janoff-Bulman R. *Shattered assumptions: towards a new psychology of trauma*. New York: Free Press; 1992.
21. Norwich JJ. *Absolute monarchs: A history of the papacy*. New York: Random House; 2011.
22. Harari Y. *Homo deus: a brief history of tomorrow*. Toronto: Penguin Random House; 2016.
23. Seminar J. (http://en.wikipedia.org/wiki/Jesus_Seminar). 2012, 2013.
24. Dutton DG. *The psychology of genocide, massacres and extreme violence*. Westport: Praeger International; 2007.
25. Douthat R. *Bad religion: how we became a nation of heretics*. New York: Amazon; 2012.
26. Lord C, Ross L, Lepper MR. Biased assimilation and attitude polarization: The effects of prior theories and subsequently considered evidence. *Journal of Personality and Social Psychology*. 1979; 37:2098-2109.
27. Metzger B, Ehrman B. *The text of the new testament*. New York: Oxford University Press; 2005.

CHAPTER 5

Islam and the Arab Conquests

"I was ordered to fight all men until they say 'There is no God but Allah."

MUHAMMAD'S DEATHBED QUOTE

Although accounts vary, Muhammad ibn Abdullah was born sometime around 570 CE in the town of Mecca in western Arabia (p 39).[1,2] He died in 632 (p 54).[3] According to Muslim legend, his Koranic revelations started one night during the month of Ramadan in 610 CE, when he was a 40-year-old merchant in Mecca. He received the first revelation from the angel Gabriel, who gave him the responsibility for inscribing the coming messages from Allah to give to mankind.

Prior to this visitation, Muhammad had taken to secluding himself in order to meditate and contemplate his life. Muhammad lived in the Sassanid Empire, which encompassed what is now the Arabian Peninsula, including Iraq, and Syria, and also Iran. Mecca was at that time essentially polytheistic,[1] and revered astral deities (the sun god, the moon god, Venus, etc.).

Religious life was focused on several themes: asceticism, apocalypse, and prophecy. As with Jesus, there were several figures at the time of Muhammad who also claimed to be prophets bearing a divine message (p 31).[1]

Muhammad would certainly have been exposed to pagan beliefs as a child. Mecca had at the centre of town a sacred, black stone and a large sanctuary to the pagan god Hubal. Mecca was also a trading centre, and thus exposed to other, non-pagan religious ideas, including Judaism and Christianity. Muhammad obviously knew who the angel Gabriel was from Christianity.

Historian Hugh Kennedy,[3] Professor of Arabic at the University of London, reports that Muhammad had made trading expeditions from Mecca to Syria and discussed religion with Syrian Christian monks. However, as Kennedy says, *"much of the story of his early life is obscured by pious legend"* (p 45).[3]

Evidence that Muhammad actually existed is essentially the same as for Jesus' existence: his presence was noted historically by scribes from outside his religious group, but little else. In Muhammad's case, in 640 CE (8 years after Muhammad's death), a Christian writer named Thomas the Presbyter wrote that Muhammad and his followers had made a raid around Gaza (p 53).[1] As historian Fred Donner put it, *"This, at least, enables the historian to feel more confident that Muhammad is not completely a fiction of later pious imagination"* (p 53).[1]

Society at the time was tribal: centred on family well-being. It was comprised of kinship groups whose existence was constantly threatened by the scarcity of meagre agricultural resources in a rocky desert. In such societies, morality is commensurate with whatever action benefits the tribe; hence, universal moral principles do not exist.[4] Kinship groups are bound together in mutual defence; belonging to such a kin group is essential for survival in a hostile desert environment (p 38).[4]

Muhammad: Visions and Influence

Muhammad himself was illiterate. The Koran itself attests to this: "*Those who follow the messenger, the Prophet who can neither read nor write, whom they will find described in the Torah and the Gospel [which are] with them ...*" (Koran 7:157). According to one of Muhammad's wives,* the first Koranic revelation occurred when the angel Gabriel visited Muhammad and ordered him to recite. Muhammad responded "*ma aqra'u*" (I do not read).

As with Christianity, Muslims believe the word of Allah was brought to Muhammad verbatim, without any alteration or change. Muhammad received these revelations as intense sounds and visions, that overcame him to the point that he could only lie on the ground, shaking and perspiring (p 40; see also[5] p 9).[1] He disclosed these revelations to his wife, then to a small group of friends, who became his first followers (p 10).[5]

In the Koran, it is emphasized that Muhammad was required only to receive the sacred text and had no authority

---

* Muhammad had several wives, including Aisha, whom he married when she was seven. The marriage may have been for official purposes only and not consummated.

to change it (10:15). Even though Muhammad had no authority to change the Koran, he was still more than a passive receiver: he received the revelations in full consciousness, witnessing in his heart the greatness of the presence of the voice of Allah.

When asked about the experience of his revelations Muhammad reported, *"sometimes it is revealed like the ringing of a bell. This form of inspiration is the hardest of them all and then it passes off after I have grasped what is inspired. Sometimes the Angel comes in the form of a man and talks to me and I grasp whatever he says"* (p 78).[5]

For Muhammad, the revelations were real, and he believed the context was objective; however, he was only able to describe the experience through metaphorical terms. As Muhammad's revelations about the Medina Jews indicates, these revelations sometimes reflected personal thoughts or reactions of Muhammad.

Muhammad described these visions as a figure who told him to preach the word of Allah to the populace. Sometimes the vision was preceded by the sound of ringing bells; at other times he heard only the voice (p 423).[7]

For around three years he brooded over these visions, confessing them only to his wife and immediate friends. He finally became convinced that the figure was the angel Gabriel, and the visions were communications from Allah. Muhammad came to view himself as a prophet in the tradition of Christ and Moses. However, his early ministry in Mecca was unsuccessful, and he was forced to flee to the nearby rival city of Medina.

What then ensued was hundreds of years of war and conflict as the new religion, Islam, spread throughout the Middle East.[3,6] Researcher Peter Townsend (p 53)[17] reports that archaeological digs failed to find any evidence supporting the existence of a city called Mecca in the area where it was supposed to have existed in Muhammad's time. And yet, other minor cities in the Arabian peninsula were found. The oldest mosques excavated (in Baghdad, Wasit, Kufa, and Fustat), all built in the early 700s, do not face toward Mecca (Townsend p 54),[17] suggesting some revision in Islamic dogma occurred between.

Epilepsy and Religious Visions

Neurologist Frank Freemon[7] ascribes Muhammad's revelations to epilepsy. Recurring epileptic seizures are reported by several neurological studies as causing religious revelations; specifically, the psychomotor seizures of temporal lobe epilepsy. These are literally self-generated micro-storms that occur in the temporal lobe area of the brain. According to Freemon, studies of epileptic patients reveal that a substantial sub-set of these patients experience religious visions if they have a religious background. Furthermore, the other symptoms reported by Muhammad (e.g. sweating and shaking) are consistent with an epileptic seizure.

Psychiatrists Jeffery Saver and John Rabin[8] describe Muhammad's spells as a "complex, partial seizure" given the descriptions of his symptoms such as pallor, appearance of intoxication, profuse sweating, falling, and visual and auditory hallucinations.[8] They cite earlier studies as suggestive of a "*distinctive, interictal (i.e. between neurological firings such as epilepsy or strokes) personality syndrome of temporal lobe epilepsy*" marked by "hyper-religiosity and intense cosmological concerns" (p 504).[8]

Other features of this syndrome include hyper-moralism, humourlessness, aggressive irritability, and hypergraphia. The latter, hypergraphia (the intense desire to write and draw), of course is not found in someone like Muhammad, who could not write. Biographical material does indicate evidence for the other symptoms.

Saver and Rabin also provide some empirical evidence connecting religiosity and temporal lobe epilepsy. The syndrome causes patients to imbue normal stimuli with "exaggerated affective tone and significance" (p 500).[8] This increased significance can take the form of religious meaning. In one previous case study, six patients with temporal lobe epilepsy had dramatic and long-lasting religious conversions after ictal experiences.

Citing a famous social psychological study by Schachter and Singer,[9] Saver and Rabin point out that identical physiological events are interpreted differently, and even experienced differently, depending on an individual's cognitive expectations. For example, pharmacologically-induced sympathetic arousal is variably experienced as anything from rewarding to stressful, depending on the cognitive set of the research subject. Neurological symptoms are similarly interpreted according to the cognitive set of the person who experiences them. Therefore, if someone has a religious orientation, they are likely to interpret the physiological signs as divinely inspired or "the voice of god."

An influential study on religious conversion and temporal lobe epilepsy[10] cited numerous cases of religious conversion that appeared to have epileptic symptomatology (such as seizures), including St. Paul and Teresa of Avila. In his classic text on brainwashing, Sargant[11] argued that emotional stress and increased suggestibility cause disruption of existing patterns of thought. This allows new patterns to assert themselves. The emotional stressors Sargant mentioned include bereavement, intense emotionalism, and lobotomy, all of which had preceded sudden religious conversions. Intense emotionalism is a part of many religious services, including Quaker and Southern Baptist services, and often involves shaking and drumming.

After reviewing evidence connecting a variety of psychological states (hallucinogens, near-death experiences, dementias) to religious visions, Saver and Rabin concluded that there was a common substrate in the limbic system for all such experiences. In his study of people rescued from cults, Wayne Sage[12] found that they reported the emotional connection to the cult's "family" was of utmost importance to them; the specific dogma was secondary. An emotional response is central to religious belief, and for this reason, strong emotions often accompany any perceived attack on one's beliefs. Psychologist Drew Westen reports a similar finding for political beliefs.[13]

The Spread of Islam

According to Professor Efraim Karsh[5] of the University of London, Muhammad's influence spread locally to Mecca's marginalia, but also to some leading families and clans. Muhammad had begun to preach about his visions around 600 CE: essentially that there was one god, Allah, and that he, Muhammad, was his messenger. The angel Gabriel had brought him Allah's word: after death, men's souls would be judged; the virtuous would go to heaven (described as a green and delightful garden, very unlike the harsh desert) and the wicked would go to a burning, scorching hell (p 45).[5]

Reactions to his preaching were mixed: some followers were attracted, but enemies rejected the idea that their ancestors may be burning in hell (p 47).[5] There was really nothing exceptional about Muhammad's claims of divine guidance. As with Jesus, there were several other poets and ecstatic soothsayers claiming divine inspiration for their preaching (p 10),[5] and Allah was already being worshiped (albeit as one main god amongst many) in southern Syria and northern Arabia. Muhammad simply elevated Allah to the status of the only god.

Also similar to Jesus, Muhammad preached equality of all believers; this challenged the tribal status quo, where leaders were traditionally treated as infallible. In this way, equality and monotheism were common themes in Christianity, Judaism, and Islam. As with Christianity, monotheism and a single set of religious practices appeared to offer a possibility of reduced conflict.

By 622 CE, matters had come to a head in Mecca between Muhammad and the existing religious leaders. Muhammad was saved by an invitation to mediate conflicts between tribes in Medina. The problems in Mecca, it seemed, were that these new ideas were seen as threatening prosperity (which was thought to derive from the adherence to older religious ideas). Muhammad left for Medina with a small band of followers in 622 CE, marking the *hegira,* or emigration, and the beginning of the Islamic era (p 46).[5]

Muhammad and his growing political base existed in Medina (then known as Yathrib) mainly as highwaymen, robbing passing caravans. A series of conflicts ensued, culminating in the slaughter of a Jewish tribe: the Banu Qurayza. Efraim Karsh, Head of the Mediterranean Studies programme at the University of London,[5] describes how *"the tribe's six to eight hundred men were brought in small groups to trenches dug the previous day, made to sit on the edge, then beheaded one by one and their bodies thrown in. The women and children were sold into slavery"* (p 13).[5]

Jews became targets of Muslims because, as Karsh puts it, the Medina Jews were Muhammad's staunchest critics: they highlighted gaps and inconsistencies in the Koran and its misinterpretation of Old Testament stories. As a result, *"The embittered Muhammad began to cast the Jews in his revelations as a devious and treacherous people"* (p 13-14).[5] In short, Muhammad's "revelations" were inspired by Muhammad's experiences, not by a message originating with Allah.

From the beginning, Muhammad was a warrior as well as a prophet, and the expansion of Islam was by armed conflict; Hugh Kennedy documents this in his book, *The Great Arab Conquests*.[3] The spread of Islam was assisted by widespread death from bubonic plague in many areas, which were subsequently easily conquered. Other empires in these areas were already exhausted by previous fighting. Islam spread by luck and historical accident.

Similarly, Christianity was also spread in large part because the indigenous populations in the Americas died through exposure to new diseases brought by the Conquistadors.[14] Neither religion won the day through theological gravitas.

The details of Muhammad's life are based on reports collected from within the Muslim community during the several centuries after his death. In the words of Fred Donner, Professor of Near Eastern History at the University of Chicago, *"these reports contained material of many kinds, based on eyewitness testimony but also miracle stories or improbable idealizations that seem to be in the realm of legend or religious apologetic*" (p 39).¹

As Donner puts it, "*The problem is that this detailed picture of Muhammad's career is drawn not from documents or even stories dating from Muhammad's time, but from literary sources that were compiled many years—sometimes centuries—later. The fact that these sources are so much later, and shaped with very specific objectives in mind, means they often do not tell us many things we would like to know more ... There is also reason to suspect that many of the incidents related in these sources are not reliable accounts of things that actually happened but rather are legends created by later generations of Muslims to affirm Muhammad's status as prophet, to help establish precedents shaping the later Muslim's community ritual, social or legal practices ...*" (p 50-51)¹

"*The vast ocean of traditional accounts from which the preceding brief sketch of Muhammad's life is distilled contains so many contradictions and so much dubious storytelling that many historians have become reluctant to accept any of it at face value. There are, for example, an abundance of miracle stories and other reports that seem obviously to belong to the realm of legend, such as an episode similar to 'feeding the multitudes' story in Christian legends about Jesus*" (p 51).¹

The Koran

According to the traditional narrative, several companions of Muhammad served as scribes, and were responsible for writing down his revelations.[5] These various codices had differences that motivated the Caliph Uthman to develop a standard version of the Koran in the 7th Century, now known as Uthman's codex. It is considered by some to be the archetype of the Koran existing today.

However, the existence of differing versions, with both minor and significant variations, means that the relationship between Uthman's codex to the text of today's Koran and the revelations of Muhammad's time is unknown. Uthman selected one text and burned all the others (p 76),[1] indicating that at this early date, perfect memorization of the original version of the Koran did not exist.

Secular scholars, such as Patricia Crone,[15] argue that there "*is no hard evidence for the existence of the Qur'an in any form before the last decade of the 7th century ... [and that] ... the tradition which places this rather opaque revelation in its historical context is not attested before the middle of the eighth.*" There is no proof that the current text of the Koran was collected under Uthman, since the earliest surviving copies of the complete Koran are centuries after Uthman himself. The oldest existing copy of the full text is from the 9th Century (p 52).[16]

Alternative versions have been found (much like the Gnostic Gospels), and these contradict the official version in critical ways. One version, found in the Grand Mosque in Yemen, was analysed by German Islamicist Dr. Gerd Puin. The text dated from a time after the supposed standardization by the Uthman codex. At present, the best estimate is that the Koran was written about 150 years after the death of Muhammad (782 CE), while the earliest existing version dates from about 200 years (832 CE) after his death (see also Crone,[15] p 3).

Kennedy describes the writing of the Koran thus: "*We have a vast number of narratives that purport to tell us what happened (in the crucial decades—the 630s and 640s). The problem for the historian is that they are mostly episodic, discontinuous and frequently contradict each other—and sometimes themselves*" (p 13).³

Crone argues that much of the classical Muslim understanding of the Koran rests on the work of storytellers, and that this work is of very dubious historical value. These storytellers contributed to the Islamic tradition during its rise. This is evident in the steady growth of information: *"If one storyteller should happen to mention a raid, the next storyteller would know the date of this raid, while the third would know everything"* (p 203).¹⁵ It is a similar problem that is found when trying to authenticate the bible.

Even one of Muhammad's earliest followers, Abdullah ibn Sa'd ibn Abi Sarh, who was recruited to record revelations, became disillusioned when his suggested changes in wording were always accepted. This led him to the recognition that the seemingly eternal word of Allah could be changed at will (p 163).¹⁷

A recent find in the library of the University of Birmingham (BBC News July 21, 2015) indicates that an earlier partial copy of the Koran might have been found. This is not a whole version, but fragments of Chapters 18 to 20 (NYT, July 22, 2015). Radiocarbon dating of the manuscript found in the university library indicates that the parchment it was written on dated from between 568 and 645 CE.

However, one Islamic scholar pointed out that parchment skins were sometimes washed and re-used. If one combines the dating of the parchment and writing style (Hijazi script, a form of early written Arabic), it suggests a writing date of around 645 to 656 CE. The manuscript is part of a collection gathered by Alphonse Mingana, a Chaldean priest who was sponsored by Edward Cadbury, part of the chocolate-making dynasty.

It is still too early to draw any lasting conclusions about this discovery. Even if the newly-found version of the Koran proved to be written only 20 years after Muhammad's death, it is hard to see how it would resolve these problems.

Crone also argues that Islamic scholars had access to the Greek, Armenian, Hebrew, Aramaic, Syriac, and Coptic literatures of their non-Muslim neighbours, translated at the end of the last century. They have been left to collect dust in libraries ever since. It is a striking testimony to the suppression of the non-Islamic Middle East that these literatures have been ignored for questions other than the chronology of conquests or the transmission of Greek philosophy and science.

From a classic Islamic view, these sources have simply gotten everything wrong: but unless one is willing to entertain the notion of an all-pervasive literary conspiracy amongst the many non-Muslim peoples of the Middle East, the crucial fact remains that they have gotten things wrong on very much the same points.

Given their wide geographical and social distribution, the Jews and Christians could scarcely have vented their anti-Muslim feelings with such uniform results. It is because of the agreement between the independent and contemporary witnesses of the non-Muslim world that their testimony must be considered. Whichever way one chooses to interpret them, they leave no doubt that Islam, like the other Abrahamic religions, is the product of an evolution in dogma (p 15-16).[15]

Islamic Hadiths

A similar problem exists with the *hadiths* (traditions). They are supposed to have *isnads* (chains of oral transmission) that originated at the time of Muhammad. The problem is that the *hadith* compilers lived, for the most part, in the late 9th Century, at least two hundred years after the death of Muhammad in 632 (p 47/312 [Kindle]).[17] Therefore, numerous contradictory collections exist: Shia and Sunni Muslims do not accept the same collections as reliable, for instance.

The *hadiths* provide what little context exists for the Koran. Even within collections, there are differing stories and "fanciful tales" (p 51)[1] that contradict portrayals of Muhammad in the Koran (for instance, whether or not he was a miracle worker). The Koran claims to be the detailed record (6:114) from which nothing is omitted (6:38). This leads to the question: why then, would the *hadiths* be important? It remains to be seen how the newly-discovered Koran fragment solves or adds to the debate.

It is observed by non-Islamic scholars that many of the stories in the Koran appear to be revised versions of earlier Christian, Jewish, or Zoroastrian parables, likely obtained by Muhammad in his travels as a trader. There are problems with the Koran's cosmology: it mentions a flat earth, around which the sun revolves (Koran 20:53, 43:10, 50:7, 35:41, 34:9). It also has little knowledge of human biology (Koran 86:6, 23:14) and appears to copy the Greek "father of medicine" Galen (130-200 CE). Muhammad's "revelations" on a person's right to the spoils of war seem more like a rationalization for his life as a caravan robber and, later, a warrior. This included the taking of sex slaves, *"those whom your right hand possesses"* (Koran 4:24).

As with the Old Testament, Muhammad accepted the rape of captured women and the massacre of men, including an infamous massacre of the Banu Qurayza Jews after the Battle of Trench (p 123-133).[18] According to Pinker, these were normative attitudes until the 14th Century, and only then did they slowly begin to change.

As far as it is possible to judge, Islam was initially welcomed because the incessant tribal wars were draining on the people; if tribes could unite under one belief system, relief was possible. This wish had also motivated Constantine to end the endless bickering of early Christian sects. As one of the Arab leaders quoted by Kennedy said, "*Our religion was to kill one another and raid one another. There were those among us who would bury their daughters alive, not wanting them to eat our food ... but then God sent us a well-known man*" (p 47).[3]

A period of incessant conquest and war filled Muhammad's life, but Kennedy argues that the campaigns of the 6th Century were not transcribed immediately. The Koran was written in the midst of a prolonged campaign that eventually spread Islam from Spain to Northern India This campaign succeeded in imposing Islam and Arabic on what had been multiple cultures and language groups.

The Caliph Umayyad Abd al-Malik (685-705 CE) decreed that Arabic alone would be the official language of this imperial empire. As with the Jews, a need existed to provide "creation myths" that explained how the Islamic Empire came into being, and to "*justify the defeat and displacement of the previous elites*" (p 14).[3]

While the Koran claims to be written in a "clear Arabic tongue" (p 56),[1] it is sporadically ambiguous. As Donner states, "*many passages remain far from clear, even in the most basic sense of what the words might have meant in their original context*" (p 56).[1]

Details of the early Islamic campaigns are sketchy.[3] As Kennedy points out, "*these accounts were edited in the ninth and tenth centuries; that is, between 150 and 200 years after the events. The Arabic narratives are rarely simple accounts ... they are actually multi-layered compositions that have gone through different stages of editing and elaboration for different purposes at different times ... oral transmission ... which preserved the memories of their predecessors ... and coloured the way in which the battles of the first Islamic conquests were remembered"* (p 15).[3]

The Muslims *"could also remember their victories as clear evidence that God was on their side, the deaths of enemies and the vast quantities of booty they amassed being evidence of divine favour"* (p 15).[3]

The next stage was the recording of this oral material, beginning sometime in the 8th Century (Crone puts the date at 782 CE). This writing process exploded in the 9th and 10th Centuries with the introduction of paper to replace parchment. These stories were "vivid" recollections, and knowledge of them guaranteed a position in court. In some cases, several anecdotes were grouped together but details were changed: events happened in different orders, different people are credited with the same heroic deed, names of commanders did not match, etc. (p 17).[3]

The final product of the Koran appears to be a composite of originally different texts that have been revised and reused (p 56).[3] Different versions of the Koran exist (e.g. Hafs, Warsh, Qalun, and al-Duri versions) and the Koran used by Shias has two extra *suras* (chapters) not read by Sunnis (p 80).[3]

Chains of storytellers were developed, called *isnads*. The chains took the form of "I was told by X, who was told by Y, who was told by Z, who was an eyewitness." This type of chain of transmission was, of course, used by social psychologists Allport and Postman in their famous study, "The Basic

Psychology of Rumour,"[19] in which sequential transmission of a complex story lost detail rapidly. As few as three reproductions (A tells B, B tells C, C tells D) generated a 65% loss of and extreme alterations to details. Famously, a straight razor in the hand of a white man in the original picture was transferred to the hand of a black man in the "terminal report."

Similarly, Frederic Bartlett asked university students to recite a ghost story to another person, who then retold it sequentially (p 158).[20] He found a strong tendency for hearers to distort or insert the information to fit their own preconceptions. Less comfortable ideas were misremembered compared to more familiar ones. In short, the story was reshaped to line up with the person's subjective notions.

One can only guess what distortions occurred in over a century of retelling for the Islamic myths. As Kennedy puts it, *"The anecdotes seem to grow details as they are handed from one generation to the next ... Modern readers will note immediately that there are some obvious problems with the procedure because it provides few ways of ensuring the reliability of the material"* (p 17-18).[3]

The Koran and Jihad

The Koran was written during prolonged Arab conquests, spreading Islam as far as Spain.[3] The spread of Islam is attributed to the historical fact that the two empires it conquered—Byzantium and Persia—were exhausted by a long series of wars between themselves. The religious creed written during these conquests would reflect the military needs of the believers. The concept of *jihad*, or Holy War, is an example of such a justification (p 48).[3]

This concept justifies religious war as "Holy" and thus necessary; the concept exists both in Islam and Christianity. The Christian concept was developed by Saint Augustine, and was used widely to rationalize the Crusades and the Conquest of the Americas.

Kennedy sees the messages in the Koran relating to *jihad* as ambiguous; some passages (e.g. 16:125) suggest "wisdom and beautiful preaching" as the means of persuasion. Others suggest "*a more militant and violent attitude towards non-Muslims*" (p 49),[3] such as 9:5, "*When the sacred months are past, kill the idolators wherever you find them, and seize them, besiege them, and lie in wait for them in every place of ambush*" (p 49-50).[3]

Townsend leans toward this latter-militant view, as does American author Sam Harris. Townsend relies on a biography of Muhammad by Ibn Ishaq, who describes Muhammad torturing a captive in order to find out where treasure was hidden (p 195),[17] taking a woman as a sex slave the same day her family was killed (p 196),[17] allowing the rape of captive women (p 197, 236, and Koran 4:23),[17] participating in a massacre of Jewish boys (p 199),[17] and the taking a wife who was only nine years old (p 206)[17] and played with dolls in Muhammad's house (p 210).[17]

Townsend uses six Sunni and four Shi'a *hadiths*, the Ibn Ishaq biography, and even the Koran itself as source material. He cites several parts of the Koran as inciting violence toward unbelievers, such as "*And slay them wherever ye catch them ... and fight them on until there is no more tumult or oppression and there prevail justice and faith in Allah*" (2:191, 2:193, 2:216, 4:95, 8:12). He also cites advocacy of domestic violence against "disobedient women" (4:34).

Townsend's book seems aimed at Christians; he never draws identical failures from the Christian Old Testament as examples when making a critical point about the Koran. For example, while the Koran advocates slaughter and sexual slavery for conquered victims, so too does the Old Testament. Both were products of their times, as was their vision of god.

Sam Harris argued in his New York Times bestseller, *The End of Faith*,[22] that war against the unbelievers, called *jihad*, is a central theme in the Koran. *Jihad* has two meanings: war against one's own sinfulness, and war against the infidel. Muslim duty, the duty of *jihad*, is *"an unambiguous call to world conquest"* (p 111).[22]

Harris cites five passages from the Koran that promote death to the infidel (p 118-123), and argues that support for *jihad* stems from these passages. To Harris, the Koran is hate literature—Islamic hatred for the unbeliever. It is based on a promise of life after death in heaven and sexual access to 72 virgins.[*] As Harris puts it, *"Islam, more than any other religion human beings have devised, has all the makings of a thoroughgoing cult of death"* (p 123).[22]

To be fair to Islam, however, the notion of Holy War was first developed by Saint Augustine in *Contra Faustum Manchaeum*, and preceded the Koran by over 200 years. Christianity and Islam have different developmental histories, with the former largely accepting separations of church and state power.

---

[*] Nothing in the Koran specifically states that the faithful are allotted 72 virgins apiece. There is a mention of "72 wives" in a *hadith*, and debate over the meaning of the term "wife" has been unresolved.

Professor Hugh Kennedy has a somewhat more pacific outlook: that although the idea of *jihad* is an important concept in Islam, questions still exist about whether *jihad* needs to be a violent or spiritual struggle; whether it can be defensive, or can be used to expand the frontiers of Islam; and whether it is an obligation or voluntary (p 48).[3]

The Koran contains passages promoting peaceful relations with unbelievers as well, such as Verse 16:125, *"Invite all to the way of your Lord with wisdom and beautiful preaching and argue with them in ways that are best and most gracious"* (p 49).[3] However, Kennedy also points out "a more militant and violent attitude to non-Muslims" (p 49)[3] such as in Verse 9:5 *"When the sacred months are past (in which a truce had been in force between the Muslims and their enemies), kill the idolators wherever you find them, and seize them besiege them and lie in wait for them in every place of ambush, but if they repent, pray regularly, and pay the alms tax, then let them go their way"* (p 50).[3] This verse, Kennedy notes, is practically a foundation text for the Muslim conquests. According to Muslim scholars, these passages were revealed later than the moderate verses. The militant verses, therefore, represent the final Muslim view on Holy War (p 50).[3]

Kennedy concludes that the Koran provided scriptural support for the idea that Muslims should fight unbelievers. The Koran also made it clear that the joys of paradise were more important than material success. In doing so, it provided the ideological justification for the Muslim conquests of Syria, Palestine, Iraq, Egypt, Iran, Mahgreb, Samarkand, and Spain (p 51).[3] The demand of Islam was straightforward: either convert or pay tribute; otherwise, we will kill you (p 51).[3]

It is clear that the idea of *jihad* and martyrdom was evident as early as 624 CE (at the battle of Badr). It was foremost amongst the motivations for the Arab conquests (p 62).[3] There were stories of men deliberately seeking martyrdom and putting themselves in danger to achieve it, including one warrior who purposefully removed his armour before plunging into hand-to-hand combat. It is difficult to understand these motivations without a true religious belief in paradise.

The other motivation for fighting was a tribal belief in the superiority of the Arab (p 63),[3] which was mentioned more frequently in the early accounts than conquest was. Arabs defined themselves as austere and honest in contrast to the decadence of the Persians.

Islamic Political Power

As Karsh argues, the very idea of an empire originated in the Middle East (Egyptian, Babylonian, Assyrian, Iranian), and for Islam, there was never a distinction between religion and state. In fact, political authority derives from Islam. From the beginning, Muhammad acted as both head of state and of church.

With Christianity, authority was also derived from god, and many modern legal practices, such as testimony under oath, still exist today. The difference is that church-state separation progressed under Christianity, despite the authority of the Catholic church. Power struggles under Christianity were ultimately lost by the church.

However, under Islam, the idea of secular authority does not exist (p 5). As Karsh[5] puts it, *"Whereas Jesus spoke of the Kingdom of God, Muhammad used God's name to build an earthly kingdom ... If Christendom was slower than Islam in marrying religious universalism with political imperialism, it was faster in shedding both notions. By the eighteenth century the West had lost its religious messianism*" (p 5-6).⁵ The westward push of Islam was stopped at the Battle of Poitiers in France (also called the Battle of Tours) in 732 CE and eventually (700 years later), Islam was pushed out of Spain.

The relevance of Islam to modern times is apparent in Western culture: since September 11th, 2001 and the attacks on the World Trade towers in New York City, Islam has been front and centre in the concept of terrorist attacks. Sam Harris sees this terrorism as a logical outgrowth of the Koran's teachings of *jihad* against infidels. Harris argues that Islamic fundamentalism has kept Muslim countries in backward-economic positions, and are thus resentful of the success of infidels.

Islamic distrust of the "western world" included resistance to the Gutenberg printing presses, and consequently led to low literacy rates in comparison to the western world. In his history of the Islamic Enlightenment, de Bellaigue[25] put the literacy rate in the 19th Century of Turkey, Egypt, and Iran at 3%, compared to 68% for men and 43% for women in England.

Graeme Wood[26] described the end times views of ISIS, the Islamic State in Syria, as a *jihad*, which would end in the existence of a caliphate in the Middle East. At least one ISIS recruiter, he cites, believed the caliphate would be established only after a battle in northern Syria with the "armies of Rome" (or any western substitute). This would be followed by the defeat of Istanbul and a battle with an anti-messiah named Dajjal, who would die. Thus would begin the apocalypse championed by Jesus (who is the second-most revered Muslim Prophet).

Prophecy and a concept of an end times are aspects of both Islam and Christianity. Both are based on unsupportable documents created by men. Both sustain belief in order to direct violence. The Islamic state is committed to purifying the world by executing large numbers of infidels, particularly in territories they currently hold. Islam was written at a time of conquest, and is thus tailored to fit the conquistador mindset.

Against the Koran: Infidels, Heretics, and Other Non-Believers

Given the extreme modern suppression of Islamic critics in the Middle East—there are countries where the penalty for "apostasy" is still death—it is interesting that some well-known heretics have existed. Jennifer Hecht cites them extensively in her classic book, *Doubt: a History*.[21]

Rationality in the form of the Greek philosophers was brought to the Middle East when the libraries of Europe were emptied by the Christians. The ideas of the Greek philosophers led to a philosophical movement called the Falsafah, which held that Allah was reason (p 221).[21] The Faylasufs (as the followers were called) disagreed with the Koran, but held that it was a valid path to Allah for those incapable of reason.

Two exceptional doubters (called *zindiq*) from that time are cited by Hecht. The first is Ibn al-Rawandi, who died somewhere between 860 and 912 CE.[21] He publicly rejected fundamental notions of Islam in a series of books, the best known being called *The Book of the Emerald*. The book is a conversation between al-Rawandi and his friend and scholar, Muhammad al-Warraq. In the book, he and al-Warraq discuss how the "prophecy" of Muhammad is simply observation and deduction, not revelations from Allah.

Al-Rawandi critiques revelation and absolute knowledge as well, pointing out contradictions between the Koran and the earlier Jewish and Christian traditions. If one religion can be wrong, they can all be wrong, al-Rawandi insists. He praises rationalism and suggests that the prophet was actively faking, using tricks to fool the audience.

He wrote other books called *Against the Koran* and *The Futility of Divine Wisdom* in which he pointed out the poverty and misery of contemporary existence and contrasted it with the notion of a caring god. By the 11th Century, most of al-Rawandi's works had been destroyed (p 226).[21] Likewise, al-Warraq was persecuted for his views and his books burned (p 224).[21]

Abu Bakr al-Razi (854-925 CE), on the other hand, was a doctor who grew famous for his generosity and intelligence. He also wrote several books critical of Islam, which asked why certain individuals (e.g. Muhammad) had been chosen by Allah and set above other people. He questioned the Koran and argued that anyone could write it: it contained no special wisdom.

Al-Razi argued that all "revealed religions" had been a disaster for humanity because of the bloodshed that they led to, pointing out that most religious authorities were cruel and despotic (p 229). He argued that the variety of religious beliefs showed that none of them could claim absolute truth. Perhaps because of his valued medical skills, al-Razi died a hero, and his books are still available. In fact, passages from al-Razi are widely cited by Hecht.

In general, however, Islam has been just as bad or worse than Christianity at silencing critical speech and writing; execution for heresy goes back further than the Koran itself. Hecht describes an execution of a heretic in 742 CE for publicly asserting the eternity of the world—as opposed to it being created by god (p 223)[21]—and another in 772 for denying the existence of a creator.

Ayaan Hirsi Ali has been the most vocal modern critic of Islam, in her books *Infidel*[27] and *Heretic*.[28] In the former, Ali recounts her early life in Muslim countries: Somalia, Saudi Arabia, and Kenya, each a horror for women. In Somalia, she was subjected to genital mutilation, a practice supported by Islam (although it predates the religion): the essential idea is to preclude women from enjoying sex. In Saudi Arabia, women cannot go out alone in public, and are literally locked in their houses. Women out alone are considered prostitutes, and thus are jailed or flogged.

Ali describes her flight to freedom, first to Holland, and then to the US: the only country where she could be protected from Muslim assassins. In *Infidel*, Ali argues that modern Islam is hopeless: it is a religion that has never accepted the Enlightenment and its moderating effects on Christianity and Judaism.

In her later book, *Heretic*, she was more optimistic that the Arab Spring signalled a growing wave of dissent within Islam. In the book, she distinguished between the Medina Muslims, who focus on the militaristic *suras* revealed to Muhammad, and the followers of the 86 less militaristic *suras* revealed earlier in Mecca, which focused on the wonders of creation and the oneness of Allah. She sees the Medina orthodoxy as needing reform, especially regarding the ideas of the infallibility of Muhammad, the literal understanding of the Koran, the priority given to the afterlife, Sharia law, and *jihad*. These areas are, in effect, the central orthodoxy of fundamentalist Islam.

In *Heretic*,[28] Ali identifies three groups of Muslims: what she estimates as 3% of Muslims who follow the more militaristic interpretation of the Koran; a smaller category of

Muslims who believe in the need for reform; and the largest category—whom she calls the "Mecca Majority"—who are neither militaristic nor reform-minded.

In a review of book, Middle East correspondent Max Rodenbeck[29] points out that the Mecca Majority have existed without serious conflict for centuries. For example, Rodenbeck argues that the practice of forced conversion is a recent phenomenon; that the Muslims who conquered Jerusalem and Persia were more tolerant than the Byzantine or Persian rulers who had preceded them. What's more, the Muslims ruled India, Greece, and Bulgaria, but never imposed Islam on those countries. The use of suicide attacks by Muslims dates back only to 1980, when it was first used by Iranians against Iraq. It was used for political purposes, as with the Japanese kamikaze and Tamil Tigers: as a last-ditch weapon against a stronger foe.

Political analyses of Muslim countries support a more diversified view of Islam; they warn against stereotyping Muslim countries as hotbeds of terrorism.[30] Instead, the Islamic terrorism of the 21st Century appears to be a "perfect storm," originating from the Islamic belief in *jihad*, everlasting life after death, and the definition of the infidel as the enemy. It is most pronounced in Arabic Muslim countries. The end times beliefs of some radical Islamic sects derive from the study of religious notions of the end of the world.

The final sparks came from socio-political forces: the grinding poverty and inequality of Muslim countries; the perceived "invasion" by the west; and the fact that, as Rodenbeck puts it, "*between 1800 and 1950 some nine out of ten Muslims happened to fall under the aggressively applied 'infidel' rule*" (p 36).[29]

It is also the case, as Rodenbeck acknowledges, that Muslim history is marked by cycles; puritan sects have periodically erupted from the hinterlands to purge the Muslim cities of corruption—as is the case with Saudi Arabia. Rodenbeck sees this as a manifestation of a felt need for reform within Islam; however, the sects themselves drive Islam in a more traditional, conservative direction.

The Koran's Influence

Since the Koran is believed by Muslims to be the uncorrupted word of Allah, no attempts have been made to edit it. This has led, in the words of Sam Pepys, to the observation that: *"One feels it difficult to see how any mortal ever could consider this Quran as a Book written in Heaven, too good for the Earth; as a well-written book, or indeed as a book at all; and not a bewildered rhapsody; written, so far as writing goes, as badly as almost any book ever was!"*[31]

The Koran is a pastiche of reminiscences, based on memory and oral retellings: from the perspective of accuracy, these are all flawed processes. Its ideas, which probably originated in Muhammad's epileptic seizures, were spread by violence before the book was even committed to print. Islam spread rapidly, in part, because it conquered empires that were already exhausted by prior wars (p 219).[21]

As Kennedy tells it,[3] the memories and narratives of the Muslim conquest (and the Koran) served as both a record of old forgotten things and the foundation myths of Muslim society (p 14). The concept of *jihad* has deep, cultural roots in Islamic tradition, although the Christian notion of Holy War, developed by Augustine of Hippo, was even older,[19,22,23] dating back to the early 5th Century.[24] Both presume that god is on the side of the tribe and justify violence by the tribe as god's wish.

REFERENCES

1. Donner FM. *Muhammad and the believers.* Cambridge: Harvard University Press; 2010.
2. Watt WM. *Muhammad at medina.* Oxford: Clarendon Press; 1956.
3. Kennedy H. *The great arab conquests.* Philadelphia: Da Capo Press; 2007.
4. Bowman J. *Honour: a history.* New York: Encounter Books; 2006.
5. Karsh E. *Islamic imperialism.* New Haven: Yale University Press; 2006.
6. Lewis DL. *God's crucible: Islam and the making of europe 570-1215.* New York: W.W. Norton; 2008.
7. Freemon FR. A differential diagnosis of the inspirational spells of muhammad the prophet of islam. *Epilepsia.* 1976; 17:423-427.
8. Saver JL, Rabin J. The neural substrates of religious experience. *Journal of Neuropsychiatry.* 1997; 9(3):498-511.
9. Schachter S, Singer J. Cognitive, social and physiological determinants of emotional states. *Psychological Review.* 1962; 69:379-399.
10. Dewhurst K, Beard AW. Sudden religious conversions in temporal lobe epilepsy. *British Journal of Psychiatry.* 1970; 117:497-507.
11. Sargant W. *Battle for the mind: a physiology of conversion and brain washing.* Cambridge: Malor Books; 1957/1997.
12. Sage W. The war on the cults. *Human Behavior.* 1976; (October):40-49.

13. Westen D. *The political brain: the role of emotion in deciding the fate of the nation*. New York: Public Affairs; 2007.
14. Mann C. *1491*. New York: Vintage Books; 2005.
15. Crone P. *Slaves on horses*. London: Cambridge University Press; 1980.
16. Gilliot C. Creation of a fixed text. *The Cambridge Companion to the Qu'ran*. Cambridge: Cambridge University Press; 2006.
17. Townsend P. *Questioning islam*. Sydney: Createspace; 2014.
18. Spencer R. *The truth about muhammad*. Washington: Regnery Publishing, Inc.; 2006.
19. Allport G, Postman LJ. The basic psychology of rumour. *Transactions of the New York Academy of Sciences*. 1945; Series 11(VII):61-81.
20. Barrett JL. *Born believers: the science of children's religious belief*. New York: Simon & Schuster; 2012.
21. Hecht JM. *Doubt: a history*. New York: Harper One; 2004.
22. Harris S. *The end of faith*. New York: Norton; 2004.
23. Russell FH. *The just war in the middle ages*. Cambridge: Cambridge University Press; 1975.
24. Asbridge T. *The first crusade: a new history*. Oxford: Oxford University Press; 2004.
25. de Bellaigue C. *The islamic enlightenment: the stuggle between faith and reason, 1798 to modern times*. New York: Liveright; 2017.
26. Wood G. What ISIS really wants. *The Atlantic*. New York: 2015.
27. Ali AH. *Infidel*. New York: Atria; 2008.
28. Ali AH. *Heretic: why islam needs reformation now*. New York: Harper; 2015.

29. Rodenbeck M. How she wants to modify muslims. *New York Review of Books.* 2015; Vol December 3:
30. Shafiq MN, Sinno AH. Education, income and support for suicide bombings: Evidence from six muslim countries. *Journal of Conflict Resolution.* 2010; 54(1):146-178.
31. http://maxwellinstitute.byu.edu Accessed in February 2017

CHAPTER 6

The Legacy of Christianity: The Past is Prologue

"Is God willing to prevent evil but not able? Then he is not omnipotent.
Is he able but not willing? Then he is malevolent.
Is he both able and willing? Then whence cometh evil?
Is he neither willing nor able? Then why call him God?"

EPICURUS, 341-270 BCE

The Greek philosopher Lucretius (94-51 BCE) wrote in his work, *On the Nature of Things*, that fear made people overly-dependent on religious authorities. This led them to adhere to superstitious and irrational beliefs instead of relying on their own experience and critical judgment. Moreover, to avoid the fear of their own finitude, people squandered their lives in trivial pursuits or became blindly obsessed with wealth, greed, or lust for power. This lack of awareness made humans profoundly dangerous and prone to unhappiness.

Such wisdom, which was in no short supply in the Greek academies, was about to disappear for a thousand years in what we now call the "Dark Ages:" times ruled exclusively by religion at the cost of reason. In her book, *Doubt: A History*,[1] Jennifer Hecht describes the slow death of intellect under the onslaught of Christianity: soon after it became the state religion, intellectuals in Florence could no longer read Greek, the language of the educated; even knowledge of the very existence of philosophy soon disappeared. It truly was, as Charles Freeman described it, *"the closing of the western mind."*[2]

By the time of Justinian (529 CE), the philosophical schools that had existed for 800 years (such as the Epicurean Garden, the Skeptic Academy, the Lyceum, and the Stoic Porch) were shut down. Philosophers and scholars moved to Persia. Historian William Manchester describes it as a time when *"intellectual life had vanished from Europe."*[3] Any public dissent from the new power of Christianity meant certain, painful death.

The threat of capital punishment was long used to motivate religious conversions; Charlemagne, the first Emperor of the Holy Roman Empire, gave his vanquished foes the option of conversion to Christianity or death. When they refused conversion, he had 4,500 of them decapitated in one morning. The Muslims would soon be following this example. In the reign of religion, mankind descended from debate and critical reasoning to forced conversion or death. How did it get this way?

The intellectual debates that characterized early Christianity disappeared entirely when it became the official state religion. No longer was it debated whether Jesus was born of a virgin or alive after the resurrection. The answers to these inquiries were now "known." Celsus, an early critic of Christianity, claimed that Christians were able "*to convince only the foolish, dishonourable and stupid and only slaves, women and children*" (p 142).[2]

Christian theologians, up to and including Augustine, argued that the Greek philosophers stole their ideas from the Old Testament (which they were assumed to have read). In fact, there is no ideal of rationality or critical thinking anywhere in the Old Testament. If any theft occurred, it was the Christian theft of Plato's idea of the Forms as a basis for unobservable religious ideals.

The physician Galen criticized Christians for their adherence to faith rather than reason, and for relying on "undemonstrated laws." It was common in the Greek world for students to go from one school of philosophy to another, listening to debates and querying the positions taken. In this world of questioning and critical thinking, Christianity, with its emphasis on faith over rationality, fared poorly. No one knew this better than Paul.

Paul and the Dismissal of Reason

Paul is frequently referred to as the founder of Christianity, since he formulated a meaning for Jesus' death (and resurrection) and acted as a leader for early Christian communities.[2] An uneducated tent-maker by profession, Paul wrote 13 books of the New Testament, or so it is claimed. Ehrman argues that seven of these are authentic and show stylistic and theological coherence;[4] the others are forgeries, differing in style and with references that indicate someone else wrote the tract.

Paul was born Saul of Tarsus in 5 CE as a Jew, and converted to Christianity after having a vision of the resurrected Christ (a light from heaven and a voice) on the road to Damascus. Paul never met Jesus in his lifetime. His conversion occurred after the crucifixion. His vision changed Saul, a self-described zealot and persecutor of Christians, to Paul. He is described as a highly emotional man who never married, had a strong personal aversion to sex (especially homosexuality),[2] and likely suffered from temporal lobe epilepsy.[5]

Before Paul, there is no evidence that sexuality was considered a social issue by Christianity. However, after Paul it became an obsession in Christian communities. What little we know of Paul comes from his letters—only some of which are accepted as his own[2,4]—and from the Acts of the Apostles.

Paul condemned philosophers and moved Christian thinking away from the rationalism of Greek philosophy. However, he was not a convincing orator, and his attempt to preach to the Greeks in Athens led to him being mocked by the sophisticated thinkers of that city (p 114).[2] *"Then certain philosophers of the Epicureans and of the Stoics encountered him and some said: What will this babbler say? ... and then Paul stood in the midst of Mars' hill and said 'Ye men of Athens, I perceive that in all things ye are too superstitious ...' And when they heard of the resurrection of the dead, some mocked ..."* (Acts 17:18-32).

Paul had no more than a rudimentary knowledge of Greek literature or philosophy, and as Freeman states *"was not an intellectual, certainly not when compared to his contemporary Philo of Alexandria who wove Plato and other Greek influences into Judaism."* Freeman speculates that, given Paul's "prickly" personality, the rejection by the Athenians may have generated his disdain for Greek philosophy.

Freeman describes Paul as being insecure and preoccupied with his own importance (p 111-114).[2] His self-identity as a Jew fluctuated with the social pressures of the times. His preoccupation with status is belied by his constant comparison of himself to other Christian leaders who had personally known Jesus (whereas Paul had not).

In his letters to the Corinthians, Paul described a "thorn of the flesh:" this is typically taken as a metaphor for his recurring infirmity, which may have been temporal lobe epilepsy. This would lead to convulsions and explain the religious visions that he describes.

"I will go on to visions and revelations ... I know a man ... who fourteen years ago was caught up to the third heaven ... and heard sacred secrets which no human lips can repeat. Of my experience like that I am prepared to boast ... my wealth of visions might have puffed me up so I was given a thorn in the flesh, an angel of Satan to rack me and keep me from being puffed up" (2 Corinthians 12, 1-9).

Neuropsychiatry has identified distinctive personality syndromes of temporal lobe epilepsy,[6,8] including hyper-moralism, deepened affect, humorlessness, irritability, and hypergraphia. In their study linking epilepsy to religious experience,[8] Saver and Rabin review medical biographies on the following religious figures, who each met the criteria for epilepsy: Paul, Muhammad, Joan of Arc, St. Teresa of Avila, and Joseph Smith, among others. They specifically see evidence for most of these in Paul, and describe his conversion to Christianity on the road to Damascus as a typical temporal lobe phenomenon.

The ecstatic, dream-like[6] state Paul describes is identical to those described by neuroscientists Bjorn Hansen and Eylert

Brodkorb in a clinical sample of patients with epilepsy.[7] Many patients in this sample describe a distinct, erotic aspect to their experience; this has led to the terms "orgasmic auras" and "ecstatic seizures." Many patients enjoyed their experiences, and tried to induce new ones through cognitive techniques.

Many religious figures appear to have had such seizures: they are clinically described as ictal experiences, and are interpreted in the context of a patient's religiosity as a religious vision. These physiological experiences occur because of strokes or seizures, typically in the areas of the brain governing emotion. As psychiatrists Jeffrey Saver and John Rabin put it, "*Patients who have culturally acquired explanatory systems of a religious character naturally tend to interpret any ictal experience as possessing religious experience*" (p 500).[8] In short, religiously-inclined people will interpret these experiences using religious symbolism.

Paul was emotional, misogynistic, and sexually repressed; he is now a seminal figure in the origin of Christian dogma. Given Paul's aversion to sexuality, any sexual aspect of the ictal experience would have been distressing for him, and further developed his repression of and disavowal of sex.

Freeman notes[2] that Paul appeared to be preoccupied with the evils of sexuality. He fulminated against "degrading passions," stressed the value of celibacy, and only accepted marriage (for others) because *"better to marry than to burn"* (p 121)—in other words, those who surrendered to sexual passion outside marriage would burn in hell.

Jesus did not seem as preoccupied with sex as Paul was. Unlike Jesus', Paul's teachings centred on the condemnation of idolatry, philosophy, and sexuality. He defended faith over reason and developed the notion that a person was merely a fragmented personality, and could only be made whole through god. Both sex and philosophy stood in the way of this wholeness.

At a time of profound ignorance, a man with epilepsy misattributed his symptoms and influenced a burgeoning religious movement. What's more, he projected his own personal infirmity into a notion of the human character. Given the various descriptions of Paul as having fluctuating identity issues, possible epilepsy, and chronic insecurity, it is quite likely that he suffered from a personality disorder: the very type that would give him the sense of being fragmented. Paul's prescription for humanity was really for himself.

The real case against reason was that Christianity, as preached by Paul, could not gain intellectual respectability amongst students in the Greek world, who had learned to question ideas. Rejecting reason solved the problem by developing adherents amongst the uneducated. As the early Christian theologian Origen* put it, *"As this matter of faith is so much talked of, I have to reply that we accept it as useful for the multitude, and that we admittedly teach those who cannot abandon everything and pursue a study of rational argument to believe without thinking out their reasons"* (p 144).[2] The essence of Christianity was that there were dogmas laid down by church leaders, and these dogmas could not be challenged; they must

---

* Origen of Alexandria (184-254 CE), was an early pro-Christian writer who defended Christianity from Celsus' early critique. Reading summations of Origen's thinking today, one is hard-pressed to ascertain what was heretical about it; he believed in an eternal, incorporeal god and a Logos (World Soul) that took the form of Jesus Christ, born of the Virgin Mary. He believed the bible was divinely inspired and that there was an intellectual argument for the existence of god.

be believed by those entering the Christian community. This authoritarian view became the official attitude of Christianity after the Nicaean Council.

Once Christianity became a political power, progress was impeded. The western world became one of magical thinking and superstition. It was a world where, as Manchester puts it, *"there were no clocks, no police, virtually no communications; a time when men believed in magic and sorcery and slew those whose superstitions were different from, and therefore an affront to, their own"* (p xiv).[3] Battle outcomes were routinely ascribed to the pleasures or wraths of god in a spectacular example of circular reasoning: we won and therefore god was pleased; we know he was pleased because we won.

Intellectual life had vanished from Europe, and even the rulers, like Charlemagne, were illiterate. According to Manchester, it was a world of incessant warfare, famines, plagues, corruption, lawlessness, obsession with strange myths, and an "impenetrable mindlessness." Only the achievements of amazing individuals, like Ferdinand Magellan, supported progress.

In this world, the Christian church struggled for power. They "borrowed" Plato's notion that truth could not be found in the material world, and applied his idea of the Forms (what existed behind the material appearances) to religious belief; hence, they distracted spiritual inquiry from empirical search. It was therefore cataclysmic to religious authorities that science, once it emerged from the Dark Ages, posited that the laws of nature were subject to measurement and explanation.

Paul's influence is still strongly felt today, especially in conservative Catholicism. Antonin Scalia, former Justice of the US Supreme Court, famously did not trust scientific evidence that contradicted his own beliefs, which included creationism, the deterrent effect of capital punishment, and the dubiousness of climate change (New York Times Magazine Dec 25, 2016). Scalia focused on "scientific uncertainty:" that science is a pursuit of objectivity, not a final decision. He used this to justify his Catholic-derived beliefs, which he described as "objective." In Scalia's mind, science was the "wisdom of the wise," and not to be trusted. Christianity had provided a belief that ensured the faithful never strayed: the belief that all non-Christian evidence was untrustworthy.

Augustine: Original Sin, the "Disease" of Curiosity, and Holy War

At the beginning of this time of profound and willful ignorance, there was Augustine of Hippo (354-430 CE). Augustine wrote the *City of God*, which argued that Rome had fallen not because of her current Christianity but because of her historic pagan sins. Augustine—arguably the most corrosive writer in all of western culture—promoted profoundly destructive ideas such as original sin, Holy War, and the disease of curiosity. He essentially argued that one should feel guilt for just being human (original sin), should not study or investigate (the disease of curiosity), and had an obligation to kill non-believers (Holy War).

Augustine is considered a major influence over Western Christianity and the philosophical founder of the Catholic church.[9] Born to a family of Roman citizens in Algeria, Augustine later wrote his *Confessions* and *The City of God*, both of which are considered central to the development of Christian dogma, especially on the concept of sin. Augustine was raised a Christian, but left the church to follow Manichaeism.

Augustine had a 15-year relationship with a woman, who bore him two sons. She remains unnamed in all sources, only referred to dismissively as "his concubine" or "his mistress" (p 56).[10] His mother was appalled by this unlawful (and sinful) union, and convinced Augustine to marry within the church. He left the mother of his children and was instead arranged to marry a ten-year-old heiress, although the marriage never occurred.*

A life of study, first at Carthage and later at Rome, led Augustine to several academies, and his fluency in Latin, ambition, and political connections (largely fostered by his mother) generated a return to Christianity when he was 31. His conversion (in 386 CE) came about when reading Paul's *Epistle to the Romans*. It was at a point where Paul advocated putting aside "*rioting, drunkenness, chambering and wantonness.*"

Augustine made modest contributions to philosophy,[10] and was concerned with the philosophical issues of evil and certitude of human thought (p 57).[10] Reading the Greek philosophers, especially the Neo-Platonists, developed Augustine's acceptance of an immaterial reality. It introduced to him the contemplation of the spiritual: the notion of wisdom.

Augustine returned to Africa and became a priest in Hippo, west of Carthage, in 391; he became Bishop in 396. This witnessed an extraordinary period of writings that now constitute the central tenets of Catholicism, including three of the most destructive ideas in western literature: original sin, Holy War, and the disease of curiosity.

---

* The wedding was postponed until she became of legal age—twelve—but Augustine broke off the relationship when she was eleven.

Mankind had an original sin: Adam and Eve ate the apple of a forbidden tree, which symbolically gave them the ability to discern good from evil. This led to their banishment from the Garden of Eden, condemning them to labour in the field and to suffer in childbirth. This "original sin" is given great weight by Augustine and the Catholic church. It is passed down through the male line, transmitted by semen. Hence, every Christian child is born into a sense of condemnation.

According to Paul, god incarnated himself into Jesus so that he could be tortured and executed to atone for the original sin of Adam and Eve. Why any of this was necessary is unfathomable to non-Christians. Was god not omnipotent? Why not just forgive the sins? What is the point of the torture and execution? And if god made Adam, Eve, and the Garden of Eden, what was there to forgive? Apparently, what required forgiveness was the exercise of their god-given free will to obtain knowledge—what Augustine later called the "disease of curiosity."

Original sin has conferred an unwarranted guilt and negative view of humanity. The self is seen as essentially evil, contaminated through semen from the "original sin" of Adam. It is considered the source of Catholic guilt about sex.

Original sin was effectively critiqued in the book *Original Blessing*[36] by ex-Dominican Friar Matthew Fox.* Fox developed a theory of "Creation Spirituality" based on a positive, celebratory view of man that included a synchronicity with nature.

---

* He was expelled for "disobedience" from the priesthood for his efforts by then-Cardinal (Later Pope) Joseph Ratzinger.

Holy War has been used as an excuse throughout human history to rape, plunder, and pillage non-Christian communities in the name of god.[11] It also includes the church's rationalizations for slavery and the Conquest of the Americas. The concept of a "just" war has been used by the church throughout history to rationalize violence and aggression against "nonbelievers:" a Christian *jihad*.

Augustine developed the idea in his book, *Contra Faustum Manechaeum*, a rebuttal to the works of the Manichean heretic Faustus. In it, he argued that a just war is one fought against the enemies of god or his representative on earth (the Catholic church). It must simply be proclaimed by a legitimate authority (i.e. the Pope), have a just cause (such as spreading god's word to heathens), and must be fought with the "right intention" (without cruelty). The just warrior restrained sinners from evil; he acted against their will, but in their own self-interest. Whoever died in fighting a just war would be guaranteed a special place in heaven.

Church sophists began to interpret scripture in line with the emerging "Christian Soldier" viewpoint; for instance, John of Mantua noted that Jesus had ordered St. Peter to sheathe his sword in the Garden of Gethsemane, but had not told him to cast it aside. Hence, according to John of Mantua, god intended the Pope to wield the laity in defence of Christendom (p 2-3).[12]

According to historian Thomas Asbridge,[13] the Catholic church tried repeatedly to implement the concept of Holy War before the year 1000 in order to increase church power. The first successful implementation was the first Crusade, launched by Pope Urban II in 1095. Promising "eternal paradise" to willing combatants, fabricating stories of Muslim violence against

Christians, and hiring stooges to be the first to "commit" in a charged crowd, Urban was able to generate 100,000 Crusaders to fight in the Holy Land. The ones who had trained as knights had a serious existential problem solved for them—now, their practice of violence in their training for combat would no longer lead them to hell.

The use of Holy War to justify violence against natives in North America is described in several sources, none more graphically than Friar Diego de Landa's[14] descriptions of torturing, massacring, and burning natives alive in Mexico on suspicion of heresy. Their unread hieroglyphic rolls were burned as well, as "works of the devil." As de Landa put it, *"they set about the business with great rigor and atrocity, putting the Indians to great tortures, of ropes and water, hanging them by pulleys with stones of 50 or 75 pounds to their feet, and so suspended gave them many lashes until the blood ran to the ground from their shoulders and legs; besides this they tarred them with boiling fat as was the custom to do to negro slaves, and with melted wax of lit candles dropped on their bare parts; all this without preceding information, or seeking first the facts. This seemed the way to learn them ... seeing these things, they fled to the forests, others hung themselves in despair, many others were left wounded, without hands or feet, and many others died of the tortures inflicted"* (p 118).[14]

Nowhere else is the problem of Christian morality made more clear: acts need not be morally justified through any weighing of consequences or compassion; they simply have to be perceived as the will of god. Of course, the authority of the church interprets what that will is. Christian morality is a non-sequitur at best, an oxymoron at worst.

The Crusades and the Inquisition

Once Christianity became the official state religion in 325 CE, all open inquiry into its central beliefs came to a sudden halt. The punishments for "heresy" were too horrible: usually death by some slow, excruciating means. But the thirst for power exhibited by the church did not stop with terrorizing the masses: it wanted power over rulers as well.

Secular kings in Europe resisted church influence. Pope Gregory (1073-1085 CE) discovered a solution to this: the threat of excommunication.[11,13] At a time when Christians believed in eternal peace in heaven or punishment in hell, this was a powerful belief, and one that came to wield political power. It was first used successfully against King Henry IV of Germany in 1075.

Henry, who traced his lineage back to Charlemagne, had "interfered in the affairs of the church" and was banned by Pope Gregory from acting against them again. When Henry resisted, the power struggle was resolved in the church's favour by Gregory's threat of excommunication. Gregory also experimented with the concept of a papal army, paving the idea that religion and warfare should be intertwined, as was later realised in the Crusades.

The Crusades, which lasted for two hundred years, were an attempt by the Catholic church to generate power vis-à-vis the Eastern Orthodox Church. To recruit troops, Pope Urban II delivered sermons, largely in France, that told of Muslim "atrocities" against Christians in the Holy Land.* He paid shills

---

* According to historian Thomas Asbridge, these atrocities were either made up or exaggerated.

to planted audience members to "run forward to commit" to an attack on the Muslims.

Social contagion, hysteria, and the wish to escape the dreadful living conditions of Europe led thousands to volunteer. The ideas used by Urban played heavily on Augustine's concept of the Holy War: he described an alien out-group as capable of cruelty toward Christians, and promised an everlasting place in heaven to those who fought.

The Crusades were nothing more than a series of slaughters where the inhabitants of besieged cities (such as Antioch, Edessa, Nicaea, Jerusalem) were tortured, raped, decapitated, and sometimes torn apart with bare hands to have their body parts paraded around the city (p 151).[13] These massacres, ascribed by historians to "bottled-up bloodlust" (p 211),[13] were perpetrated against Muslims, Jews, and other Christians. Asbridge added that, *"in the minds of the crusaders, religious fervour, barbaric warfare and self-serving desire for material gain were not mutually exclusive experiences"* (p 318).[13]

When the Crusaders slaughtered the inhabitants of the "Holy City," Jerusalem, *"they came, still covered in their enemies' blood, weighed down with booty, rejoicing and weeping from excessive gladness to worship at the Sepulchre of our Saviour Jesus"* (p 318).[13] The fall of Jerusalem on July 15, 1099 left the Holy City awash with blood, its streets littered with mutilated corpses. Eventually, when they became a health hazard, they were piled up and burned.

These massacres continued for another 200 years over at least six separate Crusades. It is estimated that the death toll for the Crusades is 1 million people,[15] with another 350,000 being killed (by the most excruciating means possible) in the Inquisition. The European Wars of Religion, fought from 1520 to 1648, over an amalgam of territory, dynastic power, and religious belief, killed about 20 million. During the same century, the Conquest of the Americas led to the death of millions, with the spoils being shared by the Spanish state and the Catholic church.[15]

The slow end of the religious wars is attributed to a sea-change in human belief that began with the Enlightenment in the 17th Century: from saving souls to saving lives.[16] The Enlightenment, driven by the writings of Voltaire and others, occurred despite the church.

The religious concept of saving souls served to disparage the temporary human existence and pit it against the eternity spent in heaven or hell. Life was cheap and death, even by excruciating means, was of minor significance.

This thinking also guided the Inquisition, which institutionalized torture in what Steven Pinker called a "culture of cruelty" (p 132).[16] Pope Innocent IV authorized torture in 1251 as a means of extracting a confession. The Catholic church was not content with citizens acting correctly; they also had to think correctly. As Pinker notes, all of the first complex societies were absolutist theocracies that punished victimless crimes (e.g. heresy, blasphemy, apostasy, adultery, and unusual sexual practices) with torturous killings such as burning at the stake or drawing and quartering.

As Pinker put in his voluminous history of violence, *"the greatest damage (from people pursuing ends that involve figments of their imagination) comes from religious beliefs that downgrade the lives of flesh-and-blood people, such as the faith that suffering in this world will be rewarded in the next"* (p 139).[16] He continues, *"A broader danger of unverifiable beliefs is the temptation to defend them by violent means ... Since one cannot defend a belief based on faith by persuading skeptics it is true, the faithful are apt to react to unbelief with rage, and may try to eliminate that affront to everything that makes their lives meaningful"* (p 140).[16]

Museums of torture in Europe contain the horrific devices used in this era to inflict the maximum amount of pain and humiliation on their unfortunate victims. As Pinker concludes, *"Medieval Christendom was a culture of cruelty"* (p 141).[16]

What causes this connection between sadism and religious belief? Is it that religious dissenters pose a threat to the organizing structure that faith in god creates? If so, heretics generate the greatest terror, and hence the greatest rage. Or is it that mankind has, more than any other animal, a talent for sadism, and that religious authority, at least in the Middle Ages, had the power to enact that sadism?

These violent, sadistic acts occur in bursts across cultures and time periods,[12] usually in wars. However, civilians sometimes enact sadistic brutality. One such example is lynching in the US south, which was often preceded by torture. In these cases, the victim again represented a symbolic threat to a central belief: one having to do with the hierarchical structure of the races.

In his classic book *Extraordinary Popular Delusions and the Madness of Crowds*,[17] Charles Mackay described the Duke of Brunswick in 1628 inviting two Jesuit priests to join him in a dungeon to witness the torture of a woman accused of witchcraft. Both the priests believed in witchcraft and in the use of torture to elicit a confession of this sin.

The Duke was not a believer in torture—he believed people would say anything to stop the pain. To demonstrate this, he told the woman that the two men accompanying him were warlocks, and that he wanted to hear her thoughts on the matter. He then instructed the torturer to increase the pain while she was on the rack. She immediately "confessed" that yes, she had seen both men turn themselves into goats and wolves, and had seen them having sex with other witches. She also "knew" they had fathered many children with heads like toads and legs like spiders.

One of the Jesuits subsequently wrote a book exposing the horrors of torturous witch trials, contributing to their eventual end. Of the 350,000 killed by torture during the Inquisition, about 60-100,000 were killed for witchcraft (p 112-113).[18]

Heliocentrism: Copernicus and Galileo

The retreat from rationality with the domination of Christianity plunged the western world into 1000 years of ignorance. During these Dark Ages, literacy was low, and no meaningful invention occurred until the Gutenberg printing press in 1439.[2] The religious attacks on science were based on an aversion to any knowledge that contravened church authority. It extended even to the 15th and 16th Centuries when Copernicus (1473 - 1543) and Galileo (1564- 1642) challenged the notion of geocentricism (that the sun and planets revolved around the earth).

Fortunately for Copernicus, he had little influence during his lifetime, and his great work was published in the year of his death (1543). This saved him from church reaction. The most the church could do in response to Copernicus was to reject mathematics.

Galileo, however, was threatened by the Inquisition to recant his ideas on heliocentrism, which were published in his book *De Revolutionibus Orbium Coelestium* (On the Revolutions of the Heavenly Spheres). Church dogma claimed that the earth was the stationary centre of the universe, and both Copernicus and Galileo were presenting an alternative to this precept. Galileo's system also replaced the circles that Ptolemy had presented with epicycles by orbits instead; these orbits were later described as "elliptical" by Kepler.

Copernicus had a theologian friend write the frontispiece to his book, stating that the theory had no implications outside the limited realm of astronomy. Greater notoriety on his part would have brought a greater threat from the Catholic church. In his history of cosmology, Arthur Koestler[19] depicted Copernicus as a coward, afraid of ridicule. Perhaps Koestler underestimated the legitimate fear of church retribution in the 16th Century.

Dominican Friar Giovanni Tolosani served the function of church advocate in the case of Copernicus; in his book *On the Truth of Sacred Scripture*, he argued that Copernicus had used mathematics in his arguments, which could not prove physical causes in nature; in essence, he denied the possibility of mathematical physics.

Tolosani never did say what could prove causality; presumably, it was church dogma. The later, even more startling cosmology presented by Einstein in his theory of relativity* derived from mathematical reasoning; the current use of quantum physics would have been impossible if we had listened to

---

* Einstein spent years developing his ideas about space-time curvature into a rigorous mathematical framework. This resulted in his "Field Equations," which accurately predicted how space and time would curve as a result of the presence of a given quantity ($E = mc^2$). Your cell phone and its GPS operate with accuracy because of Einstein.

Tolosani. Despite the current mind-boggling arguments over the nature of the cosmos, no side makes its case without mathematical proof.[20]

Tolosani's reliance on "sacred scriptures" involved a passage from the Book of Joshua, where Joshua prayed for the moon and sun to stand still, and they did (10:12-13).* As we saw in a previous chapter, the Old Testament was written 800 years after the events it depicted. Do we really believe that the laws of astronomy were temporarily suspended this one time?

Copernicus' ideas contradicted the church's depiction of the universe, but were not influential at the time; perhaps this is because they were so far outside the Zeitgeist of the times, like the ideas of quantum physics are today. Sixty years after the publication of his book, only 15 astronomers appeared to use Copernicus' system. The Catholic church had no major reaction. Tolosani's book, however, was subsequently used by Dominican prosecutors against Galileo, who also wrote a heliocentric theory. Galileo used the newly-invented telescope to show that four large moons circled Jupiter, and thus proved that bodies existed that did not orbit the Earth.

In 1615, the Inquisition placed all works advocating the Copernican system on the Index of Prohibited Books, accused Galileo of heresy, threatened him with torture, and placed him under house arrest. In 1616, an Inquisitorial

---

* This is the Joshua of Battle of Jericho fame, in which the Israelites and Joshua put Jericho under siege (Joshua 6:1-21). This was one of a series of sieges in the Old Testament that ended in (supposed) massacre. However, as Finkelstein and Silberman[25] point out, archaeological digs showed this as unlikely. This was also true for the other 30 cities Joshua was supposed to have conquered: all were uninhabited, destroyed by other means, or never destroyed at all.

commission unanimously declared heliocentrism to be "*foolish and absurd in philosophy, and formally heretical since it explicitly contradicts in many places the sense of Holy Scripture.*" There is still some debate over whether Galileo, after being forced to recant his heliocentric theory, muttered the rebellious phrase "and yet it [the earth] moves."

Anti-Semitism

Biblical scholar Bart Ehrman[21] ascribes Christian anti-Semitism to Christians' perception of the Jews' unwillingness to accept Jesus as saviour, which is the central tenet of Christianity (p 242).[21] This essentially drove some Christians to say that by rejecting god's messiah, the Jews had rejected god.

In the Gospel of Matthew, Jesus is described as being rejected by the Jews; Pilate was reluctant to order the crucifixion until urged on by Jewish crowds: "*Let him be crucified,*" (Matthew 27:22) and "*his blood will be on us and on our children*" (Matthew 27:25). These parts of Christian scripture were frequently quoted in diatribes by Christian church Fathers against Judaism as a religion (p 92).[21]

Ironically, this theme of a rejected messiah predated Jesus or Matthew in Jewish history. Early Christian writers argued that the Jewish scriptures indicated that the Jews themselves had been rejected by god. The Old Testament prophets repeatedly warned the ancient Israelites that, since they had violated god's will, he would turn on them in judgment. Amos, Hosea, and Isaiah all say that god rejected the Jews because of how they chose to live. Paul wrote about the rejection of the Jews, but believed they would all eventually become converts to Christianity (Romans 9-11).

The Gospel of John explicitly blames the Jews for the killing of Jesus (John 19-20), and indicates that the Jews are the children of the Devil: *"Ye are of your father the devil and the lusts of your father ye will do. He was a murderer from the beginning ..."* (John 8:42-44). However, once again this is based on a verbatim conversation that has been "recorded" in the Gospels between Jesus and a group of Jews at the Mount of Olives.

According to Ehrman, anti-Jewish vitriol became more extreme in the middle of the 2nd Century, with Christian writers such as Tertullian going so far as writing treatises to oppose the Jews and their religion (p 243-44).[21] But as Ehrman puts it, *"such anti-Jewish tractates continue long after the second century, becoming a steady diet for Christian readers down through the centuries"* (p 244).[21] As Ehrman points out, anti-Judaism did not exist in Rome, Greece, or any other area before the coming of Christianity. While the Roman and Greek writers maligned some Jewish customs, they did not single out the Jews for criticism.

As Christianity grew its political power with Constantine, the anti-Jewish feelings translated into action—the burning of synagogues, confiscation of properties, and anti-Jewish violence became more frequent. Ehrman sees it as ironic that a *"profoundly Jewish religion of Jesus and his followers became the viciously anti-Jewish religion of later times"* (p 245).[21] Freeman[2] describes *"attacks against Jews, especially their synagogues, were now tolerated, or even, in extreme circumstances seen as a badge of Christian commitment ... Violence and intimidation at this level and anti-Jewish legislation at the state level cold-shouldered the Jews into ... a period of long desolation"* (p 266).[21]

In the frenzy to blame the Jews, what appears to have gone unnoticed is the other Christian belief: that god sent Jesus to be crucified to "save man from his sins." In other words, Jesus' crucifixion was part of god's plan. How, then, could any humans be held accountable?

As Christianity gained political power, hostility toward Jews became an openly destructive force (p 133).[2] Freeman identifies the turning point as a moment in 388 when Ambrose of Milan persuaded the Roman Emperor not to rebuild a synagogue burned down by a Christian mob.

Steven Pinker[16] recounts how Martin Luther wrote a 65,000 word treatise called *On the Jews and Their Lies*, in which he advised Christians to set fire to synagogues and schools and to bury what would not burn; to raze and destroy Jewish houses, confiscate Jewish prayer books, forbid Rabbis to teach, abolish safe conduct on highways, and have their cash confiscated (p 141).[16]

In the year 1492, the Inquisition gave 200,000 Jews the choice to either be expelled from Spain or convert to Christianity. This action was, as usual, one part religious and one part political: the Spanish had just defeated the Muslims at Granada, completing the *Reconquista* of Spain. Torquemada, one of the Chief Inquisitors (and himself a *converso*—a Jew who had converted to Christianity on threat of death), believed that any Jews remaining in Spain would influence recent *conversos*, and thus had to be removed. Many of the expelled Jews died at sea; the luckiest escaped to Islamic Turkey, where the Sultan (Bajazet) welcomed them.*

Daniel Goldhagen[22] sees Christian anti-Semitism as fuelling the Nazi campaigns of Jewish genocide. Hitler was

---

* Current Islamic Anti-Semitism is fuelled by conflicts in Israel with the Palestinians, and is not reflected throughout history.

raised Catholic, although he had rejected Christianity as the religion of the weak. Many SS troopers were Catholic.

As Goldhagen put it, the Jew had become synonymous with the Devil in the 13th Century Christian mind (p 53),[22] and since the church had totalitarian control over European moral culture, the message of hatred for the Jews was disseminated without opposition. All calamities were blamed on the Jews, including the Black Plague.

It is this legacy of European anti-Semitism that influenced the Nazi view. Nazi propaganda films juxtaposed images of Jews and rats.* Anti-Semitic dogma was central to the European worldview. When that worldview was shattered in Germany after the loss of World War I, anti-Semitism as a model of cultural coherence grew tremendously (p 54)[22] Goldhagen argues that groups can increase their solidarity by selecting an out-group as a target for common hostilities.[23]

Sexuality

As Elaine Pagels points out in her brilliant work *Adam, Eve, and the Serpent*,[24] current social attitudes toward sexuality tend to challenge traditional Christian values; specifically, that sex is only acceptable for purposes of reproduction within a marriage. They represent a departure from attitudes that pre-existed in both pagan and Jewish communities. The pagan community accepted prostitution and homosexuality. The Romans legalized and taxed prostitution, and accepted both homosexual and bisexual relationships as a diversion from family

---

* See, for example, Peter Cohen's film, *The Architecture of Doom*

obligations. The Jewish community accepted polygamy and divorce. Meanwhile, the Christian community emphasized monogamy and borrowed the concept of sexual restraint from the Stoics; however, they institutionalized it far more, until those views became inseparable from Christian faith.

By the time of Saint Augustine's writings, spontaneous sexual desire, far from being a natural response to physical and hormonal stimulation, became "proof" of humanity's original sin. Anyone who experienced natural sexuality was then condemned to feel guilty about the reaction. These restrictive attitudes toward sex were introduced into the western tradition by Christianity. To its credit, Christianity also discouraged routine abandonment of infants and sexual abuse of slaves, both of which were still acceptable in the first two centuries of the Common Era.

Pagels traces the adoption of Christian sexual values as directly occurring during the time when Christianity became the state religion of the Roman Empire under Constantine's rule. The opinions continued with only a brief two-year interruption during the reign of Julian. Yet when either Jewish or Christian texts from the first two centuries are examined, they rarely focus on sexuality. Instead, they focus on Adam, Eve and the Serpent.

This creation myth was common in Jewish writings by 200 BCE, and specified how god commanded Adam to *"be fruitful, multiply and fill the earth"* (Genesis 9:7). This archaic story, which existed in Jewish oral culture before being written down in the 7th Century BCE,[25] was used by Augustine to argue that human sexuality was sinful, and that infants are infected with the original sin from the moment of conception.

In short, a story written at a time of profound human ignorance, and reflecting attitudes of the day, has served as an excuse for sexual repression up to the present. Homosexuals are endangered, prostitutes scorned, and Catholics carry a pervasive guilt from an apocryphal story written to generate solidarity between two separated Jewish states (Israel and Judah).[25]

Augustine also used this story to emphasize his disdain of women (after all, it was Eve who tempted Adam with the tree of knowledge) and of curiosity, since eating from the tree of knowledge is what generated shame and an awareness of evil.

To a non-Christian, since the eating of the tree of knowledge made man closer to god (Genesis 3:22), one wonders why it was a mistake. However, in Augustine's hands, both women and curiosity became disparaged, and the ensuing dissemination of Christian belief led to a view that the moral principles in the genesis myth were universally valid.

Augustine, whose biography illustrates his practiced political expedience, generated the concept of original sin to argue that morally-weak humans needed strong, external government; an idea that, not surprisingly, found immediate acceptance amongst the political powers of the day. In a later debate with Julian of Eclanum, Augustine argued that mortality and sexual desire were not "natural," but rather entered into human experience only to punish Adam's sin. We are sexually aroused and die because Adam ate from the tree of knowledge.

Pagels also cites the genesis story as influencing Christianity's view of women. As we noted above, Paul never had any intimate relationships, was misogynistic, and appeared to abhor sexuality. He fastened on the role of Eve in Genesis. She was the second sex, made from Adam's rib, and it was she who first ate the forbidden fruit and passed it to Adam.

Eve's willingness to listen to the serpent led to a long lasting view of women as credulous and easily duped (p 178).[26] These ideas affixed themselves to views of women in the patriarchal religion of Christianity and, later, to Islam. The idea that women must cover their head in church, and later in public, originated with the notion of woman as a second-class citizen.

The targeting of women during the witch hunts was first articulated by the Catholic church with the Papal Bull by Pope Innocent VIII in 1484 (*Summis Desiderantes Affectibus*). It was followed two years later by Heinrich Kramer and Jacob Sprenger's *Malleus Maleficarum,* a "guide" for finding and prosecuting witches. It targeted women because of their susceptibility to diabolical influence (p 19)[27] and their subsequent role as the cause of all misfortunes (p 105-109),[18] including male impotence.

Women were "tested" for witchcraft by being thrown into rivers. If they drowned, they were innocent. If they floated, they were witches because the water rejected evil. This was the Catholic church view of women in the 15th to 18th Century. This view of women having witch-like qualities still exists in Papua New Guinea and several sub-Saharan African countries, where they can still be burned to death on the accusation of witchcraft (p 110).[18]

Mary Daly has written extensively on the role of women in modern Christianity as second-class citizens.[28,29] Daly reviewed the history of misogyny in the Christian church, including Tertullian's statement that women "are the devil's gateway" (p 3),[29] and Augustine's opinion that women were not made in the image of god. Italian priest Thomas Aquinas defined women as "misbegotten males," and Martin Luther surmised that god created Adam as lord over all living beings, but Eve spoiled it.

In modern times, the Catholic church has consistently opposed abortion laws, and in one recorded incident, sought to have a nun excommunicated for seeking to become a bishop (while not excommunicating any priests found guilty of the sexual abuse of children). Sharia law imposes the death penalty for adulterous women, while rape is used as a form of vengeance between warring families in Islamic Pakistan. To Daly, theology simply legitimizes patriarchy; certainly, traditional Christian and Islamic thought have made scapegoats of women because they represent the temptation of sexuality.

The notion of "god the father" starts a chain of thought that women are oppressed, second-class citizens, devoid of political rights in the name of religion. Current empirical data support these arguments. In an examination of the United Nations' measures of national "Gender Empowerment Measure" (the proportion of women in managerial or professional posts, women's share of earned income, the parliamentary representation of women, and women's access to health care), John Archer[30] found that the 15 countries where women had the least political power were either Islamic or Catholic; the former being in the Middle East, the latter in Central America (the only exception was South Korea). Archer found that women's political power was inversely correlated with physical violence directed toward them.

Ironically, early Christianity made a huge impression on women, largely because it favoured monogamy and equality (of all god's creatures). Women, suffering from a lack of both, saw Christianity as guaranteeing them some order of political protection from licentious Roman mores and the double-standard to which they had been subjected. Many of the early supporters of Christianity were women, as were many of Jesus' followers: they were described as accompanying Jesus to his crucifixion, remaining faithful to him at the end, and seeing his resurrection (Mark 15:40-51, 7:24, 15:40, 16:1-8; Matthew 25:55, 28:1-10, Luke 8:1-3, 23:55, John 4:1-42, 20:1-2).

Islam, if anything, is even worse to women than Christianity. Ayaan Hirsi Ali's[31] eloquent protests in *Infidel* describe the essence of Islamic life for women: covered under burkas, requiring male consent for even basic tasks like driving a car, being stoned or flogged for adultery, and still subjected to medieval practices like female circumcision. Hirsi Ali sees sexual repression as the basis for all that is wrong with Islam, and argues that the western notion of an individualized self is absent in Islam.

Hirsi Ali argues that the Koran mandates a male supremacy and a cult of virginity for females. The result is a demand for women to cover themselves, or else they'll arouse male desire; however, there is no corresponding demand for males to self-regulate.

Hirsi Ali argues that the cause of backwardness in the Muslim world is not Western repression but Islam itself: a faith that instils contempt for the Enlightenment and secular values, teaches hatred of outsiders to children, promises a grotesque version of the afterlife, and cultivates the ideal of the religious martyr. As she puts it, the only Muslim countries that show any openness—Indonesia, Turkey and Tunisia—are the ones that resist theocracy and keep religion in bounds.

Hirsi Ali has renounced Islam: a religious crime punishable by death in many Muslim countries (prescribed by both the *hadith* and the Koran). In Holland in 2004, Theo van Gogh made a film with Ali called *Submission* about the role of women in Islam; he was killed on a street in Amsterdam for doing so.

Authoritarianism

Christianity taught people to unquestioningly accept dogma, especially when it became the "state religion." This dogma extended to moral issues: it claimed that an act was good or bad because god said so. The basis for god saying so has been dubious. It is this adherence to a moral precept that has led religious-based morality astray.

For example, the religious dictum "spare the rod and spoil the child," derived from Proverbs 13:24, imposes the morality that we must correct through punishment. However, we now know, based on the research of sociologist Murray Straus and others,[18,32] that physical abuse of children has lasting negative consequences for the child's emotional and behavioural wellbeing.[33] Social science has shown us that we do not correct but rather, exacerbate.

Christianity enforced a central dogma that enhanced its own power and rendered adherents "faithful" through fear of excommunication and everlasting hell. It suppressed alternative views: ones that were, in some cases, more life-embracing or knowledge-based, such as Greek rationality, the Gnostic Gospels, Judaism, and pagan religions. The results linger. Religious belief is a central aspect of our organized thoughts: a central belief or core idea, even to this day. As such, it unconsciously influences our thinking on a variety of social issues, from birth control to the role of women to reactions toward gays: anything that gives us a definition of and actions toward an out-group.[34]

Historical attitudes still exert their influence, although many people are unaware of the origins of their own thinking. Such core beliefs are uncompromising in individuals for their sheer neurological connectivity.[34] Socially speaking, they are intractable for other reasons, including social conformity, their ability to define in- and out-groups, and the development of shared trust.[35]

REFERENCES

1. Hecht JM. *Doubt: a history*. New York: Harper One; 2004.
2. Freeman C. *The closing of the western mind*. New York: Vintage Books; 2002.
3. Manchester W. *A world lit only by fire*. New York: Back Bay Books; 1992.
4. Ehrman B. *Forged*. New York: Harper One; 2011.
5. Landsborough D. St paul and temporal lobe epilepsy. *Journal of Neurology, Neurosurgery and Psychiatry*. 1987; 50:659-664.
6. Devinsky O. Religious experiences and epilepsy. *Epilepsy & Behavior*. 2003; 4:76-77.
7. Hansen BA, Brodtkorb, E. Partial epilepsy with "ecstatic" seizures. *Epilepsy and Behavior*. 2003; 4:667-673.
8. Saver JL, Rabin J. The neural substrates of religious experience. *Journal of Neuropsychiatry*. 1997; 9:498-511.
9. Brown P. *Augustine of hippo*. Berkeley: University of California Press; 1970.
10. Copelston F. *A history of philosophy: vol 2 augustine to bonaventure*. Garden City: Image Books; 1962.
11. Dutton DG. *The psychology of genocide, massacres and extreme violence*. Westport: Praeger International; 2007.
12. Dutton, DG. Transitional mechanisms culminating in extreme violence. Aggression, Conflict and Peace Studies. 2011; 4(1):45-54.
13. Asbridge T. *The first crusade: a new history*. Oxford: Oxford University Press; 2004.
14. de Landa D. *Yucatan before and after the conquest*. New York: Dover Publications; 1566/1978.

15. Rummel RJ. *Death by government.* Piscataway: Transaction; 1994.
16. Pinker S. *The better angels of our nature: why violence has declined.* New York: Viking; 2011.
17. Mackay C. *Extraordinary popular delusions and the madness of crowds.* New York: Harmony Books; 1841/1980.
18. Shermer M. *The moral arc.* New York: Henry Holt & Co.; 2015.
19. Koestler A. *The sleepwalkers: a history of man's changing vision of the universe.* New York: MacMillan; 1959.
20. Greene B. *The hidden reality: parallel universes and the deep laws of the cosmos.* New York: Random House; 2011.
21. Ehrman BD. *Jesus, interrupted.* New York: Harper One; 2009.
22. Goldhagen DJ. *Hitler's willing executioners.* New York: Random House; 1996.
23. Lamm H, Meyers D. Group-induced polarization of attitudes and behavior. *Advances in Experimental Social Psychology.* New York: Academic Press; 1978.
24. Pagels E. *Adam, eve and the serpent.* New York: Random House; 1988.
25. Finkelstein I, Silberman N. *The bible unearthed: archaeology's new vision of ancient israel.* New York: Free Press; 2001.
26. Ehrman B. *Misquoting jesus: the story behind who changed the bible and why.* New York: Harper One; 2005.
27. Dutton DG. *The domestic assault of women.* Vancouver: University of British Columbia Press; 1995.
28. Daly M. *The church and the second sex.* Boston: Beacon Press; 1975.
29. Daly M. *Beyond god the father.* Boston: Beacon Press; 1973.

30. Archer J. Cross-cultural differences in physical aggression between partners: A social-structural analysis. *Personality and Social Psychology Review.* 2006; 10:133-153.
31. Hirsi Ali A. *Infidel.* New York: Atria Books; 2007.
32. Harris S. *The moral landscape.* New York: Free Press; 2010.
33. Straus MA, Gelles RJ. *Physical violence in american families.* New Brunswick: Transaction Publishing; 1992.
34. Taylor K. *Cruelty: human evil and the human brain.* New York: Oxford University Press; 2009.
35. Norenzayan A. *Big gods: how religion transformed cooperation and conflict.* Princeton: Princeton University Press; 2013.
36. Fox, M. (1983) Original Blessing. Putnam: New York.

CHAPTER 7

Some Notable Heretics: From Julian to String Theory

"The whole problem with the world is that fools and fanatics are always so certain of themselves, but wiser people so full of doubts."
BERTRAND RUSSELL

From its inception, Christianity has had its critics, although, as we have seen, heresy came at some extreme personal, social, and legal costs.

Early Christianity: Celsus, Origen, and Julian

Celsus was a 2nd Century Greek philosopher, whose written critique of Christianity was destroyed fairly early on. However, we still know of its existence through the rebuttal by the early Christian philosopher, Origen, in 248 CE. Origen's rebuttal contained sections of the original text by Celsus. Ironically, without the rebuttal, we would not know of Celsus. In addition, Origen was the one who was later condemned by Christians.

In his book, *On The True Word* (written circa 177 CE), Celsus argued that there had been no virgin birth; that Jesus had a father, a Roman soldier named Pantera. He pointed out that Jesus had warned his disciples of malicious acts from others who performed miracles. Hence, "miracles" themselves were not divine, since some were the acts of wicked men. In doing so, Celsus argued, Jesus not only laid open the acts of others but also raised questions about his own authenticity.

Because the Christian church had not yet acquired state power, Celsus was spared a cruel fate. Origen considered the story of Pantera to be fabricated without evidence. Of course, that is also true for the virgin birth. Once Christianity became the state religion, however, heresy became life-threatening.

One unusual exception to this heresy rule was Julian. Set against a line of Roman Emperors who embraced Christianity, Julian, who became Emperor of Rome in 361, seems an unlikely critic. However, Julian was "a throwback, a philosopher emperor" (p 183)[1] whose philosophical leanings (like his hero, Marcus Aurelius) provided the underpinning for a wise and moderate rule.

Julian had been raised a Christian, but was dismayed by the internecine battles he saw amongst Christians. His family had been brutally treated by Christian rulers: his father and immediate family members were executed by Constantine's sons.

Julian drew upon his background in Greek rationalism to write a book called *Contra Galilaeos* in 362-363 CE. In it, he challenged what he saw as the basic irrationality of Christianity and highlighted contradictions in the Christian scriptures. For instance, only John amongst the Gospel writers accepted the divinity of Jesus. Why, Julian asked, did the other writers not also accept Jesus' divinity if he was truly the son of god?

Julian claimed that the so-called prophecies of Christ's second coming made in the Old Testament were based on misinterpretation: there was no unequivocal prophecy of the virgin birth. Time has proved him correct on that one. Julian also appeared to be aware of the misinterpretation of the Hebrew word for young girl, *alma*, into the Greek word for virgin, *parthenos*.

Julian pointed out that the Christian teachings about god were narrowly provincial—based on a sole commitment by god to the Jews—while the pagan concepts of god were much more sophisticated, and dealt with god's relationship to everyone. He also asked many questions that others were afraid to speak publicly: why did god created Eve if she was going to thwart his plans for creation? Why had he deprived Adam of the knowledge of good and evil? Why did god neglect humanity for thousands of years and then arrive to only preach to a small tribe in Israel? Why were the Greeks not also favoured by his presence if he was, as Paul argued, a universal god?

Julian rejected Christian claims to have found the truth, and pointed out that their endless arguments indicated otherwise. Greek rationality had led to advances in knowledge in mathematics, law, medicine, astronomy, and philosophy. They were greatly superior to the "faith" arguments of Christians. Why should the Christian god be the only god? Why could the Christian god not accept other gods? Surely, he argues, a supreme, caring god would want to encourage diversity. Julian noted that the acceptance of different manifestations of god was essential to a flourishing empire.

Although these were probing questions, Freeman[1] suggests, in his monumental intellectual work, *The Closing of the Western Mind*, that Julian failed to provide an alternative belief system that was widely embraced (p 184-185).[1] Common people wanted a compelling narrative, and Christian teachings supplied that. Julian also consulted oracles and reintroduced blood sacrifices, which alienated more sophisticated pagans; at the time, the moral high ground for Christianity was its advocacy of monogamy and its disavowal of animal sacrifice.

Julian was killed in battle in 63 CE after a brief (18 month) reign as Roman ruler. Julian was unique in that he was perhaps the only person to criticize Christian dogma from a position of power, and this saved him from the fate of other critics.

The Dark Ages and Erasmus

Freeman,[1] Hecht,[2] and Manchester[3] all describe the Dark Ages as a time of religious conformity, lacking any display of critical thinking. As Hecht puts it, church and state had an absolute hegemony, and by the 5th Century knowledge of Greek, the language of intellectuals, was actively discouraged by the Christian church. For centuries, the texts by Plato, Aristotle, Cicero, and the Stoics were still read about, but no longer read. Greek rationality became a diminishing flame in what Manchester called a *"world lit only by fire"* (p 2).[3]

By the 12th Century, the Catholic church had successfully challenged the authority of the state via the threat of excommunication. By 1476, the popes were living like Roman Emperors,[3] and money flowed to the Catholic church. Part of this was through the selling of "indulgences," which the Pope said applied to the suffering of the souls in purgatory. Manchester describes how peasants starved themselves and their families to assuage the suffering of their departed relatives.

It was this extreme corruption that fired up both Martin Luther and Erasmus. Desiderius Erasmus (1466-1536) was a monk who moved from Holland to England at the behest of Henry VIII. Erasmus had been educated at the University of Paris, and was there exposed to renaissance humanism. He wrote a series of works, including the *Encomium Moriae*, which argued that only human folly accounted for the absurd theological defence of certain religious beliefs: namely, original sin, the notion of a virgin birth, and that Christ's body literally existed in the communal wafer.

Erasmus also criticized the extravagance of the Catholic church and postulated that only stupidity and ignorance on the part of the faithful could explain the tolerance for this exorbitance. His next work, written three years later, assailed the "warrior pope" (p 124).[3] His works were translated into several languages and one, *Julius Exclusus*, was presented as a play in Paris. In it, Pope Julius dies and has to confront St. Peter at the gate to heaven. Peter refuses Julius entry when hearing of his list of malfeasances and hypocritical rationalizations. Julius threatens to excommunicate Peter, but Peter resists.

Perhaps as a testament to public opinion on the church, Erasmus became a bestselling author in the 16th Century. As Manchester cites in his fourteen-volume *History of the Popes*, Ludwig Pastor concedes that it was virtually impossible in those days to exaggerate the "*contempt and hatred of the laity for the degenerate clergy*" (p 129).[3]

Erasmus himself was a humanist, probably gay, and a scholar in residence at Queen's College, Cambridge, where many of his original works are kept. Because Erasmus maintained his membership in the Catholic church and worked for reform from within, he was spared the cruelty that befell other church critics.

Michael Servetus

Michael Servetus (1511- 1553) is a prime example of the church's reaction to threat—a threat that typically arises in the form of intelligent people who generate interest in their ideas. Servetus was a brilliant polymath who made major contributions in as diverse fields as astronomy, mathematics, medicine, and theology. He was the first European to correctly describe pulmonary circulation. Servetus was educated at the University of Toulouse, where he studied law.

Servetus was outraged by the pomp and luxury displayed by the Pope at the coronation of the Holy Roman Emperor Charles V in 1530. He began to publish treatises that were critical of Christian theology, especially the notion of the Holy Trinity: that god is the Father, Son, and Holy Ghost. Although this issue had been debated for centuries prior to Constantine's Nicaean Council, it was beyond criticism in Servetus' day in the church's position of political power.

Servetus argued that god does not condemn anyone who does not condemn himself through thoughts, words, or deeds. As such, he was then condemned by both Catholic and Protestant hierarchies. He was put on trial in Geneva for rejection of the notion of the Holy Trinity and his criticism of baptism: what Protestant preacher and church leader John Calvin termed "execrable blasphemies."

He was found guilty and sentenced to the stake on October 27, 1553 in Geneva. He was burned alive on a pyre of his own books and green, slow-burning wood—chosen to prolong the agony. His thinking is credited with inspiring Unitarians, who believe (as did many before the Nicaean Council) that Christ was human (e.g. Arianism).

There was widespread aversion to Servetus' execution; it marked the beginning of widespread support in Europe for "freedom of conscience" and religious tolerance. Servetus' descriptions of pulmonary circulation were greatly ahead of their time and almost lost, since the church burned all the copies of his books they could find.*

Giordano Bruno

Giordano Bruno (1548-1600) was an Italian Dominican** friar, philosopher, mathematician, and poet who was burned at the stake after an Inquisition by the Catholic church. Bruno believed in the cosmological model proposed by Copernicus: that the earth revolves around the sun. He also believed that the universe was infinite, and that there were other planets like Earth that supported life. The sun, he said, was but one star out of many, and the universe was divided into an infinite number of solar systems. This idea, which is supported by current astronomy, was unthinkable at the time; if other worlds existed with intelligent beings, what did that say about the exclusive relationship of god to man?

---

* Luckily, they missed three copies, which were hidden away for decades.
** An irony since the Dominicans were the chief Inquisitors. Pope Paul IV (1555-1559) was also a Dominican and the Grand Inquisitor. As Pinker puts it, he was "*a skilled practitioner of torture and atrocious mass murders, talents for which he was elevated to sainthood in 1712*".[15] (p 132)

Bruno became well-known for his prodigious memory; he wrote books and lectured on mnemonic techniques. He was charged with holding opinions contrary to the Catholic faith: specifically that Jesus was created by god* (as opposed to being part of the Holy Trinity), that there was doubt surrounding the virgin birth, that the bread and wine served during Catholic mass didn't literally become the body and blood of Christ, and a belief in the plurality of worlds.

An annotated copy of Erasmus—the banned writings of a secular humanist—was found in his room. The Inquisitor Cardinal Bellarmine demanded a full recantation. Bruno refused to abandon his belief in the plurality of worlds. After a seven-year trial, he was declared a heretic and sentenced to death by Pope Clement VIII in 1600 and burned at the stake.

Celsus and Julian were beyond the power of the church to punish for heresy, Bruno was not. In 1942, Cardinal Giovanni Mercati stated that the church was perfectly justified in condemning him, and in 2000 Cardinal Angelo Sodano claimed Bruno's prosecutors "*had the desire to serve freedom and the common good and did everything possible to save his life.*"[4] Cardinal Sodano reiterated that the church was justified in trying Bruno, claiming that the church "*had the desire to serve freedom.*" In the same year, Pope John Paul made a general apology for the deaths of prominent scientists due to the Inquisition.

Bruno is currently viewed as a "martyr of science" and thus compared to Galileo. A monument to him stands in the Campo de' Fiori in Rome.

---

* Admittedly, given that the Church referred to Jesus as the "Son of god," it was easy to make this "mistake."

Bertrand Russell

Philosopher Bertrand Russell (1872-1970) wrote a series of brilliant essays and lectures from 1925 to the 1950s that were critical of religion. Russell had an academic position at the City College of New York rescinded through pressure from the Catholic archdiocese, buttressed by a smear campaign that mis-represented his views. He had been scheduled to teach courses there on the philosophy of science, a topic in which he was considered a world-class scholar. He taught instead at Harvard.

In the preface to his book *Why I Am Not a Christian*,[5] Russell re-affirms his position: "*I think all the great religions of the world—Buddhism, Hinduism, Christianity, Islam and Communism—both untrue and harmful. It is evident as a matter of logic, that, since they disagree, not more than one of them can be true. With very few exceptions, the religion which a man accepts is that of the community in which he lives, which makes it obvious that the influence of environment is what has led him to accept the religion in question ... Apart from logical cogency, there is something to me a little odd about the ethical valuations of those who think that an omnipotent, omniscient and benevolent deity, after preparing the ground by many millions of years of lifeless nebulae, would consider himself adequately rewarded by the final emergence of Hitler and Stalin and the H bomb*" (p v-vi).[5]

Russell went on in his preface to decry the adulation of faith in Christianity: faith is supposedly a conviction that cannot be shaken by contradictory evidence, and yet that contradictory evidence is suppressed, since it might induce doubt. On the grounds of faith, Russell pointed out, it was held that the youth of Russia and America should not be exposed to arguments favouring capitalism and communism, respectively. The net effect of "faith" in both groups was to both enhance the belief of their absolute correctness and increase the likelihood of war, since each side saw the other as absolutely wrong.

Russell went on to say "*A habit of basing convictions upon evidence, and of giving them only the degree of certainty which the evidence warrants, would, if it became general, cure most of the ills of the world today*" (p vi-vii).[5]

Faith is, in essence, belief perseverance: a mode of close-mindedness that causes one to seek only the evidence supporting one's own beliefs and to disregard disconfirming evidence out of hand.[6] The notion of holding a belief that would be contradicted by free inquiry is common to all religions and state education. Consequently, it stunts the minds of the young and fills them with what Russell called a "*fanatical hostility to those who have other fanaticisms*".

Social psychologists Helmut Lamm and David Myers[7] examined this tendency of groups of "like minded" people to shift to a more extreme position after group discussions of a relevant issue. In groups that have a leaning toward one side of an argument and where there are no dissenters from the "other side" present in the group (or where dissent in the group is stifled), arguments are made exclusively that present one side of the issue; therefore, the information available is limited to one side of the spectrum of opinion. Hence, a "social reality" emerges that is taken as absolute.

Status in such groups is attained by being a shade more extreme than the average group member. When the group is anticipating conflict with another group, opinion shifts further away from the other group's position. When the other group can be demonized or "otherized (i.e. reduced to a stereotype of negative traits that are seen as unlike the in-group)", this polarization of each group away from each other is even more extreme.

When "faith" includes a maxim that information that is "contra-faith" should be avoided, this same type of polarizing situation exists. All information that might temper one's "faith" is excluded, and those members exhibiting the most faith are accorded the greatest status within the group. The "absolute" correctness of one's own position is heightened through the absence of any counter-argument.

At the same time, the out-group of unbelievers is otherized . For example, with regards to religion, heretics are often depicted as messengers of the devil. All commonalities between the groups are extinguished, such as that each group is human, cares about family, and cares about its place in the universe.

Russell begins his first essay in his book, *Why I Am Not a Christian*, with a definition of Christianity: that Christians believe in god, immortality, and that Christ is divine (or else was the best and wisest of men). In the past, they also had to believe in eternal Hellfire but, at least in England during Russell's time (the early 20th Century), this was no longer required by law.

Russell rejects Thomas Aquinas' 13th Century "first cause" arguments for the existence of god. The "first cause" argument is that everything has a cause, and if you go back through the chain, you come to god: the first cause. The problem, then, is who made god? If everything must have a cause, then god must have a cause. If there can be anything without a cause, it may just as well be the world as be god.

Russell also rejects the ontological argument: that, since god is perfect, he must exist because existence is more perfect that non-existence. In fact, many things, including an equilateral triangle, are more perfect in the mind than when reality intrudes on the construct. I can imagine a perfect round of golf; no one can play a perfect round of golf.

Russell gives short shrift as well to "natural law" arguments for god: that god was the "explanation" for natural phenomena, such as the course of planets. As Russell put it, *"Why did God issue just those natural laws and no others? If you say he did it for his own good pleasure, and without any reason, you then find that there is something that is not subject to law, and so your train of law is interrupted ... if there were a reason for the laws which God gave, then God himself was subject to law, and therefore you do not have any advantage by introducing God as the intermediary"* (p 8-9).[5]

Similarly is the argument of design: that everything in the world is made so we can manage to live in the world. Voltaire parodied that argument by stating that the nose was made the way it was to support eyeglasses. To Russell, *"it is a most astonishing thing that people can believe that this world with all its defects, should be the best that omnipotence and omniscience have been able to produce in millions of years. I really cannot believe it. Do you think that, if you were granted omniscience and omnipotence, and millions of years in which to perfect your world, you could produce nothing better than the Ku Klux Klan, or the Fascists"* (p 10).[5]

The moral argument for god holds that there would be no right or wrong if god did not exist. Russell counters that, if one believes in a difference between right and wrong, one has to ask if this difference is due to god's fiat. If god made both right and wrong, then right and wrong make no difference to god. If wrong came into being independent of god, then god is unnecessary for rightness and wrongness. Russell does not, however, dismiss the Gnostic argument that the world was made by the Devil when god was not looking.

An extension of the moral argument is to argue that god must exist to correct the injustices of this world. Russell's response is that all we know is this world where injustice exists; if it exists here, it is likely to exist everywhere. Hence, the moral argument is against the existence of a deity.

These failed attempts at arguing for the existence of god are ultimately irrelevant; people believe in god because they were taught to do so, and because they have a wish for protection and safety. This emotional factor is the real reason for the acceptance of religion.

Russell argues that Christ had one serious defect in his moral character: to plant the idea of everlasting punishment and a *"vindictive fury against those people who would not listen to his teachings"* (p 17).[5] A humane person would not put the fears and terrors of hell into the world. To Russell, this *"doctrine that hell-fire is a punishment for sin, is a doctrine of cruelty"* (p 18).[5] These core aspects of his character, along with some of his actions (such as drowning swine and cursing a fig tree) put Christ below Buddha and Socrates as a moral exemplar.

Russell argues vehemently against Christianity's view of itself as a moral force. *"You find this curious fact, that the more intense has been the religion of any period and the more profound has been the dogmatic belief, the greater has been the cruelty and the worse the state of affairs"* (p 20).[5]

Russell describes how every improvement in the human condition has been opposed by the church. As he puts it, *"I say quite deliberately that the Christian religion, as organized in its churches, has been and still is the principal enemy of moral progress in the world*" (p 21). As an example, Russell argues that the Catholic church's prohibition against divorce has generated numerous examples of people, (mainly women) being subjected to inhumane treatment in marriage. In fact, the church's entire view of sexuality is "so morbid and so unnatural." The concept of sin does an extraordinary amount of harm, since it grants people what they believe to be a legitimate, perhaps even noble, outlet for their sadism (p 27).[5]

Christian ethics excluded social virtue because Christianity developed in groups who had no social power (pre-Constantine), and therefore came to believe that holiness was independent of beneficent action. As Russell puts it, *"To this day conventional Christians think an adulterer more wicked than a politician who takes bribes, although the latter probably does a thousand times more harm"* (p 33).[5]

He continues to say that *"The psychological analysis of the idea of righteousness seems to me to show that it is rooted in undesirable passions and ought not to be strengthened by the imprimatur of reason; what is unrighteousness ... it is the practice of behavior that is disliked by the herd. By calling it unrighteousness, and by arranging elaborate systems of ethics around this conception, the herd justifies itself in wreaking punishment upon the objects of its own dislike, while at the same time, since the herd is righteous by definition, it enhances its own self esteem at the very moment it lets loose its impulse to cruelty. This is the psychology of lynching, and of other ways criminals are punished. The essence of righteousness, therefore, is to afford an outlet for sadism by cloaking cruelty as justice"* (p 43).[5]

Although Russell could not have known it in England, examples of the sadism hidden in religious judgment were already horribly clear in the United States. One example of such can be found in a lynching described by Dutton[9] of an African-American man named Sam Hose, who killed a white man in self-defence. After the community left church, they formed a lynch mob that tortured and burned Hose to death, and then fought amongst themselves to collect body parts as souvenirs (p 75-76).[5] Religion in the US south strongly favoured the racism practiced in that area.

Michael Shermer[10] makes a detailed argument that modern morality derived from the Enlightenment, not from any religious precepts. It was the Enlightenment that fostered compassion for others; Christianity had railed against Jews, Muslims, and women, fostered the Inquisition, profited from the Conquest of the Americas, and benefitted from slavery (which it supported via two Papal Bulls).

To Russell, religion is based on fear, a terror of the unknown, and a wish to feel protected. He does not cite Freud in this latter regard, although Freud, of course, argued the same: that religion was an illusion based on a wish to be protected, originally by parents, a father, and then a father-in-heaven. As Russell summarizes, *"A good world needs knowledge, kindliness, and courage; it does not need a regretful hankering after the past or a fettering of the free intelligence by words uttered long ago by ignorant men"* (p 23).[5]

Richard Dawkins

Evolutionary biologist Richard Dawkins led the surge of atheist arguments made in the early 21st Century. In his book, *The God Delusion*,[11] Dawkins proposed that the existence of god could be formulated as a scientific hypothesis. He then sets out to test this hypothesis: that *"there exists a superhuman, supernatural intelligence who deliberately designed and created the universe and everything in it—including us*" (p 31).⁵

Our brains evolved, according to Dawkins, to help us survive in what he calls "Middle World"—where the objects that our survival depends upon are neither very large (stars) nor very small (atoms). We perceive only a limited spectrum, and see it in ways that make evolutionary sense; however, they are not necessarily the only reality. For example, we see crystals and rocks as solid; but at the atomic level, they are composed almost entirely of empty space. The nucleus of an atom, if represented as a fly in the middle of a football stadium, has the next closest atom outside the stadium, with nothing but empty space between. As Dawkins puts it, "*Our brains have evolved to help our bodies find their way around the world on a scale at which bodies operate. We never evolved to navigate the world of atoms*" (p 368).[11]

Our decisions are not assisted by activities in the micro world of atoms. We do not see the waves of existence suggested by quantum theory; instead, we only think of solid, material things as being "things" at all. Our model of the world is regulated by our sensory data (p 371);[11] our pet dogs can smell minute differences in the atomic structure in acids that we cannot detect.

Dawkins examined the spectrum of differences between a religious and a scientific mindset. He kept a special focus on the issue of evolution versus intelligent design: that either the marvellous designs found in nature evolved to greater complexity to aid survival or were the products of god.

Dawkins calls this latter position the "god of Gaps," since any failure of science to prove every aspect of animal structure as deriving through evolutionary processes is seized upon by creationists as "evidence" that god "must have" provided the design.

While science admits the shortcomings in its explanatory ability and views these gaps as challenges for further experimentation, religion celebrates our explanatory shortcomings as evidence that we cannot grasp god's grand design.

The universe is a bewildering and complex phenomenon, and the very notion of infinity is difficult to comprehend; but does that mean that these shortcomings prove the existence of god? Not to Professor Dawkins, who rates himself as a six on a seven-point scale between certainty in the existence of god (1) and certainty in the non-existence of god (7).

Dawkins repeats a point that cannot be made too often: that the burden of proof is on those who propose a hypothesis, not those who oppose it. In court, it is the prosecution who must prove the fact of guilt. Just as one is innocent until proven guilty, something does not exist until its existence is proven—a statement true for both unicorns and gods. Dawkins restates Russell's parable of the celestial teapot: that if one asserts that a tiny celestial teapot is circling the sun, too small to be revealed by telescopes, we would want proof. Dawkins wants similar proof for god, unicorns, and Christian dogma.

While he acknowledges that there are questions science has not yet answered— such as infinity or why we exist—Dawkins rejects any claim that theologians have on answering these questions. After all, what expertise do theologians have? What have they shown us, except religious texts whose very historical and factual value is dubious? Dawkins has a similar opinion on questions of morality—do we really want our moral expertise to originate with someone who reads a book suggesting the death penalty for gathering sticks on the Sabbath?

If we reject Deuteronomy and Leviticus, then which of religion's moral values do we accept? And, if we go "religion shopping" to look for a religion that is most comparable with our own moral values, then why do we need the religion at all?

Dawkins spends more time on the issue of intelligent design, since there is far more evidence now for the role of evolution. Dawkins rejects the "god as first cause" argument because, as with Russell, it leads to the question: who made god? Furthermore, Dawkins asserts, *"Any entity capable of intelligently designing something as improbable as a universe would have to be even more improbable than the universe"* (p 120).[11] Thus the god hypothesis is *"very close to being ruled out by the laws of probability"* (p 120-121).[11]

Dawkins also explores the current notion that cultural knowledge is carried by "memes:" bits of information that act kind of like genes, in that the successful ones are passed on through a culture and evolve as time passes. These memes coexist in something called a "memeplex" (p 198).[11] These memeplexes have survival value—that is, they in some way enable the community that holds them to survive in their environment (although the argument is still being waged as to whether "random drift," rather than natural selection, operates on elements of thought and language).

To Dawkins, religious ideas survive because they are compatible with other memes that already exist in the meme pool. Dawkins views religious belief complexes as having general survival value. As he puts it, *"we survive by the accumulated experience of previous generations and that experience needs to be passed on to children for their protection and wellbeing ... there will be selective advantage to child brains that possess the rule of thumb: believe, without question, whatever your grown ups tell you, obey your parents, obey the tribal elders, especially when they adopt a solemn tone ... trust your elders without question. This is a generally valuable rule for a child but it can go wrong*" (p 174).[11] For instance, moths evolved sighting strategies based on the moon and stars, which become lethal when an artificial flame is introduced. The dark side of trusting obedience is slavish gullibility.

One example, not available at the time of Dawkins' writing, is the research of my colleague Ara Norenzayan in his book, *Big gods*.[8] Norenzayan's work argues that, in societies where no strong central authority or rule of law exists, religion becomes a central mechanism for morality. People in these cultures do not lie or cheat because they feel god is watching them. Furthermore, they believe others who believe similarly to them will also be honest for the same reason—because they are being watched by the Big god.

The key phrase here is "others who believe similarly;" the religious in-group is trusted, while the out-group is mistrusted. Norenzayan shows how Christians believe atheists are untrustworthy, even though studies show no differences between Christian and atheist research subjects on tests of morality.*

Dawkins cites other religious memes as persisting because they are compatible with the existing memeplex (e.g. you will survive your own death; if you die a martyr, you will go to paradise; heretics should be killed; faith in god is a supreme virtue). Memeplexes transmit these ideas—largely unconsciously. Natural selection does not apply to meme transmission because it

---

* In a study in the US, both Christian and non-Christian participants rated and behaved more trustingly to photos of people wearing Christian religious symbols (a cross on a necklace, Ash Wednesday ashes, etc.) than the same targets not wearing these symbols. Actual laboratory tests of honesty find no differences between Christians and non-believers.[8]

is too slow. However, it does provide the brain with its predilections and biases to readily accept the memetic content.

If the human mind is a product of evolution, then one could argue that evolution has produced a mind that believes in god (or, at least, in a supernatural agent). And why not? From an evolutionary perspective, all that is required is that the mind's errors and illusions not be fatal.

Dawkins sounds, at times, like an atheist version of the religious fundamentalism he detests. Does evolution explain everything? Jeffrey Masson points out in his book, *When Elephants Weep*,[12] that anecdotal reports exist of animals putting themselves at risk to save a member of another species.[13] Masson cites an elephant trying to extricate a baby rhino from mud, despite being charged by the rhino's mother.

In *Beyond Words*, Carl Safina[13] provides numerous examples of animal altruism, even cases of animals saving humans. This form of altruism is not supposed to happen according to evolution; not only does it confer no evolutionary advantage to the animal, it puts it at risk of dying. This anecdotal evidence is rejected by science because it relies on mere observation, but the reports are consistent and come from numerous times and places. We think animals have no concept of death, but elephants cover dead elephants and humans with soil and vegetation, while wolves only stop attacking when prey has died, not just stopped moving.

Evolution has been impressive, but one is reminded that all scientific theories are eventually supplanted by something that better explains the data—all the data. As Safina argues, *"Do humans really have a better developed theory of mind than other animals? People watching a cartoon of nothing more than a circle and a triangle moving around and interacting almost always infer a story, involving motives and personalities and genders. Children talk to dolls for years, half-believing—or firmly believing—that the doll hears and feels and is a worthy confidant. Many adults pray to statues, fervently believing they are listening. When I was a teenager, our next door neighbors kept religious statues in every room except their bedroom, lest the Virgin witness human lust. All this indicates a common human inability to distinguish conscious minds from inanimate objects and evidence from nonsense"* (p 270/412 [Kindle E-book]).

Stephen Hawking and Model-Dependent Realism

Cosmologists Stephen Hawking and Leonard Mlodinow make some stunning arguments in *The Grand Design*,[14] a book that is both brilliant and mind-boggling. In it, the authors introduce the idea of model-dependent realism: that our brains make a model of the world by interpreting data from our sensory organs. Dawkins, too, argued that our survival-derived sensorium cannot detect the nature of atoms or stars; instead, we focus on the Middle World. This sensory data can be misleading, however. For example, we currently have a paradigm of reality based on Newtonian physics that includes notions of gravitational pull from large bodies. Experiments offer a different model: a wave model called quantum physics.

In one experiment, atoms of carbon are shot at a barrier that has two slots through which the balls could pass. Behind that barrier is a screen that counts the number of hits (i.e. the carbon atoms that passed through the slots). The experimenter closes off one of the slots, re-opens it, and then does the same with the other slot.

From the perspective of Newtonian physics, we would expect the number of hits to be halved when a slot was closed. That's not what happened. Opening the second gap does indeed decrease the number of atoms arriving at some points on the test screen but, surprisingly, increases them at others. There are spots where nothing hits with both slots open, but do get hit with one slot closed. The pattern of results defies common sense, and is better explained by a wave-like effect than by any simple additive model.

As Hawking and Mlodinow put it, improved technology expands the range of phenomena we can observe; it shows nature behaving in ways that defy our Newtonian paradigm. This double-slit experiment *"contains all the mystery of quantum mechanics,"* according to physicist Richard Feynman (p 585/1850 [Kindle E-book]).[14]

Science, too, produces models of the universe; ones that make better predictions than preceding models did. No ultimate theory (which explains everything and cannot be improved upon) has yet been developed, but Hawking and Mlodinow argue that M-theory may be that Holy Grail of science.[14] M-theory is, in fact, a series of theories (p 63/ 1850 [Kindle E-book]),[14] each of which predicts phenomena in a specific area of focus, ranging from atomic to cosmological.

The arguments behind M-theory are complex and require (at least) a reading of Hawking and Mlodinow's book, but the conclusions are that we are not the only universe; instead, multiple universes were created out of nothing. That creation did not require the intervention of a supernatural being such as god, but is instead explained using natural laws. Each of these universes has many possible histories and many possible states of existence (p 82/1850 [Kindle E-book]).[14] In some other universes, electrons might be the size of golf balls and gravity might be stronger than magnetism.

Space-time has ten space dimensions and one time dimension (p 1364/1850 [Kindle E-book]);[14] seven of the space dimensions are curled up so small that we don't notice them, leaving us with our illusion of three dimensions. These curled-up dimensions have an "internal space" (where elementary particles interact) with ranges of probability for their development. These probability ranges exist up to 10 to the 500th order (10, followed by 500 zeros) for internal spaces, and each might have different internal laws and values for physical constants.

In the days when the major religions began, people believed the Earth was unique and the centre of the universe. Now we know that there are hundreds of billions of stars in our galaxy (p 1397/1850 [Kindle E-book]),[14] and a large percentage of them have planetary systems. We also know there are hundreds of billions of galaxies in the universe.

Furthermore, our universe is but one of many, and we are the product of a very unique set of circumstances that were required for sophisticated life forms. We required a universe containing carbon, and that dispersed the carbon through a supernova explosion. If we were not a specific distance from the sun, we could not exist. If our orbit was not nearly circular, we would have temperature extremes that would kill us. There is a long list of physical attributes required to make Earth habitable.

Nevertheless, habitability is possible in other locations. Planets within the so-called "Goldilocks Zone" (of habitability) have been observed since 1992, and hundreds are known to exist (p 1453/ 1850[Kindle E-book]).[14] We are not as unique as we would like to believe. We are the product of quantum fluctuations in the very early universe; the chances of our existence are infinitely small.

We are bothered by the random nature of our existence,* and we have developed belief systems to deflect this fact. This includes the belief that we are watched over by a Creator, and are the centre of the universe.

To the scientist, the laws of the universe are metaphorically like the functioning of a large watch, or rather, an infinite series of watches. As complicated as the explanation of these rules is, the explanation of rules governing a "watch maker" would be far more complicated, especially since we do not know whether such an entity even exists.

None of the above should be taken as an argument against quantum theory. Science cannot be hobbled by "common sense" restrictions. If it were, we would not currently have smart phones or GPS systems (which use Einstein's concepts of specific relativity). However, when it comes to predicting whether the common man will follow a religious explanation of the universe or quantum theory, I think the former remains a more understandable and communicable story.

---

* Social psychologist Ellen Langer did an excellent study called the Illusion of Control.[16] In this psychology experiment, she set up a numbered-ball lottery system for her subjects. There were 100 balls in the hamper and the prize was $100. After the numbers were drawn, Langer offered to buy the balls back. In cases where the experimenter chose the ball, the subjects would sell it for anything over $1—the hypothetical value of the ball (1/100). If the subjects had picked a ball themselves, they wanted more money for it. Since they had chosen the ball, they believed (at least subconsciously) that their chances of winning had increased, although they remained the same: 1 in 100. This is a manifestation of our need to believe that we can control fate.

REFERENCES

1. Freeman C. *The closing of the western mind*. New York: Vintage Books; 2002.
2. Hecht JM. *Doubt: a history*. New York: Harper One; 2004.
3. Manchester W. *A world lit only by fire*. New York: Back Bay Books; 1992.
4. Seife C. Vatican regrets burning cosmologist. *Science Now*. 2000; 21:104
5. Russell B. *Why I am not a christian*. New York: Simon and Schuster; 1957.
6. Lord C, Ross L, Lepper MR. Biased assimilation and attitude polarization: The effects of prior theories and subsequently considered evidence. *Journal of Personality and Social Psychology*. 1979; 37:2098-2109.
7. Lamm H, Meyers D. Group-induced polarization of attitudes and behavior. *Advances in Experimental Social Psychology*. New York: Academic Press; 1978.
8. Norenzayan A. *Big gods: how religion transformed cooperation and conflict*. Princeton: Princeton University Press; 2013.
10. Shermer M. *The moral arc*. New York: Henry Holt & Co.; 2015.
11. Dawkins R. *The god delusion*. Boston: Houghton Mifflin; 2006.
12. Masson JM, McCarthy S. *When elephants weep: the emotional lives of animals*. New York: Delta Press; 1995.
13. Safina C. *Beyond words: what animals think and feel*. New York: Henry Holt & Co.; 2016.

14. Hawking S, Mlodinow L. *The grand design*. New York: Bantam Books; 2010.
15. Pinker S. *The better angels of our nature: why violence has declined*. New York: Viking; 2011.
16. Langer E. The illusion of control. *Journal of Personality and Social Psychology*. 1975; 32:311-328.

CHAPTER 8

The Heretics Part 2: Psychological, Political, Moral, and Cosmological Issues of Faith

"Religion has convinced people that there is an invisible man ... living in the sky, who watches everything you do every minute of the day. And the invisible man has a list of ten specific things he doesn't want you to do. And if you do any of these things, He will send you to a special place, of burning and fire and smoke and torture and anguish for you to live forever, and suffer and burn and scream until the end of time. But He loves you. He loves you and He needs money."

GEORGE CARLIN

Freud and Religion

According to his biographer, Peter Gay, Freud was a lifelong atheist:[1] he came to university as an atheist and left with scientific arguments to support his atheism. Freud famously argued that the veneer of civilization covered man's base instincts of sex and aggression. In return for repression, civilization offered protection from both the ravages of nature and other men, and therefore a diminution of anxiety.

This bargain has, as Freud put it, "an infantile prototype:" it is the same unspoken bargain between a small child and a father, of whom he is afraid but also needs for protection. As Freud argued, "*it was natural to assimilate the two situations*" (p 20).[1] So man made the forces of nature into persons (gods) and characterized them like a father, following not just an infantile prototype but a phylogenetic one. In short, we unconsciously conceptualized the problem into terms with which we have some familiarity.

Man has a set of tasks for these gods: "*The gods retain their threefold task: they must exorcize the terrors of nature, they must reconcile men to their cruelty of Fate, particularly, as it is shown in death, and they must compensate them for the sufferings and privations which a civilized life in common has imposed on them*" (p 21).[1] In short, it became the task of the gods to even out the "defects and evils of civilization."

From there, "*a store of ideas is created, born from man's need to make his helplessness tolerable and built up from the material of memories of helplessness of his own childhood and the childhood of the human race*" (p 23).[1] The possession of these ideas protects man from the dangers of Fate, as well as from the threat of human society. In the end, all good is rewarded and all evil punished; people do not cease to exist with death, but instead begin a new kind of existence, developing into something higher. Everything that happens in this world is an expression of the intentions of a higher intelligence, who, in the end, orders everything for the best.

Freud saw these ideas as present in all religions. Today we would call this "store of ideas" a memeplex.

This store of ideas served an important psychological function: it warded off a sense of helplessness and explained the presence of earthly evil. It implied that this evil would eventually be righted. Both the human needs for control and justice were served. As Freud put it, "*it is in fact natural to man to personify everything that he wants to understand in order to later control it ... I believe rather that when man personifies the forces of nature he is again following an infantile model. He had learnt from the persons in his earliest environment that the way to influence them is to establish a relation with them, and so later on, with the same view in end, he treats everything else that he comes across in the same way*" (p 28).[1]

As we saw in Chapter 2, praying to a god is believed to generate desired results, such as end a famine, drought, or convey a victory. This is the control aspect that Freud refers to in our process of personalizing forces, which, in reality, lie beyond our control.

The early origin of a relationship to a powerful father was established because the father soon replaced the mother as the source of protection throughout childhood. When the growing child learns that he can never do without protection from strange superior powers, he ascribes those powers to the concept of a father-figure and creates for himself gods: gods whom he dreads but also entrusts with his own protection. The conceptualization of a god was a reprise of man's relationship with a father.

Religious teachings are assertions about our reality. These assertions told us something that we had not been able to discover for ourselves; however, they bear on what is most important and interesting to us. Challenging these beliefs leads to three common responses: they are the beliefs of our ancestors, they are proofs handed down from primeval times, and that it is forbidden to raise questions about authentication.

Freud dismissed these defences, saying that the prohibition of inquiry can only be based on a sense of insecurity about the religious claims. We should not believe as our ancestors believed because they were far more ignorant than us. The "proofs" handed down are "*full of contradictions, revisions and falsifications, and where they speak of factual confirmation they are themselves unconfirmed*" (p 33).[1]

Freud's conclusion was as follows: "*Thus we arrive at the singular conclusion that of all the information provided by our cultural assets it is precisely the elements which might be of greatest importance to us and which have the task of solving the riddles of the universe and of reconciling us to the sufferings of life—it is precisely those elements that are the least well authenticated of any*" (p 34).[1]

Given their lack of demonstrable foundation why do religious ideas persist? To Freud, it is because they serve an important psychological function: they are the fulfillment of the "*oldest, strongest and most urgent wishes of mankind*" (p 38),[1] the need for protection. The recognition, even if unconsciously, that our helplessness lasts throughout life, makes it necessary to cling to the idea of a father-protector. Religion persists, in short, because it fills this need for protection.

These were illusions: mere beliefs that derive from an unconscious wish—not necessarily false (as with delusions)—but highly unlikely. Freud gave, as an example, the belief in the second coming and posited *"whether one classifies this belief as an illusion or as something analogous to a delusion will depend on one's personal attitude"* (p 39).[1] Instead of living on illusions, Freud recommended scientific work, as the *"only road which can lead us to knowledge of a reality outside ourselves"* (p 40).[1]

Freud rejected the argument that belief in a god is essential for morality; that society would descend into chaos if god were rejected. He pointed out, quite rightly as future studies have demonstrated,[2] that when religious doctrines are held with unrestricted sway (e.g. in medieval times), morality was not improved. In a later work, Steven Pinker presented data showing that, up to the 14th Century, society was far more violent than it is today, despite (or perhaps because of) absolute religious beliefs and frequent daily prayers.

Freud assailed what he called "premature religious influence:" the socialization of children into religious beliefs before their intellect is developed. He also assailed the restrictive morality of religion, including the deprivation of stimulants and intoxicants. He argued that when men have given up the "infantile neurosis" of religion, they would have to admit the full extent of their helplessness, as well as their insignificance in the machinery of the universe (p 62).[1] He called the acknowledgment of these truths "education to reality" (p 63).[1]

DONALD DUTTON, PH.D.

Christopher Hitchens

Christopher Hitchens' book, *God is Not Great,*[3*] is a brilliant compilation of religious critiques by a man of amazing erudition and insight. Hitchens, sadly, died prematurely in 2011. Hitchens summarized his views on religion early in his book as *"Violent, irrational, intolerant, allied to racism and tribalism and bigotry, invested in ignorance and hostile to free inquiry, contemptuous of women and coercive toward children: organized religion ought to have a great deal on its conscience. There is one more charge to be added to the bill of indictment. With a necessary part of its collective mind, religion looks forward to the destruction of the world"* (p 56).[3]

On this latter point, Hitchens describes the *"deranged fantasies of the book of Revelation,"* as promoted in the bestselling *Left Behind* series by Tim LaHaye. At this end time, god's kingdom arrives and the great pleasures of heaven occur, which involve the pleasure (according to Tertullian) of watching the sinners being punished.

Hitchens cites the possibility of nuclear war between India and Pakistan as a possible manifestation of this view—others have cited nuclear war as a logical extension of Augustine's concept of Holy War and current notions of Islamic *jihad* (see Dutton[4]). After all, if war against the infidel promises heavenly rewards, why not make it nuclear war?[5]

There is a deep and perverse connection between death and religion; Freud argued that religion would not end until we have conquered our fear of death. Hitchens extends this to

---

* Throughout the book, Hitchens eschews capitalizing the word "god."

fear of the dark, fear of the unknown, and fear of others. On its surface, religion appears to be a panacea for fear with its promises of afterlife. Some people, for reasons not well understood, wish to destroy others to the point of their own doom: a "scorched earth" policy.

Hitchens argues that the mildest criticism of religion is also the most devastating: that it is entirely man-made. Even the men who "made religion"—the early writers of the bible, Torah, and Koran—cannot agree on what their prophets actually said or did. As we have seen, various versions of the Koran exist, while the Christian bible has been re-written many times, and still has little agreement amongst the four Gospels.

Hitchens points out that believers deem their religious teachings to be sufficient as a philosophical and moral guide, even though those teachings were written in a time of ignorance and was contradicted by later developments. This moral guide includes everything from one's diet to sexual mores, and yet rarely prohibits bad behaviour toward non-believers. The dogma is represented as all one needs to know—that a believer knows everything.

Hitchens is incensed at the invasion of religion into the public sphere, and the failure to disconnect church and state. He cites the 1996 referendum in Ireland over whether its state constitution should still prohibit divorce. The Catholic church, including Mother Teresa, fought hard to keep the divorce injunction as law; in effect, condemning an Irish woman married to a wife-beating, incestuous drunk to remain in the marriage. It basically told Protestants to accept the blessings of Rome or leave. The amendment narrowly passed.

In the next decade, the Ryan Commission Report outlined the widespread incidence of child rape by Catholic priests in Ireland. In many cases, the children were threatened with excommunication if they told anyone. Hitchens is rightly revolted by this hypocrisy.

He also outlined the pervasiveness of religious division as a cause or contributor to violence; once again, one can look to the Protestant-Catholic "troubles" in Ireland, or the religious sectarian violence in Beirut, Bombay, Belgrade, Bethlehem, and Baghdad (he just picks some "B" cities as an example).

In Belgrade, the capital of Yugoslavia, the Croats were Catholic and the Serbs Christian orthodox. In WWII, Yugoslavia became a Nazi puppet-state. The Vatican forcibly converted the Serbs, using the threat of slaughter and deportation under the command of the ruling dictator General Ante Pavelic.

In her book, *Fields of Blood*, Karen Armstrong argues the opposite:[6] her premise is that it is not religion, per se, that causes violence, but the merging of religion with politics. How could religion manifest any misbehaviour without political power? Historically, religion (especially Christianity and Islam) has sought political power and used that power to expand itself at the costs of others.

Armstrong argues that religion represents man's search for meaning; as such, it is central to human existence. But religion shapes the answers to existential questions in ways that are unsupportable, and too often it posits unbelievers as scapegoats for current maladies. It is perhaps a function of the magnitude of the questions "answered" by religion, and the niggling uncertainty of those answers, that generates the historical tendency to punish any who do not accept the given dogma.

Hitchens takes religion (especially Catholicism) to task on its policies toward contraception, which acts as an obstruction in the progress of fighting HIV and other diseases. Both Christianity and Islam have regressive views on sexuality (including homosexuality), and consequently oppose any program that encourages the use of condoms.

Any new scientific discovery can run into opposition from religious authorities. Hitchens cites Muslim resistance to the newly-developed polio vaccine in India as an example. After it was released, it led to false rumours about the ill effects of the "Western medicine." In Islamic countries, some leaders, such as Ahmadinejad in Iran, deny that homosexuality even exists, even though polls show it as a constant 10% of any population worldwide, regardless of religion or any other demographic marker.

Condom use is a necessary, but still not sufficient, means of avoiding HIV transmission. However, the religious notion is that disease, including HIV, is punishment for sin (as defined by the ancient religious notions), such as homosexuality or adultery. This antiquated attitude precludes effective prevention.

In the Middle Ages, the church thought the Black Plague was god's punishment for moral backsliding. We now know it was caused by fleas bearing a bacterium, *Yersinia pestis*. The Archbishop of London was disturbed in 1665 to notice that the faithful were dying at the same rate as all the others. Yes, superstition does not save us.

Current issues also involve immunization against other sexually-transmitted diseases, such as human papillomavirus (HPV), which can cause cervical cancer in women. The Christian church in the US opposes immunization because they see it as failing to discourage premarital sex. As recently as the Bush administration (2007), the US government would not give foreign aid to charities or clinics that offered advice on family planning.

Africans who are either Muslim or Catholic are discouraged from learning how to protect themselves from HIV. Senior clerics in several countries have told their flocks that condoms transmit HIV. Cardinal Alfonso Lopez de Trujillo, the Vatican's president of the Pontifical Council for the Family, made a video warning his audience that all condoms were secretly made with microscopic holes through which the HIV virus could pass. Given the power that these men have over their flocks, this advice is murderous.

Across Muslim Africa, female circumcision is still practised. The circumcision involves slicing off the labia and the clitoris, often with a sharp stone, and then stitching up the vaginal opening with strong twine, only leaving a small aperture to allow the flow of menstrual blood.* The result is often infection, sterility, shame, and the death of both women and babies in childbirth. As Hitchens puts it, *"No society would tolerate such an insult to its womanhood and therefore its survival if the foul practice was not holy and sanctified"* (p 50).[3]

Hitchens has a wonderfully unique take on Reverend Martin Luther King Jr,, whom he plainly admires. His opinion is that much of King's use of Old Testament metaphor to communicate his message of non-violence is purely understandable, given his training and audience of African-Americans raised in the Black Baptist church. Hitchens reminds his reader that King's journey of emancipating his people started with slavery, which was an enterprise fully supported by religion: both

---

* See also the books by Ayan Hirsi Ali[7] on this practice.

Christianity and Islam. The African-North American slave trade was never opposed by Christian churches, and the African-Mediterranean slave trade was explicitly endorsed by and carried out in the name of Islam.

As Hitchens reminds his reader, there is no country in the present world where slavery is still practised where it is not still justified by Islam (p 181).[3] The justification is a slight revision of the eighth *sura*, revealed at Medina. It states that all non-Muslims are sinners, and it is a Muslim duty to make prisoners of sinners and to make slaves of all prisoners. Augustine's concept of Holy War is not that different (see Dutton[4]).

Hitchens was influenced by George Orwell's writings on totalitarianism, and sees the ultimate totalitarian state as religiously derived—a theocracy. This is because the ultimate invasion of personal freedom—the invasion of one's thoughts—originated with the Inquisition, the original "thought police." Even current totalitarian dictatorships, such as North Korea, teach citizens from birth that the leader is a god.

Religion functions through a fear of hell and by placing impossible constraints on human motives. Theocracies, from medieval Rome to Wahhabi Saudi Arabia, are spiritual police-states. They require punishment of the flesh, incessant wrestling with impure thoughts (which become real once named), hysterical confessions of guilt, false promises of improvement, and violent denunciations of backsliders. Forms of organised hypocrisy such as indulgences (the trade of money, services, charitable work, etc. to "buy" a pardon or remission from sin) are used to buy some wiggle room. Catholic indulgences bought more time in purgatory and paid for St. Peter's basilica.

Hitchens argues that organized religions are quintessentially totalitarian: they begin with revelations from absolute authorities, and are then reinforced by fear, supported by the idealization of faith, and based on a sin ostensibly committed a long time ago. Proscriptions and regulations are then added, such as those toward sexual practices, gender relations, diet, and quotidian demands for prayer.

In effect, total obedience to these myriad regulations is impossible, and the *"resulting tyranny is even more impressive if it can be enforced by a privileged caste or party which is highly zealous in the detection of error"* (p 212).[3]

As Hitchens puts it, *"Most of humanity, throughout its history, has dwelt under a form of stupefying dictatorship, and a large portion of it still does"* (p 212).[3] Many Muslim nations, including Saudi Arabia and Iran, are religious police-states. Citing Hannah Arendt's book, *The Origins of Totalitarianism*,[18] Hitchens distinguishes between "ordinary despotism" and those states that demand citizens to surrender their private lives for the central ideology or supreme leader.

This latter type of totalitarian state has been bound up with religion throughout human history. Certainly, non-religious examples exist, such as Cambodia under the Khmer Rouge or North Korea (although, even there, Kim Jong-un is considered to be a god).

The most totalitarian dictatorships usually make the leader into a god or a being who serves as a conduit to god (e.g. the Aztecs, Oriental monarchies in China, and medieval courts in Spain, France, and Russia). In all these states, the slightest infringement of "holy duty" could bring calamity.

As Hitchens describes George Orwell writing in 1946, *"From the totalitarian point of view, history is something to be created rather than learned. A totalitarian state is in effect a theocracy, and its ruling class, in order to keep its position, has to be thought of as infallible*" (p 232).[3] To be part of a totalitarian mindset, it is only necessary to wish for your own subjection, and to delight in the subjection of others'. Orwell's insight into this nightmare of tyranny came to him in a school run by what Hitchens calls "Christian sadists."

As we noted in the preceding chapter, Bertrand Russell has also commented on the sadism of religion and its desire to enact control over other living beings. When that is combined with Augustine's notion of Holy War, which justifies conquest of non-believers, we see the risk. While Christianity's great wars of conquest are largely over, Islam continues the tradition. As I write this, a man has been sentenced to 300 lashes in Saudi Arabia for questioning the Koran on his weblog.

This sadism has served as a connection between religion and fascism to enforce a strict compliance with authority. Fascist movements in Europe arose out of the misery of World War I, mostly in Catholic countries. They generated much sympathy from the Catholic church. The Vatican had a treaty in place with Mussolini shortly after he had seized power (the Lateran Pact of 1929), one that granted them a monopoly of control over matters such as birth, death, marriage, and education. In return, it urged its followers to vote for Mussolini's party. Pope Pius XI described Mussolini as "a man sent by providence" (p 235).[3]

The Catholic church was also a reliable ally of fascist movements in Spain, Portugal, and Croatia. Mussolini rationalized his use of poison gas against the people of Abyssinia because they held an incorrect doctrine in Christianity that had been condemned by the Pope almost 1,500 years previous, in 451 CE.

John Cornwell's book, *Hitler's Pope*,[9] documents the sycophancy of Pope Pius XII to Hitler, including letters of congratulation and advice to Catholics to stay out of Nazi affairs. When the war was over, many Nazis, including Adolf Eichmann, escaped to South America on Vatican passports. The Vatican also established mutually-supportive relationships with South American right-wing dictatorships, extending their connection to fascism beyond the Third Reich (p 241).[9]

Catholicism and Nazism shared two common foes: Jews and communists. The first was historical: the Jews had been blamed for the crucifixion.* The latter was an enemy of the church because Marxism was seen as a direct challenge to religious authority; Karl Marx had stated that religion was merely the opium of the masses.

Hitler had been raised Catholic, and had often referred to his survival despite assassination attempts as proof of god's plan for him. However, he fell out with Christianity over its emphasis on compassion for the afflicted. About 25% of the SS (the Nazi party's *Schutzstaffel* troops) were practising Catholics, and yet no Catholic was ever excommunicated for war crimes; although Joseph Goebbels, the Reich Minister of Propaganda, was excommunicated, it was for the crime of marrying a Protestant woman.

Sam Harris

In his book, *The End of Faith*,[11] philosopher and neuroscientist Sam Harris argues that the greatest problem facing the world right now is religious faith. He specifically pinpoints the set of

---

* See also Daniel Goldhagen's book, *Hitler's Willing Executioners*.[10]

beliefs that include that god's book "*is the absolute truth, while your book is false and requires me to kill you and that even if I don't, you will go to hell*" (p 38).[11] Harris cites passages from Deuteronomy and the Koran where this requirement to kill unbelievers is made forcefully.

The requirement to "respect" the beliefs of others is made impossible by these central aspects of religious dogma that are central to both Christianity and Islam. Harris points out that millennia of arguments have failed to resolve interfaith disputes simply because there is no evidence to support either side.

There is no more evidence for the existence of yahweh or satan than there was for zeus or poseidon. Yet 35% of Americans polled in 1996 by the Gallup Poll, said the bible is the literal word of god and that god created the universe. Another 48% said the bible was the "inspired word of god" and certain passages need to be interpreted symbolically (p 17).[11] Hence, only 17% reported skepticism about a personal god. Some 46% of Americans polled took the literal view of god creating the world,* believing the world began after carbon dating and archaeological digs reveal that the Babylonians and Sumerians were already brewing beer (p 17).[11] These numbers are high for the Christian world; the US is

---

* Pew Research Polls (based on a US national sample of 35,071 conducted in English and Spanish) show a decline in Christianity between 2007 and 2014—from 78.4% self-reporting as Christians to 70.6%. "Unaffiliated" (made up of atheists, agnostics, and "nothing in particular") increased from 16% to 23% during the same period. The drop was most pronounced amongst young adults. (pewforum.org/2015/05/12/Americas-changing-religious-landscape/) In Canada, 24% claim no religious affiliation, equally split between atheists and agnostics.

an unusual outlier, being a nation that is both wealthy and religious—the two are negatively correlated on a worldwide basis. However, they are lower than rates of fundamentalist belief in Muslim countries.

Harris argues that Islam is a religion of militancy, and that the only world devout Muslims can envision is one in which all infidels have either been converted to Islam, subjugated, or killed (p 110).[11] Anyone who is not a Muslim is defined in the Koran as an "enemy of god." *Jihad* can be internal (or "greater" struggle, such as against one's own sinfulness) as well as external (or "lesser" struggle against the infidel). However, the struggle against the infidel is a central element of the faith. The Koran offers only one prohibition against suicide terrorism (Do not destroy yourselves 4:29), but Harris offers up five pages of quotes from the Koran advocating destruction of the infidel, describing how they are enemies of god and will burn in hell. Islam, Harris concludes, is incompatible with Western liberalism, and devout believers will be sympathetic to Islamic terrorism.

To support this claim, he offers the results of a poll of Muslims done by the Pew Research Center in 2002. The poll assessed agreement with suicide bombing of civilian targets. If we focus on the response "never justified," only a minority of Muslims polled in any Middle Eastern country concurred (e.g. in Lebanon, 12% said it was never justified, and in Jordan 26%). Countries such as Syria, Iraq, Yemen, and Saudi Arabia were not included.

Islamic states appear to represent the worst manifestations of faith as an unshakeable conviction in the unknowable; they use flogging or death as punishment for apostasy or blasphemy, and they tend toward dictatorships or theocracies.

They are rife with inequality and corruption; their political inadequacies generate rage, which gets directed outward. In general, groups with power inequities generate rage directed toward out-groups,[12] and power inequalities (as measured by the GINI index) are extremely high in Muslim countries.

Harris argues that Islamic rage is a product of believers seeing their own culture as superior while also seeing the western world as benefitting from economic largess; hence, a sense of injustice is born. According to him, the world's *"billion or so Muslims are convinced of the superiority of their culture and obsessed with the inferiority of their power"* (p 130).[11]

There are other factors. For instance, Arabs identify themselves as Islamic first and part of a nation-state second. This tendency toward religious identity helps to explain why some Western-raised Muslims—such as mass killer Colonel Nidal Hasan—would "radicalize" in later life and kill their fellow Americans.

Islam is also a militant religion, born, as we saw above, during battles and conquest. Hence, all Muslims, to the extent that they adhere to the Koran, have to believe in actions to convert infidels. The only difference between moderates and extremists is the degree to which they believe political-military action is necessary to the practice of the faith.

There is one fact that suggests Harris may overestimate the causative role of Islamic belief in current violence: virtually all suicide bombers either come from or identify with Arabic Islam. The huge numbers of Muslims in Indonesia and other countries are not involved in the violence. Hence, an interactive model of Islamic terrorism may be called for: one that involves Islamic dogma but also includes Arabic identification and socio-political issues specific to the Middle East.

As with Hitchens, Harris reviews the Catholic church's role in the Inquisition,* its failure to take any moral stand against the Nazis, and its aid to Nazis fleeing to South America.[13]

The perpetrators of torture and murder in the Inquisition were men of god: popes, bishops, friars, and priests. They were able to transform Jesus' principal message of loving one's neighbour into a doctrine of murder because they had faith—faith that they were doing god's work, which required heretics to be put to death. As Harris puts it, *"Whenever a man imagines that he need only believe the truth of a proposition without evidence—that unbelievers will go to hell, that Jews drink the blood of infants—he becomes capable of anything"* (p 85).[11]

The justification for the Inquisition' uses of judicial torture came from Saint Augustine. Augustine reasoned that if torture was appropriate for those who broke the laws of men, it was even more appropriate for those who broke the laws of god. Hence, judicial torture became a final infliction of faith.

To anyone who ascribes intelligence to the early Christian church, it was this church who argued that the truth was being elicited through torture. The last public torture and burning at the stake (a ceremony called *auto-da-fé*) took place in Mexico in 1850, about the time Darwin set sail on the Beagle and Faraday discovered the relationship between electricity and magnetism.

---

* The Inquisition started in 1184 under Pope Lucius III, although it was not officially sanctioned until 1252. Pope Innocent III decreed in 1199 that all property belonging to a convicted heretic would be forfeited to the Church, which it then shared with local officials and the victims' accusers (p 84).

Harris also examines what one might call "secondary influences:" residuals from church dogma that still plague us, such as the million dead of AIDS in Africa because of church-influenced refusals to engage in family planning. The church's "war on sin" (e.g. so-called victimless crimes such as prostitution and drug use) is another source. Licensed brothels could be established that would provide protection for sex workers, if not for church-led political opposition. Drug laws have cost over a trillion dollars to enforce, and have completely failed by any measure (such as the cost of street drugs), but are supported by churches against anything that might supplant prayer.

Harris offers an amalgam of reason, spirituality, and ethics as a requisite replacement for religion. The problem is, how do we implement this change? Faith is the conviction of facts not in evidence—and since dogma cannot be proved by evidence, evidence cannot be used to disprove dogma. Historically, the only vehicle for mass conversion has been violence and conquest: whether the conquest of the Americas by the Christian church or the Arab conquests spreading Islam from Spain to India.

Harris' concerns about Islamic imperialism may be overblown; one has to ask why did Islam not expand between the time of the Ottoman Empire until the present? The answer, it seems, would indicate a combination of Koranic dogma with current political issues, mainly deriving from Islam in the Middle East. Robin Wright's book *Rock the Casbah*[14] points out that only a small percentage of the world's 1.6 billion Muslims live in the Middle East—the extremism that has captured the world's attention is actually Arab-Islamic.

While Islam contributes to the political problems of this geographic area, such as the inequality, poverty, and general "backwardness," it has not done so in other areas, such as Indonesia. The issue has numerous causes emanating from a variety of sources to produce a perfect storm.

Stephen Hawking Revisited

Stephen Hawking introduced the world to the concept of existence as constructed by physics: multiple universes, some where our own physical laws may not apply, and others that may replicate us in a historically different way; billions of stars, which exploded in such a precise manner that could disperse carbon and heavier elements throughout space; and astronomically small odds that we evolved from the primordial stew of hydrogen, helium, lithium, and carbon. Each link in this chain was necessary for our existence; the interplay of forces had to be optimal in order for us to exist.

Computer models have been developed to show these physical progressions, and to assess minor changes in any aspect of the forces of nature (helium, lithium, beryllium, and carbon), exploding stars, supernovas, and condensation of planets within a "Goldilocks Zone" around a sun. If any minor changes in any one aspect of these processes had occurred, mankind would never have existed. Not only that, but the universe would be fundamentally different:[15] unsuitable for the existence of any carbon-based life form.

Hawking reviews various examples. After reading this work and reflecting on Einstein's dictum, *"God does not play dice with the universe,"* one has a conundrum. We understand that the existence of a god who designed the universe requires a more complicated explanation than that for the universe itself. The alternative is a dynamic picture of a developing universe of such overwhelming complexity that our existence seems to have required a billion dice throws, each of which had to come out a specific way. As Hawking and Mlodinow put it, *"Were it not for a series of startling coincidences in the precise details of physical law, it seems, humans and similar life forms would never have come into being"* (p 1533/1850 [Kindle E-book]).[15]

In the face of these mind-boggling findings from physics, the idea of a god is simpler and more compelling *prima facie*. Do we put our faith in a god (and, unfortunately, the dogma that comes with conventional religion), or do we put our faith in a set of mathematical procedures we do not understand, which create theories that defy our common sense, and have faith that these theories will not morph into something radically different (as they did when quantum theory replaced Newtonian physics)? Instead, we invent mythologies that placate us, including the myth that we control our own fate; it is far more comforting than the reality that we are improbably lucky to be here.

At the time they wrote their book, Hawking and Mlodinow were optimistic about M-theory. M-theory has the requirements for a general law of the universe: super-symmetry between the forces of nature and the matter on which they act. M-theory still has to be proven to be finite mathematically and empirically, but if this happens, the theory provides a model of a universe that creates itself. It is the unified theory Einstein was hoping to find. As Hawking and Mlodinow stated, *"the true miracle is that abstract considerations of logic lead to a unique theory that predicts and describes a vast universe full of the amazing variety that we see"* (p 1742/1850 [Kindle E-book]).

My own perspective is that arguing for or against religion based on questions of the origin of the universe is a waste of time. The true issue is that theories of the existence of the universe are simply beyond our capacity to understand. They are preposterous ideas to common sense, whether they involve a god-Maker (what preceded the god-Maker?) or a Big Bang (what preceded the Big Bang?).

Richard Dawkins

Theoretical physics delivers ideas such as quantum theory, which, according to Richard Dawkins, (citing physicist Richard Feynman) can make excellent and precise predictions, but whose assumptions literally boggle our minds.[8, 16] As Dawkins himself says, "*quantum theory is so queer that physicists resort to one or another paradoxical interpretation of it*" (p 365).[8, 16]* These include theories of multiple or infinite universes, in some of which we are already dead, others we are not yet born, and still more where we will never be born. Objects in space "exist" in that space only in the sense of wave-like probabilities. Systems have not one history, but a series of possible histories, each differing in probability and can only be determined after the fact.

We simply do not have the cognitive capacity to "appreciate" (as they say in insanity cases) these ideas. Ironically, we wind up accepting or rejecting them on faith (although that

---

* The "queerness" of quantum theory doesn't end. At the time of writing this book, a Dutch study by Ronald Hanson was published in *Nature*, which showed particles (in this case diamonds) that were separated by a great distance could instantaneously affect each other's behaviour. This was something that Einstein had referred to as "spooky action at a distance" and refused to accept. (NY Times, October 21, 2015).

faith is in scientific reasoning). We do not even know if the Big Bang was the first Big Bang or the latest in a series.

Dawkins cited physicist Lee Smolin's theory that there are "daughter universes" born of "parent universes," and recounts that "*it has been estimated that there are between 1 billion and 30 billion planets in our galaxy, and 100 billion galaxies in the universe*" (p 137).[8] Really? On what basis can we make these estimates? We do not know what is beyond the "event horizon" (the limit of our telescopic vision) in the universe. We assume it is more of the same, trailing off to infinity; but how can we merely extrapolate from what we can currently see and call it fact? And how does one extrapolate to infinity? That is an extrapolation based on faith: faith in that only more of the same exists.

Dawkins is, in the end, comparing "extravagances:" the existence of a complex god capable of making the universe with the existence of multiverses. Dawkins argues that each one of the multiverses, if it has the same fundamental laws as ours, is less extravagant (p 147)[8] than the concept of a god.

Since quantum theory makes such accurate predictions, we have a scientific obligation to take it seriously; however, it is so far from common sense that I doubt it could ever replace religion—even Einstein once remarked that he could not understand the mathematics of quantum theory. We are left with a conundrum: that the nature of the universe is beyond our present capacity to understand. We can be aware of our cognitive limitations—that we overvalue what we can see and underestimate the rest. However, the average person just cannot do the math to understand theoretical physics. That said, it will continue to dominate in the foreseeable future- as I write this, a black hole has been photographed. Originally, we only inferred their existence from mathematical equations.

The Objective-Subjective Problem

On her brilliant website Brain Pickings,[17] Maria Popova discussed the 1927 Solvay Conference. This conference brought together the most famous physicists in the word: Albert Einstein, Niels Bohr, Werner Heisenberg, and Max Planck. They were fascinated by the continuing role of religion given the advances in physics, especially Heisenberg's "uncertainty principle," which argued convincingly that any statements about physical reality had to also factor in the position of the observer into the conclusion. What did this say about religion?

The physicists were split on the answer: some insisted that the two were incompatible, since religion was a vestige of the pre-scientific world of superstition; others insisted that religion had a role to play in moral guidance that science could never supplant.

Heisenberg himself remained preoccupied with the question. In a post-conference conversation with Niels Bohr (who originated quantum theory), Heisenberg posed the question of the interface between religion and physics. Bohr responded, "*We ought to remember that religion uses language in a quite different way from science. The language of religion is more closely related to the language of poetry than to the language of science ... True, we are inclined to think that if religion deals with objective truths, it ought to adopt the same criteria of truth as science. But I myself find the division of the world into an objective and a subjective side much too arbitrary. The fact that religions through the ages have spoken in images, parables, and paradoxes means simply that there are no other ways of grasping the reality to which they refer. But that does not mean that it is not a genuine reality. And splitting this reality into an objective and a subjective side won't get us very far.*"

Bohr goes on to point out that an "objective" phenomenon, such as two events occurring simultaneously, really has a subjective aspect: they might appear simultaneous to an observer at rest, but not to another observer in motion. However, this "relativistic description" is also objective, because every observer can calculate what the other observer has perceived.

From quantum theory, Bohr argues, every physical process may be said to have an objective and subjective set of features. Religion, then, is best understood as an instrument of moral enrichment. Bohr saw physics as reducing the weight of objectivity and heightening subjectivity. Religious questions deal with our very existence, and are therefore necessarily subjective; however, they cannot be dismissed for being so. Religious teachings are complementary descriptions that convey the rich possibilities flowing from man's relationship with the central order.

As an abstract philosophical stance on empiricism, this is fine. My argument is that religious belief systems do claim some objective truth, and that this "truth" can be assessed by their ability to predict. Christian religion has consistently predicted the second coming incorrectly. Meanwhile, science and technology can send signals to satellites circling Jupiter's moons. That involves very high levels of prediction.

While it is important to accept Bohr's insights into subjectivity, it is also important to see that there is massive variation in the degree of subjectivity inherent to human belief systems. Religious systems, as we have seen, rely on dubious sources for doctrines, and make predictions that do not occur. Scientific systems generate technology that operates only when it correctly apprehends the nature of the universe. GPS systems and smart phones would not have worked in a Newtonian system; they needed to accept the time-space curve in order to be accurate.

When we gaze into the stars at night, we see numerous points of light. We know from physics that some of these may no longer exist; that we are seeing what might be the remnants of a star that exploded long ago, before its light reached the earth. We know, too, that we are limited by our own sensory shortcomings to the "event horizon:" we are astounded to see the universe through a telescope and the numerous points of light we could not see with the naked eye.

Our human capability to organize what we see also kicks in: we see patterns in the stars, and even have names for many, such as Ursa Minor, Orion, and Canis Major. Often, these patterns are in the realm of the abstract: one may look at the three stars on Orion's belt and wonder how someone else thought that represented a hunter.

If we travel below the equator, a different sky presents itself to us. This wonder is accompanied by the subjectivity of our vision, and our interpretation of patterns. These same subjective features were involved with god—a force not even seen as the stars are—but verified by tribal knowledge and accepted.

REFERENCES

1. Freud S. *The future of an illusion*. New York: W.W. Norton & Co.; 1961.
2. Pinker S. *The better angels of our nature: why violence has declined*. New York: Viking; 2011.
3. Hitchens C. *God is not great: how religion poisons everything*. New York: Twelve; 2007.
4. Dutton DG. *The psychology of genocide, massacres and extreme violence*. Westport: Praeger Security International; 2007.
5. Feldman N. Islam, terror and the second nuclear age. *New York Times Magazine*. 2006; 72-79.
6. Armstrong K. *Fields of blood: religion and the history of violence*. New York: Knopf; 2014.
7. Hirsi Ali A. *Infidel*. New York: Atria; 2007.
8. Dawkins, R. (2006) The god delusion Houghton- Miflin: Boston.
9. Cornwell J. *Hitler's pope: the secret history of pius XII*. New York: Viking; 1999.
10. Goldhagen DJ. *Hitler's willing executioners*. New York: Random House; 1996.
11. Harris S. *The end of faith*. New York: Norton; 2004.
12. Lewin K, Lippitt R, White R. An experimental study of leadership and group life. *Readings in Social Psychology*. New York: Holt, Rinehart, and Winston; 1947.
13. Aarons M, Loftus JW. *Unholy trinity: The vatican, the nazis and their swiss bankers*. New York: St. Martin's Press; 1998.
14. Wright R. *Rock the casbah: rage and rebellion across the islamic world*. New York: Simon and Schuster; 2012.

15. Hawking S, Mlodinow L. *The grand design*. New York: Bantam Books; 2010.
16. Holt J. *Why does the world exist?* New York: Liveright Publishing Co.; 2012.
17. Popova M. Nobel-winning physicist Niels Bohr on subjective vs. objective reality and the uses of religion in a secular world. (http://www.brainpickings.org/) 2018.
18. Arendt, H. (1951) The origins of totalitarianism. Schoken Books; New York

CHAPTER 9

God in the Brain: The Developmental Psychology of Religious Belief

"You cannot prove the non-existence of God; you just have to take it on faith."

WOODY ALLEN

In Chapter 7, we saw that Richard Dawkins argued that religion survived for two reasons: that the brain had certain hardwiring to make it receptive to religious ideas, and that *memeplexes*—patterns of belief and knowledge—fit this hardwiring and were passed on socially. This hardwiring was acquired through evolution. Research in human cognition now recognises that both supernatural and natural explanations for events coexist across cultures and age groups.[1]

In his book, *Born Believers: The Science of Children's Religious Belief*, Justin Barrett[2] reviews the evidence for this hardwiring that has accumulated from research in cognitive science. Barrett's thesis is that children are prone to believe in "supernatural beings," including spirits, ghosts, angels, devils, and gods, during the first four years of life. This tendency in children is a normal cognitive development and appears, according to Barrett, independently of indoctrination to a specific religion.

Barrett argues that ridiculous beliefs will not be adopted, no matter how hard one tries to indoctrinate them—he cites Pascal Boyer's[3] example that children will not come to believe that former US Vice President Dick Cheney is made of green cheese.*

A research study showed that preschoolers understand the difference between reality and fantasy: that an imagined pony cannot be touched by somebody else, for example. Boyer argued that the evolution of the human brain led to a capacity to acquire religion, although not to religion itself.** He referred to a number of beliefs that people find ludicrous in order to demonstrate that people, even children, are not generally credulous.

On the other hand, Professor Jane Risen[4] with the University of Chicago has argued convincingly that superstition or

---

* The absurdity of a belief is, of course, highly subjective. Few Christians view the virgin birth or the resurrection as absurd, while most atheists do. Many children believe in Santa Claus and a tooth fairy.

** Boyer also argues that religions as we know them are the result of historical reductions—successful ones amongst many variants (p 32/375 [Kindle E-book]). Boyer suggests an evolutionary explanation for this success.

"magical beliefs"—the belief that actions can influence events when there is no evidence for it—is actually widespread: more than half of Americans surveyed admit to knocking on wood for good luck.

People hold these magical beliefs and act accordingly, even though they know rationally that the belief cannot be true. Risen calls this "acquiescence." Risen recalls an anecdote about Nobel Prize winner Niels Bohr, who was asked about a horseshoe over his lab door. He replied that he didn't believe in superstition, but "it's lucky whether you believe or not." The anecdote indicates that even brilliant scientists may indulge superstitions.

According to Barrett, religious beliefs are different from fantasy or superstition, and they develop even in the minds of the children of atheists; it is to be noted that his evidence for this claim is largely anecdotal, and he does not entertain the issue of the development of atheism in the children of believers.

According to research in cognition, the developing human mind acquires some ideas very easily—we are much better than computers, for example, at facial recognition. We are born with natural tendencies that allow us to solve problems that are important to our survival (p 7).[2] Independently of culture, children develop what Barrett calls *"a propensity to seek meaning and understanding of their environments"* (p 8).[2] This search leads to *"beliefs in a purposeful and designed world, and an intelligent designer who is super powerful, super-knowing, super-perceiving, and immortal,"* who *"does not need to be visible or embodied and who is connected to moral goodness and is an enforcer of morality"* (p 8),[2] kind of like an invisible Superman.

This search for meaning is inherited, passed along by a brain shaped by evolution. Religious beliefs fulfill that search for meaning by offering a culturally-acceptable set of explanations. It is similar to a set of grammatical rules that Noam Chomsky and others have argued are inborn.*

Agency versus Superagency

Barrett describes the developing human brain as having a god-shaped hole, ready to receive ideas that fit a god concept (p 9).[2] This readiness is culturally widespread and not culture-dependent; however, as Barrett notes, religion is virtually a cultural universal. Certain capabilities are natural, in that we acquire them easily and automatically (e.g. we learn to speak just by listening to others and learn to walk through trial and error), as opposed to abilities that require expertise (such as doing calculus). In this sense, belief in a god is a natural capability.

Some current work in cognitive psychology supports an idea of a "god intuition" or, at least, the development of supernatural concepts stemming from intuitive psychology.[6] Developmental psychologist Paul Bloom has also shown in his book, *Descartes' Baby*,[7] that children have a natural tendency to believe in Cartesian dualism (that spirits or souls exist apart from bodies). Bloom[8] argues that "common sense dualism" stems from humans having two distinct cognitive systems: one for dealing with material objects, and one for dealing with social entities. These are an "evolutionary accident" that enables us to entertain the notion of life after death, since the soul (a social entity) is thought to survive the body.

Preschool children believe that the brain is only responsible for some aspects of life, such as math problems, but is not

---

* See, for example, Steven Pinker: *The Blank Slate*[5].

essential for pretending, loving, or brushing your teeth. These are done by people, not their brains. Children accurately report that the biological properties of a dead mouse have ceased to function, but believe that its psychological properties continue—they believe it can still feel hunger, think thoughts, and have desires.

Developmental psychology has developed very ingenious ways of studying the mind of a baby. Babies become bored and look away, or they orient themselves toward what they find surprising. Hence by measuring babies' visual focus and orientation, we can draw some conclusions about the babies' expectations and their methods of constructing their visual world. This gives us an idea of what concepts babies are born with—what their natural assumptions about the world are.

One such assumption is object constancy: that objects remain the same unless something acts upon them. For example, in a research study, babies watch a cylinder rolling down a ramp. The cylinder comes to a stop when it encounters a fixed object (called a "stopper" in the study). When babies have seen this several times, they look away from it; it is assumed they are bored or habituated.

A toy bug on wheels is then introduced at the bottom of the ramp, either away from the stopper so the cylinder would not strike it, or right next to the stopper so it would be struck. When the toy bug was struck but did not move, it caught the babies' attention. Those trials were closely watched (presumably they had seen the bug move before).

The authors concluded that 6-month-old babies divide the world into things that act (agents) and things that are acted upon (objects). At only two months, we understand that physical contact can move an object. By five months, we know something about the core properties of objects (e.g. that a shoe moves as a whole and moves on an unobstructed, continuous path). By 12 months, we know that objects must be supported to keep from falling.

In short, by studying babies' attention patterns, we can make some deductions about what Barrett calls "naive physics:" that solid objects cannot pass through one another, and that they have established rules of ordinary (versus supernatural) causation.

One aspect of this development is the concept of agency: entities that act on their environment and do not merely react. In the minds of children, this includes people, animals, computers, ghosts, space aliens, and gods. Developmental studies show that children believe these agents can move themselves, act to attain goals, and need not be visible or resemble humans. What differentiates them from objects is that they do not need to be touched in order to move.

Babies can make the agent-object distinctions by the time they are 6 months old, and the recognition of the properties of agents follows soon after that. By nine months, babies proceed beyond merely directing their attention to novel displays to pointing to things in order to direct the gaze of human agents (adults) and watch their eyes gaze to discern whether or not they are attending. In research, babies attend to agents if:

1) The agent looks human (has two eyes and a nose) or
2) Interacts with (i.e. reacts to actions of) a smaller version of itself.

The sequence of reactions appears to develop our ideas of agency. Barrett argues that when changes are observed (but no actions or agent are observed), the concept of the unseen agent develops (e.g. if the furniture in my room moved during my nap, I conclude that a parent "must" have moved them, since objects cannot move themselves). This "unseen agent" is, according to anthropologist Pascal Boyer, the fledgling god concept.[3]

Barrett cites a study by Philippe Rochat and associates.[9] They used computer-presented displays of a blue and red disc to examine the development of how we infer causality. In one display, one disc was "chasing" the other (e.g. pursuing it but never touching it). The other display was identical in the speed of the disc movement, rate of direction changes, and average distance between the discs, but the movement of the discs was arbitrary.

It was inferred that the babies perceived a causal connection between the movement of the blue and red discs on the first display. By 6 months, babies watched the non-chase rather than the chase (the latter being too predictable). By 9 months, if the roles of the discs were reversed (e.g. red chased blue, then blue chased red), the reversal caught the babies' attention. Attention was, Barrett claims, *"turned on by action that violates normal object behavior: ordinary objects do not chase, so they must be agents"* (p 36).[2]

He cited a famous study by Fritz Heider[10] that had showed college students a film of a circle and two triangles moving in and around a broken square. When asked to write down what happened, the students' descriptions included rich mental states for each of the shapes including beliefs, wants, aims, intentions, and sometimes gender roles of the triangles and circle (almost all participants described the scene as if the shapes were people).

Barrett himself did a replication of the classic study. He used an electromagnet to disperse ball bearings that participants were placing in holes on a board. The students described the ball bearings as if they were agents.

One conclusion of these studies (that Barrett seems to later overlook), is that both babies and adults infer agency in an illusory manner. Clearly the students' descriptions implied agency (intentions were attributed to inanimate objects such as geometric forms or ball bearings). This was a clear experimental demonstration of what we call anthropomorphizing: describing the actions of non-humans in human terms.[11]

Just as clearly, real agency did not exist. It was illusory causation: the students' projection of human traits onto inanimate objects. Heider himself called it "phenomenal causality" to further emphasize its (unwarranted) subjectivity. Barrett, however, says "*I do not emphasize this very human trait to make fun of it or to suggest that people are basically error prone when it comes to recognizing agents*" (p 39).[2]

In fact, Barrett goes on to describe this "hypersensitive agency detection system" (HADD) as a product of normal brain function. From an evolutionary perspective, he argues, occasionally thinking of the wind in the bushes as an agent—such as a predator—is a sound assumption for survival. Those who thought the rustling was caused by a tiger were more likely to survive than those who thought of it as the wind (since some of the latter were occasionally mistaken and eaten). From this process of natural selection, the agency detectors will flourish, and the agency-sensitive people reproduce more frequently. Thus, today, we are agency detectors.

This argument may explain the development of innate agency, but how and why would this extend to superagency? Even if we have evolved a hypersensitive agency detection system, how do we get from that to superagents who, by definition, exceed the normal cognitive rules applied to humans or other agents (including tigers)?

Since the inference of agency in the Heider studies is clearly illusory (a by-product of our evolved brain), why would superagency not also be illusory? The difficulty of this for evolutionary theorists to explain is how an illusion has ever had survival value. The answer may lie in the concept of paranoia, which is generally dismissed as a clinical aberration. Paranoia is an exaggerated fear of attack, to the point of literally "seeing" a threat where it does not exist. It is driven by fear and some dislocation of the attachment-trust system.[12]

When we consider our evolutionary past, we must remember that we lived under threat of attack by predators much larger and stronger than our ancestors. Could not extreme fear produce an extreme desire for a protective superagent? This idea, similar to Freud's notion of religion as a need for protection by a stronger other, requires only a cognitive leap into the realm of the imagined, something that humans can easily make. Once this leap is made, the resulting concept of a superagent follows easily. What is inherited, then, is not a general, unverified agent but a wished-for protector who is all-knowing. However, as Pascal Boyer pointed out, not all religions have beliefs that allay anxiety.

Developing a Sense of Meaning

Barrett argues that children are also preoccupied with the purpose of things. Developmental psychologist Deborah Keleman[13] described this eagerness to find a purpose as "promiscuous teleology." Keleman presented children with a disagreement between two fictitious characters: one argued that a variety of items were made for a purpose and the other argued that they were not. The items included a variety of living things (e.g. woman, man, tiger), biological parts (earlobe, leg), natural phenomena (clouds, iceberg) and artefacts (clock hand). Children were shown a photo of each object.

About ¾ of US 4- to 5-year-old children believed that the natural phenomena were likely made "for some purpose," as were the artefacts. The purposes given were not ones commonly taught by parents (e.g. rocks were "pointy" so animals would not sit on them). In a follow-up study, around half the children suggested that "someone" had made the natural objects, while about ¾ said "someone made animals." We get a sense here of the "unseen mover"—the unseen agent who made observed movements happen.

In another developmental study, 12- to 13-month-old babies reacted (with visual attention) to an animated rendition of a ball "creating" an ordered pile of blocks (the blocks arranged themselves after a ball approached them). However, they did not react to the same ball creating a disordered pile. When the ball had a face, no surprise was registered to the ordering of the blocks. Barrett concluded that the ball with the face (hence, an agent) was already known to create order, but a normal ball (a non-agent) could only create disorder. Hence, when it approached the pile and they arranged themselves in an orderly fashion, children were surprised.

Developmental psychologist Jesse Bering[14] has described the human tendency to seek out and postulate a meaning behind events as an "existential theory of mind." It leads to questions such as "why me?" or "what does it all mean?" These questions appear to arise in childhood.

Bering conducted what he called the "Princess Alice" experiments. Two boxes were set up on a table with a desk lamp. Children were told that Princess Alice (pictured on the wall) likes to help "good little children" win the prize that is in one of them. The experimenter asks the child to choose a box, then leaves. While out of the room, and when the child reaches for a box, the table lamp flickers (or, sometimes, the picture of Alice falls from the wall instead). Children of seven reliably changed their decision and reached for the other box. The ability to use events as meaningful signs appears before children can explain it.

Barrett cited Jean Piaget's interviews with Swiss children, which indicated that children up to age eight see the natural world as manufactured by humans. This tendency occurred before religious education. Up to this age (eight or nine) children could not distinguish between god and humans. Piaget specifies, *"when the child speaks of God ... it is a man they picture"* (p 58).[2] This may be because children already have a world peopled by super-powerful beings (parents).

More recent research has found that children believe humans make artefacts, but not natural things. One study found that British preschoolers were seven times more likely to pick god rather than humans as the origin of natural things. Other studies verify this finding, and suggest that, counter to Piaget's findings, children before the age of eight can and do distinguish god from man. In comparison, evolutionary thinking is counter-intuitive, and thus harder to teach. Notions of evolution are not demonstrated by children until the age of 10.

To summarize so far: beginning in infancy, children understand that agents can create order, but non-agents cannot. By preschool years, children believe things in the natural world to be designed and purposeful. By age four, they appear to believe that the designer of the world is not human. Barrett adds, *"these children would find the idea of God attractive,"* and thus the idea of a powerful god that created the world would come as no surprise. Correspondingly, cosmological ideas about unguided natural processes are harder to accept because these ideas fly in the face of their intuitions. Scientific thinking has to swim against the current.

One study on beliefs of the origins of nature found that children of fundamentalist parents were most likely to have creationist ideas, but children of non-fundamentalist parents still had ideas more in line with creationism than their parent did, suggesting that indoctrination alone cannot account for children's beliefs. A child's inclination to see the natural world as purposefully designed and their early linking of order with intentional agency directs them toward creationist thinking.

A designed world requires a designer, and children's understanding of intentional agents tends to orient them to the idea of a creator. As they learn of human limitations, the idea of a nonhuman creator becomes more appealing. If this idea is proposed by the socializing culture, it will be embraced readily. The natural, default position is to think that a nonhuman someone is the best explanation.

Piaget found that children attribute superpower to all adults as well as god. With experience, children learn of human limitations, which leaves god as "the strong guy." Barrett calls this process the "preparedness hypothesis." He argues that children acquire features of Abrahamic monotheism easily because their mental mechanisms easily entertain the idea of supernatural agents; in fact, they appear to presume just that until they discover otherwise. The godly properties of super-knowledge, super-perception, creative power, and immortality are intuitive to young children.

Research on children's "theory of mind" shows that before age 4-5, children assume others know exactly what they themselves know. If you put a surprise substance in a favourite container (e.g. rocks in a cereal box), the child is surprised to see the unexpected item. However, if they are asked what their friend would think was inside the box, they would answer "rocks" (because they now know the answer).

By age 5, they stop making this error and correctly attribute false beliefs to humans (e.g. that their friend would think it was cereal when, in fact, it was rocks). This pattern is not replicated for god. Somehow, god is differentiated from humans by age five.

Similar studies with other tasks have confirmed this. God is seen by five-year-old children as having super-knowledge when humans do not. Barrett argues that this is a cultural universal: that children distinguish between god and humans as soon as they can successfully predict human beliefs (about age 5). So humans would incorrectly assume cereal was the correct answer, but god would have super-knowledge and know it was rocks.

Some of these knowledge experiments were undertaken in cultures with a belief in a god or gods that were not all-knowing. The results did not vary, and hence do not appear to be a mere product of indoctrination. An anthropological study of Mayan children, for example, by Barrett and a colleague found that Mayan children differentiated gods from humans (including identifying the different gods) before the age of eight. Younger Mayan children attributed super-knowledge to all agents, even the gods that their culture did not present as all-knowing. Older children (age seven) attributed super-knowledge to gods, but not humans.

Children can distinguish between god's perceptual abilities and those of humans. Barrett states they *"can accurately predict God's mental states."* By "accurate" here, he seems to mean in terms of an all-seeing god. He dismisses this perception as based on indoctrination because it applies to senses (such as god's ability to smell) that are not typically discussed by religious teaching. Of course, they could generalize.

Barrett sums up these studies to *"tentatively conclude that three year olds 1) are capable of distinguishing between gods and people in terms of what they might know or not know 2) have a tendency to overattribute knowledge and accuracy of beliefs to others in many cases but 3) it is unlikely they attribute full blown omniscience to gods or humans ... Instead, three year old children grant super-knowledge to all agents and think they know all there is to know [full access knowledge]* (p 104).[2]

There is an element of Manichean thinking in Barrett's work: it is entirely possible for both a super-agent concept to be produced by the inherited mind as well as to have early socialized influence from parents—or, for that matter, from other children. Barrett reveals this Manichaeism when he says *"If the indoctrination hypothesis is correct, children have no special receptivity to the idea of a God with superattributes and just learn whatever they are taught with comparable facility"* (p 96).[2]

However, both could exist. I am persuaded that cognitions exist that include notions of super-agency. However, that does not rule out socialization influences. We may very well have an inherited cognitive capacity that leads us to accept a notion of a super-agent, but the socialization process directs us to the specifics of that belief. People are selectively credulous—more credulous to the concepts that ensure them acceptance by their family or social group.

Also by age five, children distinguish god's immortality from that of a friend's, although Barrett acknowledges that the concept of resurrection is difficult for children to understand. Children in Israel showed an earlier appreciation of god's immortality than of human mortality. Human mortality does not mean most people think the spirit does not survive; beliefs in ghosts and ancestral spirits is widespread. Children can understand biological properties as ending more easily than mental abilities ending.

Barrett speculates that super-knowledge, super-perception, and super-power in a deity would translate into moral goodness, but admits that the research has not yet been done. He suggests that, similar to language acquisition, there is a sensitive period for the development of the god concept in the first five years of life. He cites Piaget, *"The child of extreme youth is driven to endow his parents with all of those attributes which theological doctrines assign to their divinities"* (p 129).[2]

It seems there may also be a critical period for the interaction of the god concept and socialization. Specific religious beliefs may be most readily accepted by children who have just reached the age of understanding the god concept (about age five). Barrett himself seems to acknowledge this in parts of his book. For example, he describes how natural religion and culture interact.

It is also not clear from Barrett's argument how one gets from developing a desire for meaning to accepting a purposeful and designed world, except that we learn to explain the inexplicable in ways that have worked for the explicable. We think in terms of agents, and the agents resemble us—such as with Heider's moving geometric forms that were given human agency by observers.

The research of psychologist Andrew Shtulman found[11] that although children did assign human attributes to god, they did so even more often with other fictional characters, such as fairies and vampires. Children also attribute more psychological than physical attributes to god; god seems to be conceptualized as having a mind, but not a body. As the religious question increases to include the creation of the planet and the universe, this mode of thinking is extrapolated. If children are natural teleologists, then it may simply be that this mode of thinking for everyday events is inherited and applied to the extraordinary.

Natural Religion

Barrett defines his findings as "natural religion" and sees it as comprising the child's ability to:

1) Distinguish agents from non-agents
2) Look for agency
3) Understand that agents can purposefully pursue goals
4) Understand that agents can create order out of chaos
5) See the world as purposefully designed
6) See natural phenomena as intentionally created by a superhuman agent
7) Understand that superhuman agents know things that humans do not, and
8) Consider that these superhuman agents may be immortal.

This "natural religion" is then theologically elaborated on by culture; a child's religious culture builds on the foundation of natural religion and elaborates on it. Theological teachings are harder to understand from the perspective of natural religion, and so they require greater effort to teach. Barrett defines the less-natural concepts as including ideas about monotheism, the Christian Trinity, of god being outside of time and space, and of god having unlimited attention and grace (unmerited favour). On the other hand, animism fits more easily with natural religion.

Barrett distinguished religion from "theology," by which he means the study of ancient texts and religious dogma (a term he does not use). It is these latter, theological ideas that grow on the framework of natural religion. The theological ideas are typically more abstract, while the natural religious ideas are more anthropomorphic. In short, there are two theological concepts: an implicit anthropomorphic concept, and an explicit theological concept.

This concept of natural religion may lead to the question of whether or not religion is childish; a question that Freud answered in the affirmative.[15] Freud believed religion was an extension of a childish (and primitive) wish to be protected: a wish that extended from the mother to the father, and then to an imagined "father in heaven." Barrett sees the cognitive set about god as having properties that extend beyond this view, such as that god concepts help to order the universe and give purpose. That being said, believing in a being of order and purpose itself creates feelings of control and lessens the anxiety that Freud or Becker hypothesized. The contradiction that Barrett sees may not exist.

Barrett rather fatuously compares the belief in god to a belief in gravity: it arises in childhood but continues into adulthood. The evidence, however, is much better for gravity—or, at least, the concept of gravity (quantum mechanics notwithstanding). Barrett gets into a rather strange defence of childhood beliefs that argues that some adult beliefs are discarded as untrue while some beliefs that arise in childhood (e.g. gravity) are true. Neither of these points is convincing as an apologia for childhood notions of religion. He seems to come dangerously close to suggesting a natural intelligence in children regarding god.

It is important to note that some of the studies Barrett cites, including the famous study by Heider above, illustrate how even adults anthropomorphize the motions of geometric forms. The human capacity for misinterpretation gets lost in the vision Barrett elaborates.

One is reminded of the religious reawakening of the rhythm and blues icon, Little Richard. While touring in Australia in 1957, Richard Penniman had a religious vision that caused him to renounce the music genre and return to the church. That "vision," we now know, was him seeing the launch of Sputnik, the first space satellite.*

Barrett argues that children are not endlessly gullible: they cannot, in fact, be taught absurd beliefs or ones that run

---

* During the Sydney performance, Penniman saw a bright red fireball fly across the sky above him. He was deeply shaken. He took the event, later revealed as the launching of Sputnik 1, as a sign from god to repent from his wild lifestyle and enter the ministry. Returning to the US ten days early, Penniman later learned that his original return flight crashed into the Pacific Ocean, solidifying his belief he was doing as god wanted.

counter to a moral instinct. Nevertheless, children are taught about a virgin birth, resurrection, *jihad*, and heavenly rewards for martyrdom, which seem absurd to non-believers. Catholic children are taught that sacramental offerings become the blood and body of Christ.

A study of adult brain reactions and behaviours found that adults' brains showed a distinct reaction pattern to counterintuitive facts (such as about how the world works); however, this did not occur when counterintuitive religious facts were interpreted as metaphors rather than literal meanings.[16] Of course, that does not explain the acceptance of counterintuitive literal ideas in fundamentalists. The subjects in this study were Spanish university students who tended toward disbelief in religious precepts.*

It appears that there is something about counterfactual religious ideas that makes them unique in terms of both their phenomenal causality and brain reactivity. I believe it to be the unconscious connection of counterfactual religious ideas with attachment that makes the difference. The religious ideas are presented as consonant with a person's original social ties.

Boyer[3] argues that what is intuitive is not a "god concept" per se, but rather, a universal predisposition to interpret changes in one's environment as products of intentional agency. We represent information about supernatural beings by using a cognitive template that is normally used to represent people, and then we append one or more counterintuitive properties to that template. We then create what Boyer describes as a "minimally counterintuitive concept."

---

* They averaged 2.28 on a seven-point scale, where 1 = total disbelief and 7 = total belief (p 976).

Andrew Shtulman's research has been relevant to this notion.[11,17,18] In an early study,[11] Shtulman tested Boyer's[3] notion that supernatural beings were conceptualized as persons with counterintuitive properties. Shtulman examined college students' tendencies to attribute psychological properties (e.g. honest, talkative, awake), biological properties (alive, healthy, obese, etc.), and physical properties (heavy, hot, cold, etc.) to supernatural beings, both religious (angels, messiahs, satan, god) and non-religious (fairies, zombies, vampires, ghosts).

On average, participants attributed more human properties to fictional beings like fairies and vampires than to religious beings like god or satan. Religious beings were perceived as more believable, but believability was unrelated to human attributes. Atheists did not provide more or less attributes to god than theists did. Unbelievable beings were also anthropomorphized more strongly than believable ones, suggesting that all supernatural beings do not conform to a common template.

In a further study, five-year-old children and their parents attributed a majority of human properties to fictional beings; however, the children attributed the same properties to religious beings as well. The most-often reported property for god (by both parents and children) was that he "created life in the universe." As Shtulman concluded, *"participants provided a mixture of anthropomorphic and nonanthropomorphic properties at each age and for each supernatural being"* (p 1131).[18]

In a later study, college students were shown various properties and asked to indicate, as quickly as possible, whether each property was true of god. Both physical properties (living, breathing, possession of a heart, ears, lungs, etc.) and psychological properties (knows things, has wants, a commission of planned actions, capacity for satisfaction, happiness, sadness, etc.) were used.

Participants attributed more psychological properties to god than physiological properties.[18] They also did so faster, indicating an automatic cognitive process. From these results, Shtulman concluded that god is conceptualized as having a mind, but not a body. This is inconsistent with Boyer's[3] argument that god is perceived as a person with counterintuitive properties. Rather, Shtulman argues, his data supports the notion of god being conceptualized in a more limited manner—as an agent.

Children's concepts of supernatural beings are more anthropomorphic than their parents' were. Adult concepts of god can vary from the anthropomorphic (a wise man with a flowing beard) to the abstract (a universal force). The data also did not support Barrett's[2] claim that we hold the two distinct god concepts of an implicit anthropomorphic concept and an explicit, theological concept.

Kathryn Schulz[19] reported on the research of Shtulman and others in a piece in the New Yorker. She added Shtulman's work on plausibility to "fantastic beasts:" supernatural beings that included angels, demons, dragons, pixies, vampires, and the Loch Ness Monster (but not god). Such beings require a "foundation of fact," but from there they comprise a vast, interconnected web, where the severing of one link in a causal network still leaves the rest intact. We rely, in the end, on patterns of evidence, a grasp of biology, and theories of physics in forming our intuitions about supernatural beings.

Farias and colleagues[20] tested the notion that an adult's intuitive cognitive style (instead of an analytical style) would be related to supernatural beliefs. In two studies they assessed intuitive versus analytical beliefs with two different methods using strategies in cognitive psychology. In the first, they asked participants to choose between two jars of beads. One study was carried out with pilgrims on the walk to Santiago de Compostela in Spain. The assumption was that this may represent a group of people with what the authors called "supernatural beliefs." Their task was to grab a transparent bead from either a small or a large bowl filled with coloured beads. In the small bowl, the probability of getting a transparent bead was 10%; in the larger bowl, it varied from 6 to 9%.

Participants were explicitly told the percentages before each of four trials. 44% of the participants made the analytical choice (based entirely on better probability), 35% of them made the intuitive choice, and 23% used a mix of strategies. These analytical styles were found to not be statistically related to their answers to questions regarding their spiritual or religious identification.

The second study measured participants' speed and accuracy in associating religious and spiritual words with the categories "real" and "imaginary." In this study, using mental workload tasks and brain stimulation, no evidence was found that supernatural beliefs were related to intuitive cognitive styles. The authors concluded that socio-cultural upbringing was more important than one's "natural" or "intuitive" cognitive style in the maintenance of a supernatural belief.

My own view is that we will have limited success in trying to pinpoint a "god concept" to one small part of the brain: a structure that, while it does not function in isolation, certainly seems to be studied in isolation. The attributions of cause and effect are cognitive processes that occur in the cerebrum, the part of the brain that deals in logic. However, in the real world, the logic of attribution is constantly subjected to the powerful influence of emotion. When emotion is stirred up, the entire attribution process can be rendered irrational;[21] that is, our normal "rational" ideas of cause and effect are disturbed in seemingly irrational ways.

The rational aspect of religious dogma—specific beliefs—has been studied by neuroscience in isolation from the neural pathways that convey emotion and a sense of secure attachment (the hypothalamic functions). Attachment has profound effects on our brain functions,[22] and yet these effects operate outside of our awareness.[23] The entire structure of belief is influenced by where belief falls in this attachment neural web.

For instance, a parent whose child has gone missing in a shopping mall exhibits thinking that is quite abnormal, given their usual baseline. This is the product of a disturbance of attachment (the parent-child bond). Religious belief is usually learned during a time of familial attachment, one the child wishes to be part of and stay together with.

Religion: Inherent or Indoctrinated

If there is no heaven, and you act on these beliefs in *jihad*, you have wasted your own life and that of strangers. Religious beliefs are the most central "organizing beliefs" we hold; even political beliefs are more circumscribed than religious beliefs. It may be that natural religion shapes a willingness to adopt these beliefs, but beliefs still build upon that natural tendency. In short, theology can elaborate on natural religion to create a result that, from an outsider's perspective, is absurd. For instance, few non-Catholics believe that communal offerings become the blood and flesh of Christ.

It may also be that our hard-wiring includes some moral rules, but theological teachings can be used to convince believers that certain others do not deserve to have these rules apply to them; that committing murder against an infidel is not the same as murdering a member of the in-group.

It's a long way from the belief in a supernatural agency to a belief in Holy War or *jihad*, but Barrett is not thinking this way when he touts religious ideas as a "*wholly expected extension of the way humans are naturally put together*" (p 196).[2] Given the universality of massacres, especially prior to the 14th century,[24] one could argue that massacre is a way humans are "naturally put together." If so, some forms of nature should not be encouraged.

The "worldview" argument for religion—that it provides meaning to an indecipherable universe—continues to raise a major question: what if this worldview is simplistic and wrong? It may be intuitive—"natural religion" as Barrett calls it—but that does not make it correct. The super-agent worldview may, in fact, fit our "intuition" because of how our brains evolved. All this says, however, is that most people are limited to the intuitive type of thinking produced by a brain that evolved to aid survival—not necessarily one that evolved to entertain complex, counter-intuitive concepts.

Our eye evolved to aid survival, but it still needs aid from telescopes to see distant stars; our reasoning may require a similar boost. This is the problem we saw in the cosmological discussion in the last chapter: the notion of god is far more understandable than the concepts of quantum physics and multiple universes. The majority of people will adhere to the simpler concept.

It is curious that Barrett never cites another potential cause of children's belief in a supernatural agent: that a child's appreciation of human death develops at the same time as beliefs in supernatural agency.[25] In their book on terror management, Sheldon Solomon and his colleagues[25] cite studies of children by Sylvia Anthony, which show child curiosity about (and recognizing) human death occurring by age three.

As we saw in Chapter 3, this unique aspect of humanity, death awareness, was posited by Ernest Becker as the origin of religious belief. Believing in an immortal god and a heaven where we can go to after death softens death terror.[26] At the very age where notions of death develop, so do notions of super-agents.

In his closing chapter, Barrett argues that atheism is less frequent than we realize, and may be indicative of some form of pathology—a type of inability to develop a theory of mind, empathy, or strong social cognitive abilities. He calls this inability "male brainedness" which, in its extreme form, is described by him as a type of autism. As he puts it, *"not believing in any sort of gods may prove to be a trait that is analogous to not being able to walk"* (p 203).[2] Barrett sees this as a possible factor as to why most atheists are "white, male, highly educated" people.

Barrett seems to overlook the fact that many atheists are critical thinkers who cannot abide the strict theology of modern religion. Barrett's argument here is in line with Richard Dawkins' claim that being well-educated or having superior intellect is an antidote against infection by religious belief. Since Barrett argues that religious belief is natural, he resists Dawkins' argument. However, his own musings on atheism are not convincing. In addition to the "cognitive deficit" of "male brainedness," Barrett notes that atheists are more likely in nations that have fewer children. In doing so, he fails to mention the possible explanation that Islamic and Catholic nations have both higher birth rates and less public admission of atheism.

Barrett blames the disappearance of god on a developing notion of human power: what he terms "semisocialism" (p 211).[2] Barrett argues that children "get over" childhood fantasy characters like Santa Claus, but do not get over god. However, he presents no data on longitudinal sustenance of belief, and never follows his anecdotal children of atheists that believe in god into adulthood. It could well be that god concepts, if they are easier to sustain, do so because of social supports for religion that do not exist for Santa Claus (or other childhood super-agents).

I think Barrett's argument is convincing where he examines the aspects of childhood thinking that lead toward what he calls "natural religion" (but which could also be called "naive religion"). He is less convincing on explanations for atheism, and seems incapable of overcoming his tendency to view it mainly as a cognitive deficit accompanied by social isolation. For instance, it is hard to imagine Bertrand Russell, one of the greatest intellects in history, as suffering from a cognitive deficit.

While indoctrination may not solely account for god concepts in children, it may account both for the elaboration of religious teachings and the retention of these precepts into adulthood. Surely a natural predilection to anthropomorphize and think in terms of dualism does not make those beliefs correct; it only makes them an end product of evolution: necessary for survival, but not to conceptualize the world beyond survival.

REFERENCES

1. Legare C, Evans EM, Rosengren KS, Harris PL. The coexistence of natural and supernatural explanations across cultures and development. *Child Development*. 2012; 83(3):779-793.
2. Barrett JL. *Born believers: the science of children's religious belief.* New York: Simon & Schuster; 2012.
3. Boyer P. *Religion explained: the evolutionary origins of religious thought.* New York: Basic Books; 2001.
4. Risen JL. Believing what we do not believe: Acquiescence to superstitious beliefs and other powerful intuitions. *Psychological Review*. 2016; 123(2):182-207.
5. Pinker S. *The blank slate: the modern denial of human nature.* New York: Penguin; 2002.
6. Ullman TD. *On the nature and origin of intuitive theories: learning, physics and psychology.* Cambridge: Massachusetts Institute of Technology; 2015.
7. Bloom P. *Descartes' baby: how and why the science of child development explains what makes us human.* New York: Basic Books; 2004.
8. Bloom P. Religion is natural. *Developmental Science*. 2007; 10(1):147-151.
9. Rochat P, Morgan R, Carpenter M. Young infants' sensitivity to movement information specifying social causality. *Cognitive Development*. 1997; 12:355-314.
10. Heider F, Simmel M. An experimental study of apparent behavior. *American Journal of Psychology*. 1944; 57:243-249.

11. Shtulman A. Variation in the anthropomorphization of supernatural beings and its implication for cognitive theories of religion. *Journal of Experimental Psychology: Learning, Memory and Cognition.* 2008; 34(5):1123-1138.
12. Dutton DG, White KR, Fogarty D. Paranoid thinking in mass murderers. *Aggression and Violent Behavior.* 2013; 18(5):548-553.
13. Keleman D. The scope of teleological thinking in preschool children. *Cognition.* 1999; 241-273.
14. Bering J, Parker BD. Children's attributions of intentions to an invisible agent. *Developmental Psychology.* 2006; 42:253-262.
15. Freud S. *The future of an illusion.* New York: W.W. Norton & Co.; 1961.
16. Fondevila S, Aristei S, Sommer W, Jimenez-Ortega L, Martin-Loeches M. Counterintuitive religious ideas and metaphorical thinking: An event-related brain potential study. *Cognitive Science.* 2016; 40(4):972-991.
17. Shtulman A, Morgan C. The explanatory structure of unexplainable events: Causal constraints on magical reasoning. *Psychonomic Bulletin Review.* 2017; 24:1573-1585.
18. Shtulman A, Lindeman M. God can hear but does he have ears? Dissociations between psychological and physiological dimensions of anthropomorphism. Paper presented at: Proceedings of the Annual Meeting of the Cognitive Science Society; 2014.
19. Schulz K. Fantastic beasts and how to rank them. *New Yorker.* 2017;
20. Farias M, van Mulukom V, Kahane G. Supernatural belief is not modulated by intuitive thinking style or cognitive inhibition. *Nature/Scientific Reports.* 2017; 7 (15)100.

21. Vansteelandt K, Van Mechelen I. Individual differences in anger and sadness: In pursuit of active situational features and psychological processes. *Journal of Personality.* 2006; 74(3):871-908.
22. Mikulincer M, Shaver PR. *Attachment patterns in adulthood: structure, dynamics and change.* New York: Guilford Press; 2007.
23. Diaz MT, McCarthy, G. Unconscious word processing engages a distributed network of brain regions. *Journal of Cognitive Neuroscience.* 2007; 19(11):1768-1775.
24. Dutton DG. *The psychology of genocide, massacres and extreme violence.* Westport: Praeger International; 2007.
25. Solomon S, Greenberg J, Pyszcynski T. *The worm at the core: on the role of death in life.* New York: Random House; 2015.
26. Becker E. *The denial of death.* New York: The Free Press; 1973.

CHAPTER 10

The Social Psychology of Belief Systems

"You find this curious fact, that the more intense has been the religion of any period and the more profound has been the dogmatic belief, the greater has been the cruelty and the worse the state of affairs."

BERTRAND RUSSELL, "WHY I AM NOT A CHRISTIAN"

Social psychology is the study of universal social relations, such as how groups use power or how belief systems arise in groups. For example, a universal reaction to power accumulation is for the powerful to self-aggrandize and enhance their power advantage. For the powerless, the reaction is to band together.[1] We see the latter in the formation of labour unions and in countries with weak economies being drawn to left-wing ideologies. We see the former in dominant nations (empires) and, more recently, in the computer industry.

Banding together is a survival strategy, one of the few left to the powerless. Those operating within a hierarchical power system will explain the attributes of others in political terms: those at the top will label those at the bottom "communists," while those at the bottom will call those at the top "fascists." However, it is really a universal power dynamic being expressed; a product of the human condition that has existed in different countries at different times. The labels serve to retain social distance, and to prevent empathy for the others in the power hierarchy.

So it is with beliefs; universal social processes explain the belief systems of "cargo cults," social panics, flying saucers, doomsday predictors, and current orthodox religions. In all cases, a story develops to explain an important theme and/or inexplicable event. The story makes use of the cultural Zeitgeist and other current beliefs—a collection of ideas called memeplexes. Adherents to the story feel that they have some special knowledge that outsiders lack; they therefore earn social status deriving from this special knowledge.

For example, themes of a virgin birth and resurrection pre-dated Christianity, existing as memeplexes in their time. A sense of believers being special is an aspect of all religions. In the case of Christianity and Islam, legal proscriptions accompanied orthodoxy, which generated an ability to sanction dissenters.

The chief difference between religions and cults is that religions grew to be large—chiefly through social conditions and happenstance. In becoming the "state religion," they insisted on the truth of their dogma and used state power to punish transgressors.

All groups socialize children to their normative beliefs. Children typically possess a "natural religion"—an inborn notion of a super-agent—and this is reinforced when they grow into adulthood in a culture that ascribes to a dominant religion; research polls show that 95% of people who self-identify with a religion were raised in that religion (Pew Research Poll, 2007).

Social psychology explains this process through several threads of research: research on attachment, group formation, and group influences explain why families would have such a strong socializing influence on religious belief; research on social cognition explains why our belief systems favour the "faith" that we can control our fate; and research on intergroup behaviour explains the dark side of religion: why it has figured so frequently in divisiveness and religious war.

Anthropologist Pascal Boyer[2] argues that people are led to relax their usual skepticism against extraordinary claims, specifically those of their accepted religion, because some of the claims have become quite plausible to them. I believe this is nothing more than an attachment phenomenon; that we uncritically believe what we are told by religious instruction because the beliefs maintain the primary attachment relationships we need to survive.

When attachment is at stake, critical thinking diminishes. People freed from cults maintain that it was the social relationships in the cult, not the ideology, that was important to them.[3] They adopted the cult ideology in order to maintain the relationships in the cult.

Any initial belief system provides a neural complex against which newer beliefs are fitted. This creates a powerful neuropsychological basis for belief perseverance through a cognitive web, or "cog web." This cog web sustains religious beliefs in the face of disconfirming evidence.

Social Cognition, Belief Perseverance, and the Need for Control

In Chapter 9, we saw how the human brain is wired to perceive causality (cause and effect). Fritz Heider performed a famous study on "phenomenal causality"—the subjective interpretation of events. In that study, Heider showed moving geometric forms to research subjects. The subjects then told a story about the objects in motion, reading human motives into these objects. Heider demonstrated how we "anthropomorphize" (read human features and motives into non-human forms), even in something as simple as moving geometric shapes. The brain does this to create some order out of the chaos reaching our sensory receptors. We impose familiar patterns on our sensory world in order to generate a sense of predictability and control.

Evolutionary psychologists describe that pattern recognition has survival value, especially when recognizing the pattern elicits a response.[4] For example, a rustle in the trees is a pattern that may signal the presence of a predator, and a cautious response may save the perceiver. If we assume that over hundreds of thousands of years, cautious people survived and less caution didn't, then we can see the evolution of a brain that makes cautious errors—that is, assumes "false positive" cause and effect patterns. The brain would evolve to assume agency (the presence of predators), even when no direct evidence existed. Along similar lines, it might also assume the presence of gods when no evidence existed. What Barrett and Boyer do not explain, however, is how we get from agency to superagency by evolutionary processes.

The need for control in human cognition was nicely demonstrated in a study by Ellen Langer[5] at Yale University.

In this study, research subjects were either given a lottery ball at random or were told to reach in and pick a ball. The lottery balls were redeemed for cash by the experimenter. Research subjects who chose their ball wanted more money back for it than those who received the ball at random. Of course, all the balls were random choices, even when the subject reached in and chose the ball. However, the illusion of control kicks in for the personally-chosen balls, which generates the higher asking prices. Chosen balls are seen as having a higher chance of winning and hence, demand more value.

We want to believe that the outcomes of our choices are under our control, and that we've made the correct ones. When the result of our choice is less than stellar, we cognitively upgrade that result (called cognitive dissonance reduction) to preserve our personal self-image of a person who makes good choices.[6] In short, the research shows that any freely-made bad choice produces an aversive state of cognitive dissonance. This dissonance can be reduced by re-evaluating the choice in a positive direction (dissonance reduction).

Our ensuing re-evaluations constantly re-affirm our need to think of ourselves as good decision makers. As social animals, we harbour a need to believe in our ability to make good choices; the future appears dreadful otherwise. We quickly descend into a state of powerlessness when we lose confidence in our decision-making ability, even if this is an illusion. In the Langer study, it is clearly an illusion: the likelihood of choosing a winning ball from the batch is no higher than if a ball is selected for us by an experimenter. Objectively, we have the same chances in each case, but our subjective landscape changes.

When we read the physical history of the planet by Hawking and Mlodinow in *The Grand Design*,[7] describing all the chance astronomical events that had to line up in order to lead to our existence, it is hard to escape our essential powerlessness. Sixty-five million years ago, an asteroid crashed into the Yucatan, leading to the devastating climate effects that killed the dinosaurs. Without their extinction, it is doubtful that our mammalian ancestors would have survived and evolved into *Homo sapiens*. Similarly, if we made a prediction one year before your parents met that you would be born, your life would have seemed highly improbable at that time.

This "retrospective prediction" is something hard for us to grasp, in part because it shows just how improbable we are and how much chance has played a part in our lives. In the face of this, an illusion of control is essential to maintain ourselves. It is hard to see people, *en masse*, abandoning the security that comes from religious belief for the precarious, capricious universe presented by science; it undermines our illusion of control.

Langer later demonstrated the positive effects of the illusion of control[8] by examining nursing home residents' feelings of happiness and self-worth. Those who were given some choice over their living conditions were happier than those who were not; this happiness persisted in an 18-month follow-up. In this case, residents were given a simple choice of whether they wanted a plant to care for. The control group were given a plant by the staff. It was the choice, not the plant caring *per se*, that made the difference. The simple choice extended to life expectancy, with 30% of the no-choice residents dying of natural causes before the follow-up (18 months later), compared to 15% of those given the choice.

Numerous other studies confirm the importance of feeling in control of our lives. However, this essential feeling resides in us in a world where we have little control over larger events: war, crime, natural disaster, illness, and death itself. Religion offers a sense of control: when people pray, they expect certain outcomes. When these are met, they thank god; when they are not, they say, "god works in mysterious ways." Hence, they never have to conclude that prayer is useless and, by extension, that they are powerless. It brings to mind Herbert Benson's meticulous study on prayer's lack of effect on the outcome of cardiac patients. It is possible that religion persists in individuals because it creates an illusion of control.

Psychologist Kenneth Pargament and his colleagues[9] examined patterns of coping with stressful life events. Pargament assessed the types of coping mechanisms used by participants and developed a scale for religious coping. The positive factor on this scale involved:

1) Thinking about how one's life was part of a larger, spiritual force
2) Looking to god for strength and support
3) Working with god to get through the hard time
4) Thinking about sacrificing one's own wellbeing and living only for god
5) Trying to find a lesson in the crisis, and
6) Believing the victim(s) to be at peace with god in heaven.

These forms of positive religious coping both provided a means of stress reduction (especially 1, 4, and 5, which give meaning to a stressful event) and were related to health and adjustment. Pargament found that participants in his study reported using these positive religious coping forms more than negative forms (such as blaming people for incurring god's vengeance). Hence, it could be argued that stress reduction acts as a reinforcing aspect to religious belief. This may be a placebo effect, but it is an effective placebo effect.

Anthropology has also concluded that mankind as a whole cannot tolerate chaos; as we saw in Chapter 2, Ernest Becker viewed this as the origin of sacrifices to gods to ensure good harvests, protect the tribe in war, etc.[10] Religion provides a set of central beliefs that, in turn, generate feelings of belonging to a group and control over fate. As we described in Chapter 2, Solomon and colleagues[11] tested Becker's ideas in their own social psychology experiments. By exposing research subjects to images or thoughts of death, Solomon and his colleagues revealed the essential centrality and immutability of a religious worldview. Subjects exposed to mortality salience became more convinced of the correctness of their central social tenets—the socializing belief that served to buffer them from death terror. They also came to prefer their own in-group after exposure to death imagery: Jews preferred Jews, Christians preferred Christians, etc. Whatever their culture held as a central value became more valued after exposure to death imagery.

Culture can be thought of as a security blanket against death terror. Religious beliefs also diminish death anxiety. For these reasons, such beliefs are central to our sense of wellbeing. They both serve as an organizing blueprint for other, more restricted beliefs. They emotionally assure us, at an unconscious level, that we are well and will live, if not forever, into the foreseeable future.

It is for this reason that violence to "infidels" is so great. They represent a contradiction of death-denying beliefs, whose contradiction raises anxiety unconsciously; it forces us to embrace our creaturely finitude. The culture that raises us, and the central beliefs of that culture, constitute a transcendent reality—one that symbolically represents our own immortality.

Lord and associates[12] and Lee Ross[13] performed several experiments where people with strong beliefs—for example, in the effectiveness of capital punishment—were exposed to findings that either supported or contradicted their belief. These studies had little effect on their beliefs, and in some cases, caused a "boomerang effect" (i.e. the belief the study contradicted was strengthened). Subjects rated the studies that supported their pre-existing beliefs as more valid than the ones that contradicted them.

Of course, as we saw in Chapter 4, the most typical cognitive strategy to support existing beliefs is to either ignore or denigrate opposing arguments. For example, in his defence of Catholicism, Ross Douthat denied the value of the scholarship of Bart Ehrman and Elaine Pagels, lumping them into the same category as novelist Dan Brown. Ehrman and Pagels' work goes to the very basis of Catholic legitimacy; Brown is a novelist. So really, what is unrealistic in the Lord and associates study is that the subjects are even exposed to opposing arguments at all. In the real world, these are tuned out.

The Brain and Religious Belief

New patterns of belief are accepted when they "feel right;" in other words, when they fit in with existing patterns of thought. Neuropsychological studies indicate that sensory information, such as what we see and hear, reach the emotional centres of the brain (the amygdala and the limbic system) twice as fast as they reach the conscious section (the frontal lobe).[14] Hence, the emotional centre of the brain has a head start on new information.

These emotional centres also mediate religious experiences[15] and our reactions to political beliefs.[16] The beliefs that feel right—those that are accepted on an emotional basis—lead to a search for confirmatory information to support the belief. This is what social psychologists call "confirmatory bias," a type of belief perseverance[12] in that disconfirming information is either rejected or ignored.

The philosopher Sir Francis Bacon put it well in 1620 in his *Novum Organum*: "*The human understanding when it has adopted an opinion draws all things else to support and agree with it. And though there may be a greater number and weight of instances to be found on the other side, yet these it either neglects and despises, or else by some distinction sets aside and rejects, in order that by this great and pernicious predetermination the authority of its former conclusion may remain inviolate.*"

In short, we accept new evidence because of how well it integrates into the patterns of beliefs that we already have. The central beliefs that make up our cogweb then act as a giant blueprint for specific beliefs to follow. We then proceed to bias our search for confirmatory information. In some religions, like Christianity, the human process of confirmatory bias is revered as faith, and critical thinking is disparaged.

Belief without evidence is called faith. As we have seen, Sam Harris sees faith as the origin of socially-induced evil: the way he sees it, once you can get someone to believe something without evidence, you can get them to do anything. Morality becomes based on what "god demands."

Of course, religion is more than just one belief. It is a set of guiding beliefs into which all common behaviours can be fitted and interpreted. Neuropsychologist Kathleen Taylor has examined the neuropsychological basis of central beliefs,[17,18] focusing on what she calls "core ideas." These ideas are characterized by the importance of the belief (how much of our thoughts or actions are based on it), its connections to other ideas, its closeness to sensory inputs, and its links to internal signals (e.g. the emotional meaning of the central belief).

Central beliefs have synaptic connections in the billions. Any new stimuli proceed from the peripheral nervous system to the cortex. The further along the stimulus gets, and the more relevant it is to one's central beliefs, the more emotional interference it encounters. This means that if the new information contradicts our beliefs, sense of control, attachment security, or our death-denying defences, it is quickly neutralized.

Central beliefs are "ethereal,"[18] ambiguous, and very well-connected to internal signals. Their ambiguity makes them hard to challenge with rational debate. Indeed, religious arguments are quintessentially emotional, and are typically based on emotional associations, such as loyalty, family, and tribal existence. These central beliefs have a wide spectrum of influence over any specific beliefs, and typically generate an indifference to conflicting evidence. An example of such can be seen in the Catholic indifference to paedophile priests, dismissing them as "few bad apples" when the numbers show a greater problem.*

Our central beliefs operate without our direct awareness, but still colour our perceptions of our more specific attitudes

---

* For more details, see the Ryan Report, published in 2009 in Ireland.

and beliefs. We might also call them "general assumptions." The entire set of beliefs and associations is what makes up the cogweb.[18]

Beliefs that rely on sensory inputs (i.e. empirical beliefs) are weaker because these inputs constantly change. Beliefs associated with strong emotion are not in flux along with our changing reality, nor do they need to be disturbed by errors of thinking; their power is fuelled by the third source of neural signals: the visceral body. Hence, these beliefs only need to change when feelings change. It is for this reason that cult members taken from pathological cults by "deprogrammers" say that the content of the cult's dogma was irrelevant to them. Only the relationships—the feeling of being in a family—mattered.[3]

In fact, as signals from our external senses travel the neural pathways, they are intercepted by internal signals from neurons connected to other, non-sensory detectors. This means that our subjective feelings transform our sensory perceptions before they even reach our conscious awareness.

As Taylor puts it,[18] *"ethereal ideas gain their strength from signals which may have little or nothing to do with the way the world is at that time ... rather than from signals deriving directly from that world which could act as a useful reality check. As such, cogwebs do not rely for their potency upon external information, arguments based on that information will have little or no impact ... it is this quality of faith, impervious to reason and reality, which makes ethereal ideas potentially so lethal"* (p 141).[18]

New information is either adopted or rejected, not on its empirical validity, but on how it resonates with our existing attitudes. Political psychologist Drew Westen made this point about political attitudes, which obey the same rules.[16]

Studies of cognitive dissonance examine what happens when a person is forced to examine their personal choices when those choices are revealed to be inconsistent with a particular form of central belief: that person's self-image.[6] When this happened, people re-evaluated their choice in a positive direction; the alternative was to experience an unpleasant disjunction between their current behaviour and their concept of self, called an "aversive arousal."

This aversive arousal is what we feel when we are exposed to any information that confronts our central beliefs. In fact, aversive arousal is all we feel; we are unaware of the interaction between the current information and our pre-existing cogweb. This is the reality of the unconscious: not the sexual cauldron envisioned by Freud, but rather a set of unchallenged, broad assumptions about how things are that direct our thought.

If the current confronting information does not resonate with the cogweb, it results in the aversive subjective state. Social psychologists have shown how people will go to extraordinary lengths to change their perceptions to regenerate consistency, even to the point of evaluating painful shocks as less painful, hunger states as more tolerable, or boring experiments as interesting.[19] To prevent themselves from seeing their choice as a bad decision, they re-evaluated it as a good one (or at least, a not as bad one), so that their choice does not contradict their identity as a person who makes good decisions.

We are naturally conservative in our search for information, and wish for confirmation rather than new information. The reason for this is neurological: the new information must resonate with our cogweb, or it produces the discomfort described above. In effect, we personally practice the legal principle of *stare decisis:* judging every new finding on its ability to fit with the old.

Therefore, assuming that someone with fundamental religious beliefs reads this book, I do not believe they would be persuaded by it; instead, they would dismiss the evidence presented as the "wisdom of the wise," as Paul would put it. A central valuing of faith protects religious belief from empirical disconfirmation.

Martin Luther was well aware that reason was religion's archenemy, and he frequently warned of its dangers. Dawkins cites him as stating, *"Reason is the greatest enemy that faith has; it never comes to the aid of spiritual things. Whoever wants to be a Christian should tear the eyes out of his reason ... Reason should be destroyed in all Christians"* (p 190).[20]

Luther need not have worried so much. Reason has its impact on individuals, but not by directly contradicting an individual's belief system (because of the built-in resistances of belief perseverance). Instead, it offers a socially-accepted alternate view of reality, which has impact over time. We see more people who self-describe as non-believers in the modern world (pewforum.org places the US percent of "unaffiliated with any faith" as 16.1% in 2007 and 22.8% in 2014).* Some of this is a product of what is now socially acceptable, while some is the availability of an alternative framework.

Consider the development of a religious cogweb in a hypothetical Christian family: the family reserves Sundays as a day of togetherness and worship. They go to church in the

---

* The majority of this group report "nothing in particular" as their religious affiliation; only 3.1% of the 22.8% describe themselves as atheists (pewforum.org).

morning, they have a meal together after church, they reserve the day for togetherness. The stresses of the week are put aside. Perhaps they play or spend time watching sports after the meal. All of these positive emotions and associations are connected in a neural network that may encompass both the religion's traditions and connections to security, hope, and optimism. The specific elements of proof for the doctrines may recede and be less relevant. The feelings of attachment or appreciation, of "being blessed," are paramount. In times of stress, the images attached to these feelings can be called forth and serve to soothe and inspire.

No argument from rationality, including the ones I have made here, will supersede these feelings. The strength of beliefs derives from neural patterns being activated; the result is a neural network of associated beliefs. Any new beliefs that we appreciate are those that cause clear patterns that fit easily among the network we already have. For this reason, the vast majority of adult religious beliefs are what were acquired as a child.[21]

In most cases, a person adopts their parents' religious belief network with few variations; generally, those variations are caused by cultural changes. Young people today may, for example, adhere to a parent's Abrahamic belief system while dropping a religious aversion to homosexuals. This requirement that new beliefs must be assessed through the existing neural network means that we are typically conservative when it comes to our religious beliefs. Radical change is possible, but unlikely, as the Pew Research Polls indicate. It is for these reasons that the majority of people retain the beliefs that they were raised with. In general, people are not going to abandon the positive feelings generated from this cogweb, particularly for a set of beliefs that say there is no immortal purpose, that the universe is random, and that we are lucky to exist.

When a new belief fits into existing patterns, it also encounters the emotional response of attachment theory. Many have beliefs that we share with our parents, to whom we once turned to for security and support. Attachment theory and the research stemming from it[22-24] show that the most powerful emotions relate to our attachment to a stronger, wiser other. During early development, we form strong attachments to our caretaker. At that time, our brain is growing rapidly: doubling in size in the first year of life.[25] Our neural structures are expanding at the very time that attachment is paramount. This becomes a lifelong impetus for attachments, later manifested in group loyalties.[26] Children who experience stress have what psychologist John Bowlby called their "Attachment Behavioural System" activated: they experience physiological arousal that is only reduced by physical contact with their attachment base—typically a parent. This attachment bond has survival value, and is a powerful human motive.

For instance, soldiers who have experienced the threat of death in battle maintain bonds with their fellow soldiers for decades after seeing conflict.[27] Promises of reunification after death with beloved others are central to some religions, including Christianity and Islam, and have been used to generate compliance with religious war edicts.[28] Some adults, in the face of dissolution of an important attachment, kill themselves or others.[29]

In a less-lethal sense, the power of attachment works to foster the acceptance of the religious beliefs of one's parents. This is through the positive associations of "family feelings" of closeness, a sense of social stability, and unconscious aspirations to maintain the social attachment necessary to survival. The social force of attachment generates continuity of religious beliefs across generations.[30]

A study of Christians in Sweden found that securely-attached people scored highest on what the authors called "socialization-based religiosity:" the extent to which the participants adopted their parent's religious standards.[22] The authors concluded that parent-child attachment has a major effect on religiosity.

It may be, as Barrett argues, that the initial concept of god as a supernatural agent occurs without parental influence; however, beyond the early years, the shaping of one's central beliefs is influenced by attachment. This central structure is difficult to change once formed, simply because it has too many neural connections: it is a full neural network that shapes more specific attitudes into a religious perspective.

Change is still possible, but is only experienced by a small number of people, such as scholars dedicated to the truth—Charles Freeman and Bart Ehrman come to mind—or those who have disconfirming emotional experiences (such as the loss of a loved one) that challenge their notion of the existence of a just god.

John Bowlby himself reconciled psychoanalysis with evolutionary theory, showing that attachment provides a link between survival and group influence; the acceptance of the driving principles of a group is perceived as protecting the individual. People who join cults are really looking for a substitute family,[3] and may or may not be mindful of the central dogma of the cult. When they leave the cult, the dogma is abandoned; it was the set of relationships that held the appeal.

Group Dynamics and Faith

Although less of a focus in current times, the area of social psychology in the 1950s called Group Dynamics (a concept applied to Mrs. Keech's cult in Chapter 1) explains how groups influence the beliefs of their members, nurture a central dogma, and sanction dissenters.

The twin motives that drive people to adhere to group influences are the sense of belonging to or being part of a group (especially one that they see as special) and the status that they are afforded in that group. Group Dynamics also shows how groups become more extreme when left to their own devices, creating a social reality called "groupthink." It does so because voicing opinions that are slightly more extreme than the group's central dogma earns status within the group.[31] As more people jockey for power within the group, each moves to a more extreme position, and the group as a whole follows.

In a series of carefully-controlled experiments done in the 1950s, Stanley Schachter,[32] Leon Festinger,[33] and their colleagues showed how pervasive conformity is in groups and how those groups reject dissenters.* Another famous study from that era, by Solomon Asch[34] found that, even on the most basic of judgments, individuals would give in to group opinion in the majority of test trials. Later examination of this phenomenon found that individuals, faced with the task of choosing an

---

* The rejection of dissenters by groups is seen quite clearly with religion. For instance, atheists are the least-highly regarded religious affiliation in the US because their belief—that there is no god—is the most radically different from Christianity. Even Muslims—despite the perceived threat from Islamic terror groups—believe in a god.

obvious answer based on their own perception or an incorrect, socially-influenced answer, showed increased anxiety as their turn to choose approached. Once they gave the socially-influenced answer, their anxiety diminished.

Small informal groups, in other words, have extraordinary power over individuals: this power increases along with that group's ability to satisfy the individual's needs for status, identity, and sense of belonging. We see this in the reactions of sports fans who dress in team colours, and whose emotions rise and fall with the team's fortunes. We also see it with religion. We saw it with Mrs. Keech's group in Chapter 1: the members earned status within the group if they accepted the group's central dogma and took committing actions that were consistent with it.

Groups form in three basic ways: through the common identification of people (e.g. a person sees themselves as an American, a Muslim, or both), through the satisfaction of social needs (e.g. for identity, belonging, status) and through emotional connections (e.g. how some people weep when their national anthem, a symbol of group identity, is played after a sports victory).

Groups draw in people with a pre-existing affinity for the group's ideology, and then further shape that ideology once the person is in the group.[35] Groups have enormous impact on the formation of a person's "social reality"—the set of perceptions and attitudes favoured by the group.

For example, in a famous examination on the impact informal groups have on their members, Leon Festinger and his colleagues[33] studied military personnel returning to college at the Massachusetts Institute of Technology in 1946. Since these subjects were assigned to housing units by the college, the aspect of personal selection seen in most real-world groups was removed. Still, within a short period of time (18 months), cliques had formed. These cliques generated influence over the attitudes of their members. The capability of these groups to exert social pressure (i.e. their ability to generate complete adherence to the group's opinion) was directly related to how they mediated social needs for their members.

This ability of groups to direct the views of their members is called group cohesiveness. Highly-cohesive groups create active channels of communication through which a communality of information is shared. A "bubble" develops of shared information: the central dogma of the group.

In some cases, the central dogma is adhered to because of the emotional relationships of the group. Wayne Sage[3] studied the beliefs of cult members who had been kidnapped from cults and "deprogrammed" (i.e. confined and forced to listen to the cults' beliefs being specifically challenged by a professional "deprogrammer"). Those who gave up their cult's dogma said they did not care what the cult believed: that it was the social/emotional relationships, the sense of belonging to a family, that mattered. This level of belief adherence is called "identification" by group dynamics, since it depends on the individual's identification with a specific group, and lasts only as long as that relationship does.

Some cults struck a deeper chord, however; their influence was accepted because it felt intrinsically "right" to the individual—in other words, it resonated with or even expanded on their pre-existing beliefs (their cogweb). Thus for some, religious dogma is held to be beyond criticism.

As groups develop even greater relevance for real-world consequences, the ability of the group to shape the perceptions of individual members increases to the level of what social psychologist Irving Janis labelled as groupthink:[36] *"a mode of thinking that people engage in when they are deeply involved in a cohesive in-group, when members' strivings for unanimity override their motivation to realistically appraise alternative courses of action"* (p 37).[36]

The characteristics of groupthink include an illusion of absolute correctness, as well as a collective rationalization against any outside opinion that might cause the group to temper its position. These groups have an unquestioned belief in their own moral superiority, and tend to possess negative stereotypes of out-group members. They direct heavy pressure on dissenters, and those dissenters learn to self-censor, leading to a shared illusion of unanimity. Many of these groups have self-appointed "mind guards" who act to censor adverse information.

Janis' main focus was on policy groups, especially US foreign policy decisions. In general, groups exhibiting groupthink fare poorly and make worse decisions—historically, they have been more likely to be egregiously wrong.

One clear example, although written after Janis' work, was the Bush-Cheney decision to invade Iraq. Documented in excruciating detail by James Risen,[37] the story of the policy decisions reads like a clinical text on groupthink: dissenters were simply fired or demoted, and the resulting decision to invade Iraq as "payback" for the attack on the US World Trade Center* is considered by many to be the worst foreign policy decision in US history.

---

* Worse yet, it was an attack they were not involved in, as most of the terrorists were from Saudi Arabia.

By comparison, J. F. Kennedy's policy-making on the Cuban Missile crisis, which involved groups giving alternate assumptions and a wide range of debate, is historically credited with averting a catastrophe; the push by some US Generals, notably Curtis Lemay, to bomb Cuba almost certainly would have triggered nuclear war with the USSR.

Social psychology, however, has focused mainly on religious cults, such as the cult of Mrs. Keech we saw in Chapter 1. Cult dynamics include secrecy, an unquestioned authority, and a non-empirical belief system that is typically knowable only through a pathway to the leader.

These dynamics also appear in larger, organized religions, but are not subjected to the same scrutiny. The practice of excommunication, used as a weapon by the Catholic church,[38] emphasizes that religious groups have their own power so long as they can pretend to be a gatekeeper on the path to god. The horrific penalties exacted on "heretics" throughout history show the enormous power religion has had. For literally a thousand years (from 400-1400 CE), defiance of religious dogma was an automatic death sentence: it was 1,000 years of groupthink.

In his brilliant book, *Sapiens: A Brief History of Humankind*,[39] historian Yuval Harari describes groupthink as the "inter-subjective:" as *"something that exists within the communication network linking subjective consciousness of many individuals"* (p 182). This inter-subjectivity does not rely on the beliefs of an individual, who will die, but instead transcends such potential loss. Harari lists law, money, nations, and gods as examples of the intersubjective.

According to his analysis, this intersubjectivity was the advantage that *Homo sapiens* had over Neanderthals;

however, it was also the driver of *sapiens*' lethality. Harari points out that anthropological work places incursions of *sapiens* in areas where massive extinctions soon occurred, either of Neanderthals, other *Homo* groups (e.g. *Homo erectus*), or large mammals. Exactly why *sapiens* developed this advantage remains a mystery; Neanderthals had larger brains than we have. The best theory to date is that an accidental genetic mutation did the trick. We got lucky and developed better language and cognitive skills—Neanderthals didn't.

This was yet another fortunate happenstance in the history of mankind to accompany the numerous essential changes described by Hawking and Mlodinow that allowed our life.[7] For some reason, *sapiens*' brains evolved between 70,000 and 45,000 BCE, making us capable of advanced language, adaptation, and the ability to learn from others. Our brains evolved, which allowed *Homo sapiens* to coordinate socially in groups of more than 150. We did so, says Harari, by developing common myths rooted in the collective imagination of all citizens. These myths were necessary; they bound people together through shared beliefs. Mere discussion of factual events could not have served the same binding process.

The cognitive revolution that produced the capacity for these intersubjective beliefs allowed our survival. Because of this, we believe in communal myths as though they had objective truth. One of these communal myths is religion. In fact, believing the intersubjective has objective truth is necessary to give it its binding power.

As Harari points out, communal myth allows two Catholics who have never met to cooperate to fund a hospital or join a crusade: because they both believe that god was incarnated in human flesh and allowed himself to be crucified to redeem human sins. Similarly, Israel was united through the communal myths produced in the Old Testament.

Judicial systems are also rooted in common myths: the myth that laws, justice, and human rights exist. Harari describes the "legal fiction" of a limited company, which has a legal existence but no physical one. The same thing applies for gods and demons: they exist so long as an imagined reality exists. Yet none of these exist in any objective sense. Their force in the world depends solely on the ability of others to persuade us that they exist.

As Harari puts it, *"Ever since the Cognitive Revolution, Sapiens has thus been living in a dual reality. On the one hand, the objective reality of trees, rivers and lions; and, on the other hand, the imagined reality of gods, nations and corporations. As time went by the imagined reality became evermore powerful"* (p 516/6831 [Kindle E-book]).

A larger form of groupthink has fostered evolution and promoted social cohesion, despite the fact that, as far as we know, there are no gods in the universe outside of the human imagination.

The Cultural Transmission of Ethereal Ideas

Citing Susan Blackmore's book, *The Meme Machine*,[40] Katherine Taylor[17] refers to Dawkin's concept of the memeplex: a constellation of ideas that is passed down in a culture through generations because it has some survival value. This is Harari's "intersubjective." One can easily see how the invention of arrowheads or the wheel had survival value. Memes are *"ideas that are good at getting themselves copied"* (p 196).[20]

A gene pool is an environment in which each gene is selected. Because each gene is selected in the presence of others in the host environment, groups of co-operating genes emerge. Selection of genes is based on the compatibility of the individual gene with the gene complex. Meme pools are less structured than gene pools, but the meme pool is still part of an environment of ideas—a Zeitgeist. Each meme is a survivor in the presence of other members of the memeplex.

For this same reason, Dawkins argues, some religious ideas survive because they are compatible with other ideas in a memeplex (e.g. that there is life after death, that heretics must be punished, or that there are events that the scriptures describe that are beyond our reason). In the early stages of a religion's evolution, simple memes survive by virtue of their universal appeal to human psychology (e.g. life after death satisfies a craving for immortality).

In later evolutionary stages, the development of elaborate dogma is explained by the theory of memeplexes: that various memes that are mutually compatible will come together to form elaborate collections. The notion of compatibility with an existing landscape of ideas is reminiscent of Kathleen Taylor's notion that new ideas are accepted when they "feel right" because they resonate with the existing structures of the cogweb. Of course, some religions evolve more than others; Christianity has gone through numerous re-writings, while Islam is still pretty much in its original form.

There are also examples of innovation that go far beyond the existing memeplex, and even, sometimes, contradict it. The best examples are Einstein's Special and General Theories of Relativity, which so altered our view of the universe from Newtonian physics that it is a miracle they were even conceived of, let alone published. It appears that Einstein's brilliance was recognized among the physicists of his day.[41] To date, Einstein's theories stand as the pinnacle of human cognitive capacity.

There are also moral ideas that exist universally, without specific religious dogmas. For example, the idea that other members of a group who are in danger must be aided. This is held cross-culturally in societies with vastly different religions,[2] so the specific connection of belief to morality is complex. According to Boyer, religion helps make these general moral codes intelligible to adherents (p 217/375 [Kindle E-book]).

It is the memeplex that delivers the social function of cohesion in large groups as described by Harari, even amongst strangers who know only that another person shares their group. It is the memeplex that allowed *Homo sapiens* to change their social behaviour without waiting for genetic alterations to occur.

In archaic civilizations, only genetic change altered behaviour. *Homo erectus* appeared about two million years ago and used stone tool technology. It never underwent any further genetic alterations prior to extinction, and the stone tool use remained for all of its two million years. *Homo sapiens* has been able to change social behaviour rapidly, repeatedly, and without genetic or environmental change.

With these insights, we can begin to see a theory of religion. It began in *Homo erectus*, who had the cognitive skills to be curious and the language skills to assert theories. The curiosity was over the inexplicable: the origin of life, and the experiences after death. Early cave paintings depict this search. As groups grew larger, religious lore began to aid in group cohesion; more cohesive groups had better survival chances.

The themes of early religion, such as virgin birth and resurrection, survived as memes. These memes were used anew by new religions. Christianity picked up these themes (likely from Judaism or Egyptian religion) and recast them as the story of Jesus. When Christianity came into being, Messianism was a central political theme, so it too got integrated in with the virgin birth and resurrection. There have always been splendid storytellers, and Jesus and Muhammad were capable of generating devoted followers through their stories, actions, and circumstances. Political events spread Christianity and Islam far and wide and both became state religions, which furthered their sustainability.

In addition to the political and social reasons for adherence, a neural one operates on an individual level. Neural connections bridge the gap between beliefs and feelings of group solidarity and belonging. We think it unseemly to challenge someone's "deeply held" religious beliefs, even if they only parrot what they were taught at a child.

The Future of the Moral Arc

There is a sign of progress in human moral history, as Steven Pinker[42] and Michael Shermer[43] have pointed out. Before the 14th Century, sadism (both toward man and animal) was normative. Pinker provides numerous bloodcurdling examples of morality in earlier times: routine uses of torture, rape, slavery, and horrific punishment for apostasy. The Inquisition, for instance, was a product of its times.

Shermer describes a science behind morality: that it is now possible to analyse the factors that serve to promote a utilitarian regard for human and animal rights. This moral arc involves the greatest natural rights for all sentient beings: actions that increase their survival and success.

This moral arc, as described by Shermer, requires a scientific approach simply because morality requires empirical evidence for consequences. Child abuse is a prime example: before the development of social science techniques, extreme physical punishment of children was commonplace, and the admonition "spare the rod and spoil the child" was ascendant. Now we know, through the research of sociologist Murray Straus and others, that children who are physically punished by their parents are more likely to subsequently break the law and to use physical violence against others.[44] This knowledge has to factor into any decision to physically punish a child. The punishment may, in the short term, stop an undesirable action, but it will also create long-term effects that are deleterious to the child's flourishing.

Hence, a truly moral reaction depends on information that derives from analysis and reason. Slavery required the wilful ignorance of slaves being human. Now we know better. We can also now grade countries on their success (such as through their financial success or their capacity to honour the human rights of all citizens).

Shermer presents data from numerous indicators of Gregory Paul's Successful Societies Scale[43] a measure of a country's social health that includes incarceration rates, life expectancy, sexually transmitted disease frequency, family planning and fertility, sustained marriage rate, alcohol consumption, life satisfaction, corruption indexes, per capita income, income inequality, employment levels, and others. Each country is rated on a nine-point scale. Paul also quantified religiosity of relatively well-off countries (Australia, Austria, Canada, Denmark, England, France, Germany, Holland, Ireland, Japan, New Zealand, Norway, Spain, Sweden, and the United States) by measuring the extent that citizens believed in god, were biblical literalists, attended religious services at least several times a month, prayed at least several times a week, believed in an afterlife, heaven, and hell. Countries were ranked for religiosity on a ten-point scale.

The United States, according to these findings, is by far the most religious and the most dysfunctional. The US has the highest rates for homicide, incarceration, and abortion. It is tied with Sweden for divorce. Despite the "American Dream," on Paul's scale it is only the sixth most upwardly mobile.

In another study, the Organisation for Economic Cooperation and Development correlated the earnings of fathers and sons in various countries. If they were highly correlated (on a measure called "intergenerational elasticity"), then the sons made about the same amount as their fathers—that is, they were not economically mobile. In the US, the correlation is .47: about the same as the UK, Italy, or Switzerland. In Denmark, Norway, Finland, Canada, Australia, Sweden, and New Zealand, the correlations were in the .15 to .29 range; thus showing more upward economic mobility than the US.

Shermer points out that correlation is not causation, but asks why the US—the most religious country in the western world—has a combination of measures scoring high on social pathology and low on economic mobility. He attributes the data to different patterns of social capital between the US and more secular countries. Social capital is the connections amongst individuals: a society's social networks and the norms of reciprocity and trustworthiness that arise from them. In less religious societies, social capital is produced by secular institutions; in the US it is produced by religious affiliation. The US form of social capital does well for religious groups, but not for outsiders.

One other theory for the data pattern is that in societies with high levels of social pathology, people turn to religion for support. In the US, extreme individualism contributes to a general sense of insecurity—the US leads the world in per capita consumption of anti-anxiety and anti-depressant medications.[45] Hence, in the US, religion serves as a buffer against this stress. No other well-off country in the world has the US's level of religiosity.

Cross-cultural studies by psychologist Michael Bond and his colleagues[46,47] assessed the relationship of religious faith to people's subjective wellbeing across cultures. They used the World Value Survey, a multinational survey conducted in 2009 to investigate basic values of people in several countries. One of the beliefs assessed was support for religious socialization. They defined this support through participants' reaction to the statement, *"Here is a list of qualities that children can be encouraged to learn at home. Which, if any, do you consider to be especially important?"* Support was assessed by the percentage of people in any given country who listed religious faith (one of 10 qualities given) among the qualities they saw as important.

In national cultures where socialization for religious faith was more common, spiritual practice was subjectively related to well-being. Where support for religious socialization was less prevalent, this relationship was reversed. In the US, polls showed a 51.4% level of support for religious socialization—higher than all countries except Muslim or other Catholic ones.

This outlier status of the US is consistent with, but does not prove, Sherman and Berman's speculations. Across cultures, there is no clear proof that religious practice improves subjective well-being; however, it is considered as such in countries where socialization for religion is relatively commonplace. The historical association of religion in the US with individualism suggests a theory: that individualism creates high levels of anxiety, which result in religiosity.

The Happy Planet Index, which measures the ecological footprint, life satisfaction, and life expectancy of countries, rates the USA as 105th of 151 countries assessed. No other country in the world is both so rich and so unhappy, both ecologically and socially. These findings are consistent with Shermer's theory that religion is an attempted panacea for the country's ills. What, then, is the antidote?

REFERENCES

1. Ng SH. *The social psychology of power.* New York: Academic Press; 1980.
2. Boyer P. *Religion explained: the evolutionary origins of religious thought.* New York: Basic Books; 2001.
3. Sage W. The war on the cults. *Human Behavior.* 1976; (October):40-49.
4. Shermer M. *The believing brain.* New York: Times Books; 2011.
5. Langer E. The illusion of control. *Journal of Personality and Social Psychology.* 1975; 32:311-328.
6. Festinger L. *A theory of cognitive dissonance.* Stanford: Stanford University Press; 1957.
7. Hawking S, Mlodinow L. *The grand design.* New York: Bantam Books; 2010.
8. Langer E, Rodin J. The effects of choice and enhanced personal responsibility for the aged: A field experiment in an institutional setting. *Journal of Personality and Social Psychology.* 1976; 34:191-198.
9. Pargament K, Magyar G, Benore E, Mahoney A. Sacrilege: A study of sacred loss and desecration and their implications for health and well-being in a community sample. *Journal for the Scientific Study of Religion.* 2005; 44(1):69-78.
10. Becker E. *Escape from evil.* New York: The Free Press; 1975.
11. Solomon S, Greenberg J, Pyszcynski T. *The worm at the core: on the role of death in life.* New York: Random House; 2015.

12. Lord C, Ross L, Lepper MR. Biased assimilation and attitude polarization: The effects of prior theories and subsequently considered evidence. *Journal of Personality and Social Psychology.* 1979; 37:2098-2109.
13. Nisbett R, Ross L. *Human inference: strategies and shortcomings of social judgment.* Englewood Cliffs: Prentice-Hall; 1980.
14. Raine A. *The anatomy of violence.* New York: Vintage Books; 2013.
15. Saver JL, Rabin J. The neural substrates of religious experience. *Journal of Neuropsychiatry.* 1997; 9(3):498-511.
16. Westen D. *The political brain: the role of emotion in deciding the fate of the nation.* New York: Public Affairs; 2007.
17. Taylor K. *Cruelty: human evil and the human brain.* New York: Oxford University press; 2009.
18. Taylor K. *Brainwashing.* New York: Oxford University Press; 2004.
19. Zimbardo P, Cohen A, Weisenberg M, Dworkin L, Firestone I. The control of experimental pain. *The Cognitive Control of Motivation.* Glenview: Scott, Foresman & Co.; 1969.
20. Dawkins R. *The god delusion.* Boston: Houghton Mifflin; 2006.
21. Kirkpatrick LA, Shaver P. An attachment-theoretical approach to romantic love and religious belief. *Personality and Social Psychology Bulletin.* 1992; 18(3):266-275.
22. Mikulincer M, Shaver PR. *Attachment in adulthood: structure, dynamics and change.* New York: Guilford Press; 2007.
23. Bowlby J. *Attachment and loss: attachment.* New York: Basic Books; 1969.
24. Bowlby J. *Attachment and loss: separation.* Vol 2. New York: Basic Books; 1973.

25. Schore AN. *Affect regulation and the origin of the self: the neurobiology of emotional development.* Hillsdale: Erlbaum; 1994.
26. Baumeister RF, Leary MR. The need to belong: Desire for interpersonal attachments as a fundamental human motivation. *Psychological Bulletin.* 1995; 117(3):497-529.
27. Elder GH, Clipp EC. Wartime losses and social bonding: Influences across 40 years in men's lives. *Psychiatry.* 1988; 51(May):177-198.
28. Dutton DG. *The psychology of genocide, massacres and extreme violence.* Westport: Praeger; 2007.
29. Dutton DG, White, K. Attachment insecurity and intimate partner violence. *Aggression and Violent Behavior.* 2013; 17:475-481.
30. Kirkpatrick LA, Shaver PR. Attachment theory and religion: Childhood attachments, religious beliefs and conversion. *Journal for the Scientific Study of Religion.* 1990; 29:315-334.
31. Lamm H, Meyers D. Group-induced polarization of attitudes and behavior. *Advances in Experimental Social Psychology.* New York: Academic Press; 1978.
32. Schachter S. Deviation, rejection and communication. *Journal of Abnormal and Social Psychology.* 1951; 46:190-207.
33. Festinger L, Schachter S, Back K. *Social pressures in informal groups: a study of community housing.* New York: Harper & Row; 1950.
34. S. A. Studies in independence and conformity: A minority of one against a unanimous majority. *Psychological Monographs.* 1956; 70.

35. Haslam SA, Reicher S. Beyond the banality of evil: three dynamics on an interactive social psychology. *Personality and Social Psychology Bulletin.* 2007; 33:615-622.
36. Janis IL. *Groupthink.* 2nd ed. Boston: Houghton-Mifflin; 1982.
37. Risen J. *State of war.* New York: Free Press; 2006.
38. Asbridge T. *The first crusade: a new history.* Oxford: Oxford University Press; 2004.
39. Harari Y. *Sapiens.* New York: Random House; 2014.
40. Blackmore S. *The meme machine.* New York: Oxford Uiversity Press; 2000.
41. Clark R. *Einstein: the life and times.* New York: The World Publishing Company; 1971.
42. Pinker S. *The better angels of our nature: why violence has declined.* New York: Viking; 2011.
43. Shermer M. *The moral arc.* New York: Henry Holt & Co.; 2015.
44. Douglas EM, Straus MA. Corporal punishment experienced by university students in 17 countries and its relation to assault and injury of dating partners. Paper presented at: European Society of Criminology; August, 2003.
45. Berman M. *Why america failed: the roots of imperial decline.* Kindle Books; 2014.
46. Leung K, Bond M. *Psychological aspects of social axioms: understanding global beleif systems.* New York: Springer; 2013.
47. Lun V, M. HB. Examining the relationship of religion and spirituality to subjective well-being across national cultures. *Psychology of Religion and Spirituality.* 2013; 14, 104-128.

Coda

In Chapter 1, we examined how social belief systems can develop from scratch, and how the "cargo cults" in the Pacific Islands bore all the hallmarks of a religious belief: a "magical" event that required an explanation, a central dogma that purported to offer that explanation, and a group that adhered to the explanation.

The doomsday cult studied by Leon Festinger[1] revealed how these complexes come to be formed: a small coterie of the "exalted" have close access to the leader, and within the group status is conferred on the most committed members of the cult. The sense of belonging to an elite group and possessing status in that group is what motivates the actions of followers. The doomsday beliefs in the Festinger study caused group members to commit to their beliefs by quitting school and jobs to await the coming apocalypse.

Religious belief systems have predicted doomsdays or second comings as far back as pre-Christian times (the coming of the messiah to free the Jews from Roman rule had been predicted for centuries). No prediction has ever been quantifiably fulfilled. This strongly suggests a flaw in the belief systems themselves, and points to an unusual and paradoxical feature of human cognition: that we sometimes strengthen our beliefs when evidence disconfirms them.

Festinger applied this understanding to the disconfirmation that occurred to Jesus' disciples when he was crucified.

Now, the event is viewed as central to the Christian belief: that Jesus died for our sins (and that we are inherently sinful). This process, called cognitive dissonance, also explains the tendency of early Christians to proselytize. Christianity has, of course, a built-in principle that inoculates its followers against disconfirmation: the adage that "god works in mysterious ways." It prepares the faithful for disconfirmation, and to accept the evidence without questioning their faith.

In Chapter 2, we examined the early origins of the Abrahamic desert religions (Christianity, Judaism, and Islam). At a time when female fertility was seen as a magical ability to create life, god was worshipped as a woman. In Marija Gimbutas' archaeological studies[2] of Old Europe and Middle Eastern religion, the central focus of religion was on creation: creation of the earth and of the individual. These themes still gather our attention. Gimbutas shows how in these cultures female deities were worshipped for 20,000 years.

The goddess of life was the central deity from 7000-5000 BCE. She was transformed in later religions as Ishtar, Gaia, and Aphrodite, although these religions were now polytheistic, featuring both male and female gods. Only after mankind made the causal connection between intercourse and pregnancy did patriarchal religions come into being (such as with the gods Aten and Yahweh), sometime around 5000-2000 BCE.

In any event, our image of god has always been a projection of human self-image: a man-made god. Nowhere is this more evident than in the jealous, violent god of the Hebrew bible: a god who advised genocide, slavery, and rape, which were consistent with the values of the day.

Freud believed god was an illusion, derived from our deep-seated need to be protected by a stronger, wiser other.[3]

When we express this wish it is rarely answered (such as with prayer). Any baseball fan sees opposing players crossing themselves before a game—only one set of prayers can be answered. Herbert Benson and his colleagues[4] studied the effects of prayer on the recovery of cardiac bypass patients; prayer had no effect on recovery from the surgery. Christians tend to dismiss the failure of prayer by "god works in mysterious ways." In fact, there is no evidence supporting the elevation of prayer over any other superstition. Yet religious people continue to believe.

Ernest Becker viewed religion as man's answer to his fearful awareness of death. Many religions, including the desert religions reviewed in this book, have a comforting concept of the afterlife. Current research by Sheldon Solomon and his colleagues[5] indicates that the Freudian notion of a need for protection may be deeper and more pervasive than what even Freud imagined, and may stem from our own awareness of death. Becker saw this as a terrifying awareness that we denied in order to suppress our fear. This denial of death included, but was not limited to, religions that promised an afterlife.

The very associations of religious institutions are transcendent, with cultural practices that appear permanent; this generates a sense of our own immortality. Numerous studies of mortality salience show that when confronted with death awareness, we tend to adhere strongly to both religious beliefs and cultural values to improve our sense of transcendence.

Early Christianity was an era of great debate amongst Christians. This all changed in 325 CE when Constantine, the then Roman Emperor, converted to Christianity. He convened the Nicaean Council and settled the disputes for the time being. Christian churches then became tax-free and politically powerful—dissenters were now routinely put to death.

There is some debate about the existence of Jesus, and several writers claimed that Osiris or Zoroaster were earlier versions of the "Jesus myth:" virgin birth, resurrection, and godliness. In fact, a "virgin birth" was a common way of implying importance in those days, and Alexander the Great, among others, was said to be of virgin birth. Many of these realizations occurred when the Rosetta Stone was discovered in 1799, allowing Egyptian hieroglyphics to be deciphered.

Bart Ehrman[6] made a strong case for Jesus' actual existence, just not in the form of Christian myth. Jesus was mentioned by both Roman and Jewish historians, although as a cult leader, not as a messiah. He was a victim of his own success, becoming a threat to the Jewish religious establishment; they subsequently pushed Pilate for his death as they had with an earlier "messiah," Menahim.

The crucifix story signified the theme of necessary suffering and, hence, compliance and conformity to political powers. At that time, Christianity had become closely identified with Roman power; it had transformed to what biblical scholar Tom Harpur[7] called Christianism. Whereas early Christianity viewed the resurrection as a symbolic event, Christianism viewed it as a historical fact.

Charles Freeman views the sightings of Jesus after the crucifixion as hysterias. A more likely explanation is that Caiaphas, fearing a burgeoning political movement, had the body removed by priests. Once Christianity became the state religion, however, it was futile (and lethal) to argue these points.

In Chapter 3, we examined the basis for the Old Testament, a document written in 700 BCE about events purported to have happened in 1300 BCE. It was, as comedian Bill Maher likes to say, *"a collection of Jewish folk tales."* The Old Testament was written about 600 years after the events it depicts; all indicators suggest it was in order to unite the Jewish states of Israel and Judah, and thus has a mythic quality that serves this purpose. Archaeological digs reported by Finkelstein and Silberman[8] do not support the Old Testament fables.

The dialogues in the Old Testament—for example, between god and Moses or god and Abraham—cannot have been known verbatim given the lapse of 600 years. The same can be said for dialogues between Jesus and his disciples, written in Greek at least 30-40 years after they originally transpired in Aramaic. Less critical scholars have tended to accept "oral transmission" as a given reason. However, early studies on rumour done by psychologist Gordon Allport[9] and his colleagues showed how quickly any veracity is lost in chains of oral transmission. Studies of the accuracy of human memory make the claims of early religions highly dubious.[10] More critical scholars, like Patricia Crone in her studies of Islam,[11] point out its dubious veracity; there were no witnesses to Muhammad's conversations with the angel Gabriel.

The fables in the Old Testament are simply that; unfounded stories written to unite Jews by featuring creation myths about them. A unified religion (i.e. belief in Yahweh) was seen as a means to generate this unity. Until the 17th Century, it was taken for granted that the scriptures of the Old Testament were divine revelation, and it was believed that Moses wrote the Books of Moses himself, including Deuteronomy.

In the 17th Century, textual analysis noticed literary asides that indicate later revision. By the 19th Century, biblical scholars doubted Moses had any hand in writing the Torah, and it was now clear that several versions of these books existed, including two conflicting versions of genesis. There were also two different given names for god: Yahweh and Elohim. The current thinking is that the present biblical text is a constellation of the various source texts. Scholarship was boosted by the 1799 discovery of the Rosetta Stone, which allowed the deciphering of Egyptian hieroglyphics. It allowed us to reconcile evidence from Egyptian, as well as biblical, sources.

Starting in the mid-19th Century, archaeological excavations of the Middle East revealed that there was some historical basis to the Old Testament; however, there were way too many contradictions between the archaeological finds and biblical narrative to indicate that the bible was historically accurate. The Israelite conquests described in the bible were extremely unlikely given the power of the Egyptian kingdom at that time. More likely, these stories were written to reflect the views of the King Josiah of Judah in the 7th Century; they provided an ideological validation for his political ambitions to unite the two existing Jewish states.

There is, in fact, no historical evidence for the existence of either Abraham or Moses. The historical evidence suggests that the Jews emerged in Canaan, were displaced, and became a separate tribe by choice. The Israelites did not conquer Canaan; they emerged from it, and the conquest myth was created 600 years later. Included in the creation myth was a god—Yahweh—a being borrowed from an earlier Egyptian god and named after a Canaanite place: YWH, in Midian.

Some similar problems exist with the factual basis of the New Testament, as we reviewed in Chapter 4. For instance, it was written in Greek at least 30 years after the crucifixion; neither Jesus nor his disciples were literate, and they spoke Aramaic; there were no eyewitnesses to Jesus' "verbatim" conversations with his disciples.

Greek and Roman sources have nothing to say about Jesus; there are no birth records, accounts of his trial or death, reflections on his significance, or disputes about his teachings (p 148).[6] There are numerous sources from the period, and yet there is no 1st Century source, of either Greek or Roman origin, that mentions Jesus (p 148).[6] He didn't seem to be that important.

According to biblical scholar Bart Ehrman,[6, 12-16] the Christian bible has been repeatedly rewritten, typically to embellish events to later fit new Christian dogma (e.g. that Jesus was born of a virgin and resurrected). There are no copies of the originals remaining, and they are known to exist simply because others referred to them.

In Chapter 5, we saw that the same problems exist with the Koran. Secular scholar Patricia Crone puts its writing at 150-200 years after Muhammad's death. The oldest existing copy is from the 9th Century; Muhammad died in 632. It was written, as was the Hebrew bible, to achieve political ends: Islam was in the middle of a series of conquests, spreading its influence from Spain to Persia. Muhammad had been a trader, who was exposed to religious ideas from Christianity, paganism, and Judaism in his travels between Mecca and Syria.

As with Jesus, Muhammad competed during his time with other self-styled prophets. His status was elevated when he was asked to come to Medina to mediate conflicts in that town. There is some thought that his revelations conform to epileptic seizures (as did Paul's).

Of note here is that all three of the desert religions were based on writings that occurred a long time after the death of their leader and the events depicted. The best current estimates are 30-40 years for the Christian New Testament, 600 years for the Hebrew bible, and 150-200 years for the Koran. All of these religions refer to "oral tradition" as the transmission from the original events to the writing.

However, as we showed in Chapter 4, personal memory and chain communications are notoriously unreliable. They inevitably are coloured by the beliefs of the communicators in the chain. Some of the earliest studies in social psychology demonstrate this.[17] It seems that a process like this would have coloured the transmission of the writing of religious texts.

Experimental tests of memory indicate that it is notoriously flawed; the reports of verbatim dialogues in the bible and Koran cannot be accurate. They have no witnesses for dyadic conversations, and even if they had occurred, too much time elapsed before the writing of them for an accuracy to be had. The two thousand years of conflict, murder, and forced conversions between Christians, Jews, and Muslims is based on sets of beliefs that are inherently questionable, yet steadfastly endorsed by their believers.

Morality

What becomes of morality if it is not guided by a religious basis? Both Sam Harris[18] and Michael Shermer[19] are clear on this point: true morality is fact-based. As we examined in Chapter 6, it is primarily a question of knowledge and secondarily a question of values.

The knowledge aspect is made clear by the witch hunts of the Middle Ages: people believed in the supernatural, and that witches caused evils such as the plague. In the context of their beliefs, their actions made sense. But they were woefully misinformed about the facts. In the days before microscopes, ignorance drove actions and moral decisions.

Harris cites the modern-day results of religious influence, such as the 19 US states that still allow corporal punishment in their school systems. This practice is based on the religious notion that to "spare the rod spoils the child."* In fact, sociologist Murray Straus' research (and that of others) has shown repeatedly how corporal punishment of a child increases their subsequent likelihood of violence and criminality.[20-22] The biblical proverb backfires because people were ignorant of social science when it was written. In most Western jurisdictions, the courts have ruled against parents who invoke religious beliefs to refuse their children medical care. In effect, the courts have ruled that modern medicine's knowledge of the facts about the child's infirmity are superior to the parent's religious knowledge.

Shermer[19] traces the "moral arc"—an improvement in normative morality—and views that the moral condition of humanity has improved; not because of religious belief, but because of science. When religious belief prevailed, it was considered acceptable to torture people to "save their souls from hell." We know pain as fact, but there is no factual support for hell. As we saw above, western culture fell into a 1,000-year "closing of the western mind," when religion superseded Greek advances in rationality. It began with the elevation of Christianity as the state religion in the 4th Century.[24] This

---

* Based on Proverbs 13:24, *"He that spareth his rod hateth his son; but he that loveth him chasten him betimes,"* 20:30, *"The blueness of a wound cleanseth away evil,"* and 23:13, *"Withhold not correction from the child; for if thou beatest him with the rod, he shall not die."*

lasted through the suppression of Copernicus and Galileo, but eventually the truth began to win out. During the Dark Ages, torture was acceptable, and rates of everyday violence were much higher than at present.[23]

Shermer dates the improvements to moral progress as beginning with Copernicus' *On the Revolutions of the Heavenly Spheres* in 1543, and the publication of Isaac Newton's *The Principia* in 1687. The scientific revolution slowly began to generate a change in the study of knowledge; it was now more acceptable to use evidence and reason to make decisions, including moral ones. The Enlightenment, with its values on reason, liberty, and natural rights, had begun. Voltaire demolished the validity of the use of torture as means of gaining knowledge. These ideas were disseminated by the newly-invented Gutenberg printing press; in the past, the church had controlled all information.

Religion has a dismal moral record: the Catholic church ran the Inquisition, benefitted financially from the Conquest of the Americas, and supported slavery. Capuchin missionaries were excommunicated for calling for the abolition of slavery, and many Catholic orders and Popes owned slaves.[24] When the church did take a stand against slavery, it was only applied to free, Christian slaves. Papal Bulls such as the *Dum Diversas* (1452) and *the Romanus Pontifex* (1454) sanctioned slavery, which they called "perpetual servitude;" they used derivative arguments from Augustine's concept of Holy War to rationalize the practice. Pope Pius XII (Eugenio Pacelli) was strongly criticized after World War II for never taking any public moral stand against the Nazis,[25] and for supplying Vatican Passports to Nazi leaders fleeing to fascist countries in South America: the so-called "Ratline."

The Irish Commission to Inquire into Child Abuse (CICA or Ryan Report),* published in 2009, was so critical of Catholic priests sexually preying on innocent boys that Ireland almost voted the church out of a Catholic country. A study by John Jay College in New York found that for every priest who was a perpetrator of child rape, ten others covered up for him. The Christian Brothers successfully sued to have no individual priests named in the Ryan Report, and no criminal convictions followed.

Religious-based moral systems have not worked, and they cannot work. This is because they simply impose a moral dictate "from god" that, in reality, is a projection of the religious person's belief system. For example, those who carry signs reading "god hates fags" are simply using a religious voice for their own twisted hatred. Yes, they can cite the Old Testament warnings about "Sodom and Gomorrah," but this tells us only that in 7th Century BCE, certain Jewish writers were offended by homosexuality.

In fact, when people who engage in extreme acts against homosexuals are studied it is mental illness, not religion, that is found to drive their actions,[26] even when they claim some religious authority. The illness includes "*inner conflicts about sexual functioning associated with shame and rage (that) leads to paranoid attacks*" (p 131).[26] These people have woven shards

---

* The report was based on interviews with 1,090 former residents of Irish schools and reformatories. Detailed in 2,600 pages, the report describes child rape, the whipping of orphaned and disabled children, and the threat of excommunication by pedophile priests to silence their victims. Ninety percent of interviewees reported physical abuse, and fifty percent reported sexual abuse.

of religious themes into their overall rage toward a target group. The "voice of god," in short, came from them.

Religious moral systems also cannot work because they are essentially tribal systems: outsiders (the infidels) are historically and routinely mistreated compared to the "faithful." Hence, there can be no universal laws because the non-tribe has different prescriptions applied to them than the tribe.

Finally, religious moral authority cannot work because it is essentially authoritarian, and yet derives from an authority whose very existence is unproven.

Shermer[19] posits a better moral approach; one based on maximizing *"the survival and flourishing of sentient individuals."* This humanist-utilitarian view respects the personal autonomy of sentient beings (including animals), unlike religious-based morality, which has sought to control people's thoughts and actions. We might call this a secular humanist system based on science: a system on knowing, through reason, what causes what effect, and which of those effects will generate the best outcome for the greatest good. This would immediately stop the mindless persecution of victimless crimes, and begin a period of morality based on evidence.

The systems that serve us best are those very systems that have attempted to reduce subjective bias: science and the adversarial system in law. A religion that can tap into an emotional sphere is valuable, so long as it does not attempt to confer a dogma whose basis is ephemeral and dubious.

Spirituality and morality without dogma is now finally a possibility. We need to reinstitute the Gnostic idea that spirituality occurs through self-enlightenment and freedom from illusion—including freedom from religious illusion.

The Perseverance of Religious Belief

One might ask why, given the dubious nature of evidence for religious doctrines, they persist into the 21st Century. One reason was given by the work of Ara Norenzayan:[27] that religious belief has a central notion that god is always watching. At one time, this served to prohibit any behaviour that might anger god. Since these were usually also actions that were socially unacceptable, god became a moral force for conventionality.

Since believers thought others would act similarly to themselves, god became a force for social trust, a form of glue that cemented an in-group of believers. Of course, it also sealed the fate of infidels. Harari's work[28] reinforces this; religious beliefs are part of the intersubjective, which serves as the social method of enhancing group cohesiveness. At the individual level, religious teachings are part of a myriad of neural connections called a cogweb.[29]

How is it that these specific desert religions have endured for so long? There are, of course, numerous reasons, including political power, socialization of followers, and punishment of infidels. However, another reason is the work and fear involved in challenging a central belief that encompasses all we know.

As an example, consider Ross Douthat's book, *Bad Religion: How We Became a Nation of Heretics.* In it, he blames the social strains put on Christian orthodoxy as the problem. Much of Douthat's argument is well taken: the amalgamation of orthodoxy with unfettered capitalism detracts from the religion's original message and corrupts it with current fads. Douthat is adamant that he has retained his belief in orthodoxy, and yet his voluminous bibliography makes it clear that he has been exposed to a broad spectrum of heretical ideas along the way, including Bart Ehrman, Elaine Pagels, and Sam Harris.

However, Pagels and Ehrman are lumped together with novelist Dan Brown and labelled "accommodationists," while Harris is labelled as a "polemicist." But in no case are any of their ideas revealed, taken seriously, or challenged. They are simply dismissed as part of a current Zeitgeist. But Paul's ideas were also a part of a social movement or Zeitgiest; one far less informed that those of the present.

Absolute truth may exist, but everything we know about the human brain and all we know about human social influence points to the opposite conclusion: that bias and subjectivity generate beliefs, which are falsely viewed as being objectively true. Douthat demonstrates how intelligent, well-read people operate to sustain beliefs: through failing to engage in heretical questions and by applying a double-standard to heretics and founders of the orthodoxy.

It is for this reason that I doubt that anything revealed above will change the minds of deeply religious people. The work of Ernest Becker explains why. Religious belief systems generate large conceptual nets of ideas: a cogweb. Thus, notions of morality and who constitutes an in-group and who an out-group are all nested within a belief system. Such systems are notoriously difficult to change.

As Kathleen Taylor describes them, these central beliefs[29] have the greatest number of synaptic connections in the brain. As we saw in Chapter 10, they also connect to centres governing emotion. Therefore, the acceptance of new ideas depends on how well those ideas fit in with our already-held beliefs. The ideas that resonate with our *cogweb* of beliefs produce feelings of rightness. This does not, of course, make the ideas that fill the cogweb accurate, and as we have seen in this book, most are without evidence. But they suit our sense of self and lessen our death anxiety. They have also now become a part of our culture—something that transcends our existence and represents infinity in our minds.

That does not mean that these broadly-held beliefs cannot change; as we have seen, there is an epistemological arc that parallels the moral arc. It started with Copernicus and the rebirth of science and proceeded to the present, where atheistic ideas can circulate without punishment. This book is a rational argument that contradicts religious dogma. Each reader will find their own path from here.

From the cognitive transformation that began our rapid evolution, we stand at a critical time of human progress. We have the possibility of science making illness a thing of the past. We also have the impending threat of annihilation via nuclear war or climate change. Our scientific prowess is remarkable, but our cognitive process is still too wedded to the tribe and irrational beliefs.

One possible way to evolve is to drop the intersubjectivity based on ancient myth and begin a new, shared perspective that acknowledges the universality of the human condition. This book has attempted one small step in that direction.

References

1. Festinger L, Riecken H, Schachter S. *When prophecy fails*. Minneapolis: University of Minnesota Press; 1956.
2. Gimbutas M. *Goddesses and gods of old europe 7000-3500 B.C.* Los Angeles: University of California Press; 1982.
3. Freud S. *The future of an illusion*. New York: W.W. Norton & Co.; 1961.
4. Benson H, Fusey D, Sherwood JB. Study of the therapeutic effects of intercessory prayer (STEP) in cardiac and bypass patients: A multicenter randomized trial of uncertainty and certainty of receiving intercessory prayer. *American Heart Journal*. 2006; 15:934-42.
5. Solomon S, Greenberg J, Pyszcynski T. *The worm at the core: on the role of death in life*. New York: Random House; 2015.
6. Ehrman BD. *Jesus, interrupted*. New York: Harper One; 2009.
7. Harpur T. *The pagan christ*. Toronto: Thomas Allen; 2004.
8. Finkelstein I, Silberman N. *The bible unearthed: archaeology's new vision of ancient israel*. New York: Free Press; 2001.
9. Allport G, Postman LJ. The basic psychology of rumour. *Transactions of the New York Academy of Sciences*. 1945; Series 11:61-81.

10. Lynn SJ, McConkey KM. *Truth in memory*. New York: Guilford Press; 1998.
11. Crone P. *Slaves on horses*. London: Cambridge University Press; 1980.
12. Ehrman B. *Lost scriptures*. New York: Oxford University Press; 2003.
13. Ehrman B. *Misquoting jesus: the story behind who changed the bible and why*. New York: Harper One; 2005.
14. Ehrman B. *Forged*. New York: Harper One; 2011.
15. Ehrman B. *Did jesus exist? The historical argument for jesus of nazareth*. New York: Harper One; 2012.
16. Ehrman BD. *Jesus, interrupted*. New York: Harper One; 2009.
17. Allport G, Postman LJ. The basic psychology of rumour. *Basic Studies in Social Psychology*. New York: Holt, Rinehart & Winston; 1965.
18. Harris S. *The moral landscape*. New York: Free Press; 2010.
19. Shermer M. *The moral arc*. New York: Henry Holt & Co.; 2015.
20. Straus MA. *Beating the devil out of them: corporal punishment in american families*. New York: Lexington; 1991.
21. McDonald R, Jouriles EN, Tart CD, Minze LC. Children's adjustment problems in families characterized by men's severe violence towards women: Does other family violence matter? *Child Abuse & Neglect*. 2009; 33:94-101.
22. Douglas EM, Straus MA. Corporal punishment experienced by university students in 17 countries and its relation to assault and injury of dating partners. Paper presented at: European Society of Criminology; 2003.
23. Pinker S. *The better angels of our nature: why violence has declined*. New York: Viking; 2011.

24. Rodriguez J. *The historical encylopedia of world slavery.* New York: ABC-CLIO; 1997.
25. Cornwell J. *Hitler's pope: the secret history of pius XII.* New York: Viking; 1999.
26. Murphy D. Homophobia and psychotic crimes of violence. *The Journal of Forensic Psychology & Psychiatry* 2006; 17:131-50.
27. Norenzayan A. *Big gods: how religion transformed cooperation and conflict.* Princeton: Princeton University Press; 2013.
28. Harari Y. *Sapiens.* New York: Random House; 2014.
29. Taylor K. *Cruelty: Human evil and the human brain.* New York: Oxford University Press; 2009.

Index

A

Abraham 78
Afterlife 119
Alexander the Great 100
Allah 136-137
Woody Allen 251
Anthropomorphizing 258
Ayaan Hirsi Ali 158, 192
Gordon Allport (and
    Postman) 92-93, 149-150
Amenhotep III 65
Anabaptists 7
Anti-semitism 184-187
Apocalypse 5
Karen Armstrong 70
Apocalyptic prophecy 29
John Archer 191
Hannah Arendt 234
Karen Armstrong 46, 54, 230
Thomas Asbridge 175
Solomon Asch 296
Aten 50
Attachment 282, 295
David Attenborough 1
Augustine 172-175, 189, 240
Authoritarianism 192-193

B

Babies, visual focus 255
agents and objects 255

attention patterns 256
Sir Francis Bacon 289
Banding together 280-281
Justin Barrett 252-272
Frederick Bartlett 158
Ernest Becker 44, 275, 287
Belief perseverance 27
Bisexuality 187
Herbert Benson 36
Susan Blackmore 302
Paul Bloom 254
Jesse Bering 260-261
Niels Bohr 246-247, 253
Michael Bond 309
Book of Daniel, predating of
    30
John Bowlby 295-296
Pascal Boyer 46, 259, 269, 271,
    282
Paul Boyer 29
Giordano Bruno 203-204

C

Canaan 86-91
Camel bones 83
Cargo cults 1
George Carlin 223
Catholic Church,
    authority of 121-123
    Donation of Constantine
    122-123

causal inference 257-258
Chak Muul 45
Charlemagne 165
Child abuse by priests 229-230
Celsus 197-198
Noam Chomsky 254
Christian ignorance 131
Christian mysticism 17
Christian sadism 235
Cognitive web/ cogweb 12, 292
Cognitive dissonance 11
Constantine 69,126-129, 185
Need for control 283-284
Copernicus 181-183
John Cornwell 235
Counterfactual ideas 269
Creationism in children 262
Patricia Crone 144-145, 149
Crucifixion as disconfirmation 10
Crucifixon and resurrection 113-118
Crusades 177
    First crusade 175
Cuban Missile crisis 301

D

Mary Daly 190
Dark ages 165, 200-202
Richard Dawkins 2, 211-217
The Day the Earth Stood Still 25
Death anxiety 50
Death terror 44-46, 286
The Denial of Death 44
Deprogrammingp 24

Disease as punishment for sin 231
Dissociative states 115
Dominicans 203
Fred Donner 135, 142
Ross Douthat 129, 288

E

Egyptian Book of the Dead 54
Bart Ehrman 32, 69, 100, 103, 121, 185, 296
Elohim 81
Elvis sightings 116
Encomium Moriae 201
End of Faith 236
End Times 5, 155
End of Days 6
Enuma Elish 52
Einstein 182
Riane Eisler 59
Epicurus 164
Epilepsy and religious visions 138-140
Erasmus 201-202, 204
Evolutionary psychology 283
Extraordinary Delusions and the Madness of Crowds 34
Excommunication
use of 177, 301
Existential theory of mind 260
Exodus 84-86

F

M. Farias 271-272
Female circumcision 232
Female deities 51
Leon Festinger 5, 296, 298

Israel Finkelstein 76
Forging of gospels 110-123
The Forms 166, 171
Matthew Fox 174
Charles Freeman 107, 165, 185-186, 296
Frank Freemon 138
Friar Diego de Landa 176
Freud, as atheist 224
   On Religion 224-226
   God as paternal protection 224-226
   Socialization of children 227

G

Gabriel 134
Galileo 181-183
Gallup Poll
   Re existence of God 237
Peter Gay 224
Epic of Gilgamesh 57
Marija Gimbutas 51
Gnostic Gospels 68, 101
Daniel Goldhagen 186-187
Jeff Greenberg 47
Group dynamics 296
Groupthink 300-301
The Guardians 14

H

Hadiths 146-148
Hammurabi's code 78
Happy Planet Index 310
Yuval Harari 68, 301
Tom Harpur 63
Sam Harris 151 – 152, 236-242, 289
Stephen Hawking 217 -220, 242 -244, 284- 285, 302

Jennifer Hecht 156, 165
Heliocentrism 181-184
Heaven's Gate 28
Hegira 141
Fritz Heider 257-258, 283
Werner Heisenberg 246
Christopher Hitchens 109, 228-231
Hitler 186-187, 236
Hitler's Pope 235
Homosexuality 188-189, 231
Hypatia 67
Hypersensitive agency detection system 258

I

Illiteracy 100
   Of Muhammad 136
   of Jesus 106
   of Charlemagne 171
   of Jesus disciples 99
Illuminati 6
Illusion of control 46, 285
Indulgences 233
Inquisition 178-179, 183, 186, 240
Intercessory prayer
   Failure of 37
Intersubjective 301
Irenaeus 99, 107
Ishtar 57
Islam
Spread of Islam 142, 148
Battle of Poitiers 153
Influence of earlier religions on Islam 147
Islamic doubters 156-158

J

Irving Janis 300
Julian Jaynes 59
Warren Jeffs 22
Battle of Jericho 86-87, 183
Jesus brothers 109
Jesus seminar 124
Jews as critics of Islam 142
    Mass slaughter of Jews by Mohammed 141-142
Josephus 61, 104
Jihad 150, 153 , 155, 159, 238-239
Julian, Roman Emperor 198-200
Pope Julius 201

K

Efraim Karsh 140-142, 154
Marion Keech 13
Deborah Keleman 259
Hugh Kennedy 135, 142, 144-145, 151, 153
J.F. Kennedy 301
Koran
    early version 143, 144
Uthman's codex 144
Partial finding 145
Recording of 149
Isnads (chains of storytellers) 149-150
Death to infidels 150-152

L

The Late, Great Planet Earth 35
Timothy LaHaye 22, 29-36
Ellen Langer 283-285
Cristine Legare 48
Little Richard 268

Hal Lindsey 35
Elizabeth Loftus 93-94
Lucretius 164
Martin Luther 293
Lyceum 165
Steven Jay Lynn 94, 115

M

Charles Mackay 4, 34, 180
Ferdinand Magellan 171
Magical beliefs 252-253
Maleus maleficarum 190
Malinowsky 48
William Manchester 165
Marduk 53, 64
Gerald Massey 65
Maya 45
Kevin McConkey 94, 115
McMartin preschool trial 3
Mecca 134-135
Memes 214, 302-304
Memeplex 214, 225, 251, 304-305
William Miller/ Millerites 8
Leonard Mlodinow 217-220, 242-244, 284-285, 302
Islamic misogyny 158-159
Monogamy 188
Montanus 6
Moses 75, 80
Muhammad 134
    Exposure to pagan beliefs 135
    illiteracy 136
Marriage to nine year old 151
Advocacy of domestic violence 151
Muhammad's revelations 134
Muslim atrocities 177

N

Natural religion 266-268, 281-282
Neanderthals 301-302
Nicaean Council 69
Ara Norenzayan 215
Nostradamus 22

O

Organization for Economic Cooperation and Development (OECD) 308
Origen 69, 170, 197-198
George Orwell 234
Osiris 64

P

Elaine Pagels 101, 118, 187-188
Pattern recognition 283
Kenneth Parmagent 286
Paul 31, 166
Gregory Paul 307
Sam Pepys 160
Pew Poll 237, 238, 293, 294
  Of Christian religious knowledge 131
Phenomenal causality 258
Jean Piaget 261-262, 265
Steven Pinker 60, 147, 179, 186, 254, 305
Pliny the Younger 105
Prophecies 4
Post-diction of Christian "prophecies" 32
Battle of Poitiers 153
Pork, proscription on 90
Proselytizing 11
Thomas Pyszynski 47

Q

Quantum theory 244-246
Willard van Orman Quine 12

R

Paul Radin 70
Amaury de Reincourt 58, 63
Retrospective prediction 285
Henry Riecken 5
Jane Risen 48, 252
Pat Robertson 22
Edward Robinson 82
Phillipe Rochat 257
Max Rodenbeck 159
Rosetta Stone 64
Lee Ross 288
Bertrand Russell 75, 197, 205-211, 235, 276, 280

S

Carl Safina 216
Sabbati/ Sabbati Zevi 7
Wayne Sage 24, 140, 299
Satanic Panic 3
Sananda 14
Saver and Rabin 138, 139
Antonin Scalia 171
Schachter and Singer 139
Katherine Schultz 271
Scientology 13
Sea People 88
Second Coming 6
Michael Servetus 202-203
Shlomo Sand 90-91
Michael Shermer 211, 306-308
Andrew Shtulman 266, 270-271
Skeptic Academy 165
Siblings, of Jesus 109

Son of God 44
    Plato as 44
    Alexander the Great as 44
    Augustus Caesar as 44
    Pythagoras as 44
Sicario 61
Neil Silberman 77
Sheldon Solomon 47, 275, 287
Slavery
    taking of sex slaves and Islam 147, 151
    Catholic church and slavery 324
Son of god, as explanation 100
Spooky action at a distance 244
SS (Schutzstaffel) as Catholics 236
Stanley Schachter 5, 296
Successful Societies Scale 307
Superagency 254, 264

T

Tacitus 105
Kathleen Taylor 290-292, 303
Temporal lobe epilepsy 139, 168-170
Ten Commandments 79
Terror management 48
Theory of mind 260, 263
Torture 179-181, 240
Paul Tobin 85
Peter Townsend 137, 151
Troy, Trojan Wars 86

V

Vatican passports 236
Verbatim conversations 94-95

Jeffery Viktor 3, 115-116
Virgin birth 64, 108, 199

W

Julius Wellhausen 83
Drew Westen 291
When Worlds Collide 5
Witch hunts 190
Graeme Wood 155
World view defense 50
Wisdom of the wise 31
Robert Wright 47, 54
Robin Wright 65, 70, 241

Y

Yahweh 75, 81

Z

Zealots 61
Zoroaster 64

72 virgins 152

About the Author

Don Dutton is Professor Emeritus in the Department of Psychology, University of British Columbia. He is also the author of several books including *The Abusive Personality*, *Rethinking Domestic Violence*, and *The Psychology of Genocide*.

www.ingramcontent.com/pod-product-compliance
Lightning Source LLC
Chambersburg PA
CBHW030902080526
44589CB00010B/107